Finding Birds in the
National
Capital Area

Finding Birds in the National Capital Area

A Smithsonian Nature Guide

Claudia Wilds

Smithsonian Institution Press
Washington, D.C.

Library of Congress Cataloging in Publication Data

Wilds, Claudia P.
    Finding birds in the national capital area.

    (A Smithsonian nature guide)
    Includes index.
    Supt. of Docs. no.: SI 1.20:B53/2
    1. Bird watching—Washington Metropolitan Area.
2. Bird watching—Virginia. 3. Bird watching—Maryland.
4. Bird watching—Eastern Shore (Md. and Va.) 5. Bird
watching—Delaware. I. Title. II. Series.
QL683.W37W54   1983   598'.07'23475   82-600348
ISBN 0-87474-959-X

Printed in the United States of America

Designed by Alan Carter

Illustrations by Doreen Curtin; maps by Kai Yee.

The paper in this book meets the guidelines for permanence and durability of the
Committee on Production Guidelines for Book Longevity of the Council on Library
Resources.

Frontispiece: Peregrine Falcon.

For
Ives and Evan
Lola and Ted
whose friendship is reward enough
for taking up birding

Contents

SOUTH OF CHESAPEAKE BAY

SPECIAL PURSUITS

APPENDIXES

Maps of the **National Capital Area** and the **District of Columbia and Arlington County** can be found at the back of this book.

This book is the outgrowth of a series of articles prepared for the *Audubon Naturalist News*, the newsletter of the Audubon Naturalist Society of the Central Atlantic States. The society is an independent, regional natural history and conservation group based in Washington, D.C., and 95 percent of its members live in the National Capital Area.

The society's strong program of field trips has been, in recent years, the best introduction available to the birding sites of the region, and many of the locations described here are on its calendar of regularly scheduled bird walks.

These and several other areas were brought to my attention as editor of the Voice of the Naturalist, also sponsored by the society. This weekly telephone recording of news for birders features the locations of rare or hard-to-find species sighted in the region, reports of migration and invasions of irruptive species, and sites that local birders are finding especially productive.

A number of chapters are the direct result of asking a regular contributor to the Voice for a tour of a favorite locale. A few sites are included because a listener to the Voice or a reader of the *News* or a friend feared that I was overlooking a place that he wanted to share.

Regardless of source, the selections are a reflection of my own knowledge and prejudices. There may be superb birding sites in Virginia southwest of Washington or in Maryland northeast of Washington or along the lower Potomac, but I do not know about them. The very occasional sightings reported from these areas are almost always of species that are just as easy to see elsewhere close to the capital. By contrast, while I like to think that the reader has an abundance of land-bird sites to choose from, my own preference for water birds and for coastal habitats, especially my affection for Chincoteague, is hard to miss.

No attempt has been made to treat with evenhanded thoroughness all the worthwhile locations in the area. Good birding spots in and around other towns and cities are included only if they are of particular interest or so fruitful that they merit a special outing or stopover on travels from the District of Columbia. Several excellent publications, listed in Appendix B, cover other sites both within and beyond the range of this book. In particular, Hawk Mountain in Pennsylvania and Cape May in New Jersey, though visited regularly by Washington area birders, are so thoroughly described elsewhere that I could not bring myself to repeat readily available information.

This may be as good a point as any to mention the mileage problem. Almost every route was checked at least once, and some were run in three different vehicles. Even the shortest distances may be 0.1 mile off from your odometer; on longer stretches a 0.1 mile discrepancy for every 3 miles or so appears to be entirely normal. Wherever possible, road names or numbers or other landmarks have been included to minimize confusion, and Kai Yee's careful maps may do more than prose can to get you where you want to go.

Acknowledgments

When I began looking at birds in 1970, one of my most joyful discoveries was a delightful, lucid, and informative series of articles collectively called "Where to Go," written by Carl W. Carlson and published in the *Atlantic Naturalist* in the 1960s. They guided me flawlessly through dozens of the finest birding areas near Washington, giving me continuing pleasure for several years. Gradually, interstate highways and condominiums paved over some of the nesting sites and migrant traps Carl described. Only his resistance to updating and compiling his fine series made the present book a reasonable undertaking. Though none of his articles was used as a direct source, they must all be acknowledged as the basic course on finding birds around Washington that inspired this effort, and as a model impossible to emulate.

For many of the sites described herein I am heavily indebted to local birders, who generously shared their knowledge of specific areas, some spending an entire day or several of them supplying not only a deluge of information but the greater gift of companionship. My fervent thanks go to Jackson Abbott (Alexandria), Roger Anderson (Long Branch), Harry Armistead (Blackwater, Hooper Island, Elliott Island, Deal Island), John Bazuin (Loudoun County, Lake Anna), Rick Blom (Baltimore Harbor, Baltimore County, Fort Smallwood, St. Mary's County), Dan Boone (Washington County), Terry Boykie (Long Branch), Dave Czaplak (District of Columbia), Owen Fang (Alexandria), Tony Futcher (District of Columbia), Delores Grant (Meadowside), John Gregoire (Jug Bay), Evan Hannay (the Pulpit, geographic research), Kerrie Kirkpatrick (Linden Fire Tower), Valerie Kitchens (Long Branch), Floyd Parks (Kent County), Bob Patterson (Jug Bay, Merkle), Bob Ringler (Baltimore Harbor), Stan Shetler (Algonkian Park), Jim Stasz (map for Back River Sewage Treatment Plant), Len Teuber (Myrtle Grove, Oxon Hill Children's Farm, Highland County, Shenandoah National Park), Bill Thomas (Long Branch), Barry Truitt (Virginia Coast Reserve), Craig Tufts (Claude Moore Center), Keith Van Ness (Seneca Creek), Dean Weber (Garrett County), and Hal Weirenga (Sandy Point, Deal Island, owl-finding).

I am especially grateful to Joy Aso and John Malcolm, two volunteers who divided the tedious job of checking the mileages and directions for most of the trips in this book. Between them they drove nearly 3,000 miles, and then transcribed notes, sketched maps, and drafted improved directions. I also thank Sharon Malcolm for navigating for John on some of his trips and for being so patient while he went off to check other routes.

Finally, I wish every author had good fortune equal to mine in having an ally like Eve Bloom, my typist, counselor, and friend, who saw to it that a thousand ambiguities and inconsistencies bit the dust.

The Region
and Its Birds

More than a quarter of the species of birds that inhabit or regularly visit the continental United States and Canada may be found in the course of a year within the Washington Beltway. As many again, more than 350 in all, may be seen within a four-hour drive of the District of Columbia.

The location of the national capital on the line between piedmont and coastal plain, less than three hours away from both 4,000-foot mountains and ocean beaches, offers bird watchers of the Washington area an exceptional variety of habitats in which to study birds. Nine major National Wildlife Refuges and innumerable national, state, and regional parks and wildlife areas provide assurance of permanent access to important sanctuaries throughout the region.

Nearly 200 species are regular nesters in the region, ranging from Saw-whet Owls, Hermit Thrushes, and Nashville Warblers in far western Maryland to Wilson's Plovers, Sandwich Terns, and Red-cockaded Woodpeckers in southeastern Virginia. More than half of them breed in the counties around the beltway, and Washington itself offers nesting Fish Crows, Veeries, Prothonotary Warblers, and Louisiana Waterthrushes, among other species.

Migration goes on virtually nonstop, reaching ebb tide only from mid-December to mid-February and from mid-June to early July. A remarkable number of major migration routes converge on the region or pass through it: the mountain ridges, the Potomac, and the Susquehanna rivers, both shores of the Chesapeake Bay, and, of course, the Atlantic coastline.

Raptors, especially buteos, use the ridges mainly in fall, passerines in both fall and spring. Waterfowl and gulls are the most conspicuous migrants on the rivers in fall and early spring, but in May one can see thousands of nighthawks and swallows moving steadily upstream, and riverside trails are alive with transient passerines. Loons, waterfowl, and raptors stream up or down the shores of the Chesapeake and are often easy to see where the width of the bay is constricted. The coast is incomparable for its abundance of migrating loons, gannets, cormorants, herons and ibis, Snow Geese, Brant, sea ducks, falcons, shorebirds, and fall swallows and other passerines. Aside from these principal flyways, mirgrant passerines seem to blanket the area, appearing in every faintly appropriate habitat, most abundantly close to streams and marshes.

The importance of the region as a wintering ground lies overwhelmingly in the habitats of the coastal plain, attested to by the concentration of wildlife refuges and the high species totals on the Christmas Bird Counts, especially in southern Delmarva (the Chincoteague and Cape Charles counts each averaging more than 160 species). High numbers of waterfowl—swans, geese, sea ducks, and diving ducks in particular—are to be found mainly on the Eastern Shore but, for many species, in the sheltered waters from Baltimore and Washington to Point Lookout as well. Raptors are plentiful both on the coastal plain and in the piedmont. Huge flocks of gulls gather on beaches, breakwaters, sandbars, landfills, sewage treatment plants, farm fields, and golf courses all around the coastal plain and at selected sites in the piedmont near the Fall Line and open water. Hundreds of thousands of crows, blackbirds, grackles, cowbirds, and starlings are distributed throughout the lowlands of the region. Among the wintering finches and sparrows abundant everywhere but on the Allegheny Plateau, the invading House Finch is now as common as the American Goldfinch. The unpredictable arrival of irruptive species like Evening Grosbeak, Pine Siskin, and Common Redpoll lends anticipatory excitement to winter land birding.

Thus, for resident and visiting birders alike, the National Capital Area offers fine opportunities year-round. The pages that follow attempt to provide useful information about the landscape, habitats, and weather that one can expect in the region and a species-by-species sketch of seasonal and geographic abundance, preferred habitats, and likely locations.

The heart of the book is the section on birding sites. Those closest to Washington are grouped geographically, but most birders are likely to sample no more than two or three in a morning or a day. Beyond the suburban counties, suggested tour routes—most of them measured from the Washington Beltway—describe excursions suitable for a day or a weekend or, in combination, several consecutive days of good birding.

The appendixes contain information about local ornithological and natural history societies, maps, and other publications, and activities for birders in the National Capital Area.

2 Geography and Climate

THE REGION DEFINED

The region covered by this book has a configuration like a gerrymandered congressional district, reasonable for birding out of Washington, but perhaps bizarre-looking to readers from the rest of the country. It includes sites in all parts of Maryland and Delaware, the Virginia piedmont and mountains north of an east-west line just below Charlottesville, and the Virginia coastal plain close to Washington, south of the James River and east of the Chesapeake Bay.

The North Carolina Outer Banks are beyond the National Capital Area by any rational definition but birders do go there from Washington and published information about the way to bird the Banks is all too scanty. Though included in the book, they should be viewed as in an adjacent region with a somewhat different avifauna.

PHYSIOGRAPHY AND HABITATS

The region is divided into five well-defined and traditional physiographic provinces, two of which have been lumped here for ornithological simplicity. Those at the western and eastern extremes have the most distinctive habitats and bird life, but each shares many characteristics with its neighbors.

The Allegheny Plateau. This highland province, covering almost all of West Virginia, reaches its eastern outpost in Maryland's Allegany County along the ridge of Dan's Mountain. On the Maryland plateau the valley floors do not sink below 1,500 feet; in Garrett County they average 2,500 feet, and the ridges and peaks that rise above them are modest. Maryland's highest mountain, with its summit in the extreme southwest corner of the state, is Backbone Mountain, only 3,360 feet high. The hills and valleys here are somewhat randomly oriented, not strongly parallel as they are further east.

The mountains, except for their rocky summits and sheer cliffs, are typically covered with second-growth oak, maple, and pine, though some of the north-facing slopes have stands of hemlock. The wide valleys, known locally as "glades," are mostly bluegrass pasture land, though many are under cultivation. Along the streams, notably at Swallow Falls, one can find groves of hemlock, spruce, and pine. Deep Creek Lake provides major man-made still-water habitat for migrant water birds.

Unique for the region are the boreal bogs of heath and sedge-meadow, broken by scattered rhododendron and alder bushes and clumps of spruce, hemlock, birch, and maple; the most famous is Cranesville Swamp on the border with West Virginia.

Dividing the plateau from the next province to the east is the Allegheny Front, an escarpment on a virtually straight northeast-southwest line from Cumberland, Maryland, to Bluefield, Virginia, entirely to the west of northern Virginia.

Ridge and Valley (including the physiographically distinct Blue Ridge). The outstanding characteristic of this province is the tightly folded landscape shaped into a series of long ridges and valleys in parallel lines, all running northeast-southwest. In the west the valleys are narrow, but east of Clear Spring in Maryland the broad Hagerstown Valley marks the northward extension of the Valley of Virginia, up which the two forks of the Shenandoah meander to their junction at Front Royal. To the east of this valley the Blue Ridge marks the eastern boundary of the province in Virignia. In Maryland the lower counterparts of the Blue Ridge are South Mountain and Catoctin Mountain, with the Middletown Valley in between.

The entire province is much higher in Virginia than in Maryland, with most ridges above 3,000 feet and some peaks over 4,000 feet. Harrisonburg in the Shenandoah Valley lies at over 1,900 feet and Monterey in a valley west of Jack Mountain is exactly 3,100 feet above sea level.

In Maryland, on the other hand, the altitude of the valleys is no higher than most of the piedmont, at 500-600 feet, and the highest ridge, just east of Cumberland, is Warrior Mountain at only 2,135 feet.

The broader valleys are heavily farmed; the valley floor is under cultivation and the slopes are rich in apple orchards. The narrower western valleys are usually bluegrass pastures or hay fields, with boggy marshes near the headwaters of highland creeks; relatively little land is still under the plow, and abandoned fields are easy to find.

The habitats of the Blue Ridge and the western Virginia ridges are quite similar to those of the mountains of the Allegheny Plateau. The northern conifers are less common, however, and the bogs are missing. Even the lower highlands in Maryland, rising steeply from the flood plain, provide the altitude and climate that attract species to the oak-beech-hickory forests that are rare or absent from similar habitat to the east.

The bottomland woods along the Potomac in this province and the next, all the way from Cumberland to Washington, are traversed by the old Chesapeake and Ohio (C&O) Canal and the highly accessible towpath beside it.

The Piedmont. The national capital lies on the edge of this gently rolling plateau province. The western limit runs along the foot of the Catoctin Mountains in Maryland, jogs west to Harpers Ferry, and continues along the base of the Blue Ridge. In the east the piedmont ends at the Fall Line, where the soil changes from clay to sand and the rivers tumble through rocky rapids to the navigable tidal waters of the coastal plain. Interstate 95, curving south through Wilmington, Baltimore, Washington, and Richmond, runs just above the Fall Line from the Delaware River to the North Carolina border.

The piedmont is divided by two great rivers, the Susquehanna and the Potomac (and its tributaries), and by four other important streams, the Gunpowder, the Patapsco, the Patuxent, and the Rappahannock. Virtually all the still waters of the province are in manmade reservoirs, recreational lakes, and farm and fish ponds. All the rivers—especially the Potomac and the Monocacy, which flows into it—are bordered by outstanding examples of flood-plain forest, dominated by giant sycamores, maples, elms, and hackberry. Georgetown Reservoir in Washington and Lakes Frank and Clopper in Montgomery County, Maryland, are among the closest lakes to the capital. Piedmont marshes of exceptional interest are at Hughes Hollow, Summit Hall Turf Farm, and Lilypons.

Where it has not been paved over, the province, with an altitude that ranges from 300 to about 800 feet, consists of active and abandoned farmland and of forest and woodlots in various stages of succession. Cropland, hay fields, and pastures and turf farms, divided and edged by bird-rich hedgerows, line the back roads of nearby Loudoun County in Virginia and western Montgomery County and southern Frederick County in Maryland.

Recently abandoned farmland is marked by fields of broom edge and goldenrod, dotted with red cedar and saplings of red maple and other hardwoods. The red cedar and, more locally, Virginia pines grow into solid groves. In later years deciduous trees invade the shaded understory, then take over: oak, beech, hickory, and tulip tree, with red maple, dogwood, redbud, and sassafras among the trees in the understory.

The forested areas increase as one heads south in Virginia and the proportion of pines to hardwoods expands as well.

Coastal Plain. Slashed into three distinctive sections by the Chesapeake Bay and the James River, the coastal plain is marked by the narrowest range of altitude (0–300 feet) and the greatest diversity of habitats in the region.

The Western Shore (a term normally applied only to Maryland west of the Chesapeake Bay) shares almost all of its characteristics with the Virginia shoreline from Arlington to Hampton. The somewhat hilly landscape near the Fall Line flattens out in the south, close to the bay. Upland oak-hickory forest is typically found inland; swampy bottomland woods and pine stands (mostly of Virginia pine) are extensive. The predominant farmland is in row crops, including tobacco, with relatively little pasture or hayfield habitat. Fresh to brackish marshes are scattered throughout; the finest wild rice marshes in the east line the Patuxent near Jug Bay, but Baltimore County, Dyke Marsh, Sandy Point, and Point Lookout all offer excellent habitat for rails, marsh wrens, and herons. Wooded swamps range from Mason Neck to Myrtle Grove to an isolated bald cypress swamp in Calvert County. The convoluted shoreline of Baltimore County, along with urban environments like landfills and sewage plants, attracts gulls and waterfowl in great numbers.

The nearly level Eastern Shore (a term interchangeable with the Delmarva Peninsula) is under cultivation from end to end wherever there is sufficient drainage and the land is unprotected.

Among the interspersed patches of bottomland forest two distinctive habitats draw avian specialties. The stands of loblolly pine increase in abundance southward from their northern limit between Kent Island (at the east end of the Chesapeake Bay Bridge) and Rehoboth, Delaware; they are readily accessible at Blackwater and Chincoteague refuges. Bald cypress, loblolly pine, water oak, and red bay mark the extensive and famous swamp along the Pocomoke River, especially interesting near the Delaware-Maryland line.

The superb marshes of Delmarva range from the huge freshwater marshes on either side of the Chesapeake and Delaware Canal to the tidal marshes that line Delaware Bay and both sides of the peninsula from Rehoboth and Cambridge south.

Off the shore of the lower bay numerous wooded islands, marsh islands (locally called "tumps"), and sandbars are the nesting sites of many of the region's colonial water birds. The shoreline itself is so dominated by long, twisting creeks, bays, coves, and inlets that it is one of the nation's greatest concentration points for wintering waterfowl.

The ocean beaches from Cape Henlopen to Ocean City are primarily a human playground, enhanced for winter birders by two jetty-lined inlets that provide (along with the Chesapeake Bay Bridge-Tunnel at the tip of Delmarva) the region's principal rocky-coast habitat.

The coastal islands from Assateague south, with their miles of beaches, dunes, salt marsh, tidal flats (and, on some, pine woods), are not only major water-bird nesting areas but a crucial stopover for mirgrant shorebirds and a highway for southbound raptors.

Finally, the brackish impoundments of the federal and state wildlife refuges, found the length of Delmarva, are important to tens of thousands of birds all year, populations that change markedly with the season and the variations in water level.

Southside Virginia, that part of the coastal plain south of the James River and the Chesapeake Bay, is conspicuously more southern than the rest of the region, warmer and wetter, with regular avian residents and visitors that are rare to accidental farther north. The remaining undeveloped land east of the Elizabeth River is similar to the swampiest, marshiest stretches of Delmarva. To the west the Great Dismal Swamp, intersected by dykes along canals, is a vast and beautiful southern swamp of bald cypress, tupelo, and white cedar. The sandy farmland south of the James is largely devoted to peanut growing, but the feature of greatest ornithological importance is the broken loblolly pine forest in Sussex County that is home to most of Virginia's small population of Red-cockaded Woodpeckers.

CLIMATE

The Washington climate is both temperate and humid, a condition that makes for a green, lush environment, but one in which the cold is dank and penetrating and the heat sultry and oppressive. The range of temperature in any one year is typically 0°–100° F, except in the highlands, where it may drop to −30°. Near the coast and Chesapeake Bay the thermometer rises above 90° an average of twenty days a year; in the piedmont and the valleys and lower ridges around thirty-five days; and on the Allegheny plateau and the high western ridges ten days or less. In winter the coastal temperatures drop below freezing fifty days (south) to 100 days (north) a year; on the plateau about 160 days.

If the extremes are painful, the norm is tolerable: an average July day in Washington ranges from 69° to 87° and an average January day ranges from 29° to 44°. Spring and fall are usually long and pleasant, particularly April, May, October, and November, but temperatures can fluctuate sharply.

There are some 100 days a year with measurable precipitation, totaling 35–47 inches. Norfolk averages ten days with snow cover, Washington about twenty, Garrett County about seventy. Rain is more common in summer when thundery tropical air masses move in from the southwest; but one year in three the summer weather is dominated by "Bermuda highs," when a high-pressure system stays immobile just off the coast and severe drought afflicts the region, especially the coastal plain.

The humidity is almost always high, from a low average of 60–65 percent in late winter and early spring to a high average of 75–80 percent in late summer and early fall. At dawn on an August morning on the coast it can easily be higher than 95 percent.

Species to Look For **3**

The region treated in this book covers not only diverse geographical provinces but a substantial range of latitude and climate as well. The abundance of any one species may vary as much from east to west and south to north as it does from month to month, and any precision on arrival and departure dates would have to be based on a much smaller territory.

The species accounts that follow are based primarily on the Maryland and Virginia checklists and on bird lists of a dozen refuges and parks, including Bombay Hook. The Delaware checklist is still in preparation, and the North Carolina Outer Banks are too far south to share many of the patterns of the Delmarva coast. (The Outer Banks should not, as noted earlier, be considered within the National Capital Area but the focus of an extraterritorial expedition.)

These descriptions of the species that are found with some regularity in the region only suggest the likely provinces, habitats, and months in which to look for each of them. The recommended locations, except where a species is listed as locally common or uncommon, are by no means the only ones in which to look. A species listed for Loudoun County, for example, is as likely to be found in southern Frederick County or rural Montgomery County; birds found along the C&O Canal can be expected in parks across the Potomac River.

For species that are common and widespread on the coastal plain and in the piedmont, only a few sites close to Washington are mentioned; some birds are so universal that any neighborhood with appropriate habitat will do.

Most of the birds that are summer residents of the mountain counties are found at another season much closer to the nation's capital. Many Eastern Shore species have a vastly more restricted range, and some are virtually confined to the coast itself. Birds listed in "Delmarva refuges" are as likely to be in Blackwater as Chincoteague; birds in "coastal refuges" are much more reliable within a mile or so of Delaware Bay and the Atlantic Ocean. Marsh nesters are especially selective and are often absent from entire areas that look no different from the ones where they are reliably present.

The terms "common," "uncommon," and "rare" are necessarily vague, partly because of the size of the subregion to which any of them may be applied, partly because the published sources use the terms quite differently. In general, it pays to pick up a local bird list in any refuge or park that has one and to seek out the birders on the staff for exact information on particular species. (A pleasant new local phenomenon is the increasing number of naturalists, especially in county and regional parks, who are interested in and knowledgeable about birds.)

Eager listers may notice an absence of exotic species, including all Old World waterfowl except Eurasian Wigeon. Barnacle, Lesser White-fronted, and Egyptian Geese, Common and Ruddy Shelduck, Garganey Teal, and Tufted Ducks are among the many reported waterfowl that the keepers of the state checklists regard with cautious skepticism. In view of the numerous collectors and breeders of ornamental waterfowl in the area, such species are likely to remain "uncountable" indefinitely.

The Species (in the standard taxonomic sequence of *The A.O.U. Checklist of North American Birds,* 5th ed., 1957)

Common Loon Common from October to May, chiefly in coastal waters and Chesapeake Bay; also inland lakes and rivers in migration. A few oversummer. Cape Henlopen, Ocean City, Chincoteague.

Red-throated Loon Common from October to May in coastal waters and Chesapeake Bay. More common offshore, less common in sheltered waters than Common Loon. Cape Henlopen, Ocean City, Chincoteague.

Red-necked Grebe Rare from November to April, most often seen in March, in coastal waters, Chesapeake Bay, and tidal rivers. Chesapeake Bay Bridge-Tunnel, Baltimore Harbor, Potomac River from Wilson Bridge to Mount Vernon.

Horned Grebe Common, but perhaps decreasing, from October to May, chiefly in coastal waters and Chesapeake Bay. Cape Henlopen, Ocean City, Chincoteague, Craney Island.

Eared Grebe Very rare visitor, usually near coast. Craney Island, Chincoteague. Recorded from August to April.

Pied-billed Grebe Common from September to April, rare in summer, chiefly in sheltered fresh and brackish waters throughout region. Tidal Basin, Roaches Run, Georgetown Reservoir.

Northern Fulmar Rare and irregular well offshore, chiefly from December to March.

Cory's Shearwater Uncommon well offshore from May to October.

Greater Shearwater Uncommon in spring, rare in summer and fall, well offshore, chiefly in May and June. Occasionally seen from shore, especially after storms.

Sooty Shearwater Uncommon well offshore in late May and early June, rare through August. Occasionally seen from shore.

Manx Shearwater Rare well offshore, with sightings in all seasons.

Audubon's Shearwater Rare well offshore from June to August; more common off North Carolina.

Leach's Storm-Petrel Rare offshore from mid-May to mid-October.

Wilson's Storm-Petrel Common offshore from May to September.

Brown Pelican Rare in southeast Virginia from April to November; casual farther north; common on North Carolina coast.

Northern Gannet Common offshore from late October to April; abundant November, March, and April. Frequently seen from shore and Chesapeake Bay Bridge-Tunnel, occasionally in Chesapeake Bay during migration.

Great Cormorant Rare but increasing in recent years, from October to May. Usually on breakwaters and channel markers near coast.

Regular at Cape Henlopen, St. George Island, Chesapeake Bay Bridge-Tunnel. If not at St. George Island, try Point Lookout.

Double-crested Cormorant Abundant in migration, chiefly March-May and September-November, uncommon to rare throughout the year, mostly along the coast, especially in southeast Virginia. Shearness Pool at Bombay Hook, Ocean City Inlet, Chincoteague, Hunting Towers.

Anhinga Accidental on coastal plain, usually seen flying overhead. Recently resident at Stumpy Lake.

Great Blue Heron Common all year on coastal plain, uncommon elsewhere. Marshes, vegetated shores of ponds, lakes, streams. Typically solitary except near breeding colonies. Roaches Run, Pennyfield Lock, Myrtle Grove, Deal Island, all refuges.

Green Heron Common and widespread from mid-April to mid-October, rare in winter, in marshes and swampy woods. Kenilworth Aquatic Gardens, C&O Canal, Lake Frank, Dyke Marsh.

Little Blue Heron Common in summer along coast from April to October, uncommon to rare inland in spring and late summer. Marshes and impoundments. North Assateague, Chincoteague, Back Bay, Bombay Hook; Dyke Marsh, Hughes Hollow, Lilypons in late summer.

Cattle Egret Common on Delmarva from April to early October, especially with cows, horses, deer, and near breeding colonies at both ends of Assateague. Uncommon to rare elsewhere. Chincoteague and roads near coast.

Great Egret Common and widespread from April to October in Delmarva marshes, southeast Virginia refuges, and along lower Potomac; uncommon to rare in winter. Rare spring visitor inland, uncommon in late summer and fall. All coastal refuges, Baltimore Harbor, Miller's Island Road, Point Lookout.

Snowy Egret Abundant from April to September in Delmarva marshes, uncommon to rare in winter. Rare in spring and after breeding inland. All refuges on Delmarva and marshes along Western Shore of Chesapeake Bay.

Louisiana Heron Common to abundant from mid-April to mid-October along coast, uncommon to rare in winter. Uncommon in southern Maryland, rare inland. All coastal refuges, Point Lookout.

Black-crowned Night Heron Common from mid-April to early November near coast, locally common to rare all year all over coastal plain, rare elsewhere. Coastal refuges, Baltimore Harbor, National Zoo.

Yellow-crowned Night Heron Uncommon and local near coast, rare and local inland, from April to mid-October; rare in winter near southeast coast. Chincoteague, Hughes Hollow, Sycamore Landing

Road, Loudoun County along Potomac River and Maryland shore opposite.

Least Bittern Uncommon from May to September, in freshwater marshes on coastal plain; rare and local elsewhere. Dyke Marsh, Hughes Hollow, Lilypons, coastal refuges, Deal Island.

American Bittern Uncommon in migration, late March to late April and mid-September to late October, rare the rest of the year, in brackish and fresh marshes. Waterfowl sanctuary near Pennyfield Lock, Deal Island, coastal refuges.

Wood Stork Rare and irregular, mostly in summer, in southeast Virginia; casual vagrant in rest of region. Marshes, swampy lakes, impoundments.

Glossy Ibis Common to abundant along coast from late March to mid-September; uncommon to rare visitor inland, mainly mid-April to mid-May. Marshes and muddy fields. Coastal refuges.

White Ibis Rare and irregular postbreeding visitor, mostly in years of southern drought, on coastal plain and in piedmont; some spring records. Has recently bred in southeast Virginia. Most birds are immatures, in small groups or as singles with Glossy Ibis. More likely in coastal refuges, but has turned up at Summit Hall Turf Farm, on C&O Canal, in suburban creeks.

Mute Swan Locally common all year, mostly on Delmarva, in sheltered bays, ponds. Eastern Neck, Chincoteague, Assawoman refuges have well-established feral populations; single birds often escape from captivity.

Whistling Swan Common to abundant on Eastern and Western Shores, November to April; uncommon to rare migrant and winter visitor inland; rare in summer. Sheltered bays, rivers, ponds; cornfields. Eastern Neck, bays from St.Michaels to Cambridge (Maryland), West Ocean City Pond, Back Bay.

Canada Goose Abundant from late September to mid-April on coastal plain, locally common to rare elsewhere. Small, scattered breeding populations present all year (e.g., Dyke Marsh). Merkle Wildlife Management Area, all Delmarva refuges.

Brant Locally common along coast from late October to late April, around jetties, oyster beds, marsh banks, tidal flats. Cape Henlopen, Ocean City, Chincoteague.

Greater White-fronted Goose Rare winter visitor, found in flocks of wintering Canada Geese. Bombay Hook, Remington Farms, Blackwater.

Snow Goose Abundant from November to March in coastal refuges (white form), Blackwater (predominantly blue form). Marshes, sand and mud flats. Bombay Hook, Blackwater, Assateague, Back Bay.

Fulvous Whistling Duck Rare and irregular visitor at all times of year, generally near coast, most often in ponds and freshwater marshes.

Mallard Common to abundant in winter, rare to uncommon in summer throughout region. Population constantly being increased by released birds. Roaches Run, Lake Frank, marsh near Chain Bridge, duck ponds everywhere.

Black Duck As widespread and almost as common as Mallard all year, especially near coast. Dyke Marsh, Jug Bay, all refuges.

Gadwall Common from September to April on coastal plain, uncommon to rare in piedmont. Locally common in summer. Bombay Hook, Deal Island, Chincoteague, Back Bay.

Pintail Common from September to April, mainly near coast; often abundant in November and March. Bombay Hook, Chincoteague, Back Bay.

Green-winged Teal Common October to April on coastal plain, uncommon elsewhere. Rare on Delmarva in summer. Dyke Marsh, Hunting Creek, all refuges.

Blue-winged Teal Common from mid-March to April, September to late October on coastal plain, uncommon elsewhere. Uncommon and local or rare in summer, rare and irregular in winter. Pennyfield Lock, Lilypons, Deal Island, refuges.

Eurasian Wigeon Rare and irregular from October to April among flocks of American Wigeon, mostly on Delmarva. Coastal refuges, Remington Farms, Deal Island.

American Wigeon Common on coastal plain from mid-September to mid-May, uncommon elsewhere. All refuges; ponds, freshwater marshes.

Northern Shoveler Locally common near coast from mid-September to April, rare inland. Marshes, ponds. Bombay Hook, Blackwater, West Ocean City Pond, Chincoteague.

Wood Duck Common throughout region from March to mid-November, rare in winter. Ponds and swampy woods. C&O Canal, Lilypons, Mason Neck.

Redhead Uncommon on coastal plain from mid-October to April and in piedmont in migration, rare elsewhere. Sometimes in flocks of Canvasbacks in ponds, lakes, sheltered coves. Baltimore Harbor, Lake Anna, West Ocean City Pond, Silver Lake (Rehoboth).

Canvasback Locally common from November to April, mostly on coastal plain; uncommon in piedmont and as migrant in ridge and valley province. Sandy Point State Park, West Ocean City Pond, Silver Lake, Georgetown Reservoir.

Ring-necked Duck Common on coastal plain and in piedmont from mid-October to April; common elsewhere in migration, uncommon in winter. Rivers, lakes, and freshwater marshes. Great Falls, Lake Anna, Back Bay; Georgetown Reservoir in migration.

Greater Scaup Fairly common on coastal plain from mid-October to April, common in migration; rare elsewhere. Bays, coastal waters (often near jetties), rivers, lakes. Chesapeake Beach, Hooper Island, Ocean City Inlet, Chesapeake Bay Bridge-Tunnel.

Lesser Scaup Common on coastal plain from October to April; common elsewhere in migration, uncommon in winter. Ponds, rivers, lakes, and sheltered bays. Baltimore Harbor, Potomac near Wilson Bridge, Lake Anna.

Common Goldeneye Common from November to April on coastal plain, uncommon elsewhere. Bays, rivers. Sandy Point, Point Lookout, Eastern Neck, Ocean City, Chesapeake Bay Bridge-Tunnel.

Bufflehead Common to abundant from November to April; uncommon west of piedmont. Lakes, rivers, bays, ponds. Potomac River (try Fort Hunt to Mount Vernon), Chesapeake Beach, Bombay Hook, Point Lookout.

Oldsquaw Common from November to April along coast and in Chesapeake Bay, uncommon to rare elsewhere. Ocean City Inlet, Chesapeake Bay Bridge-Tunnel, Hooper Island, Point Lookout.

Harlequin Duck, Common Eider, King Eider All three rare and local from November to April at coastal jetties. Cape Henlopen, Indian River Inlet, Ocean City Inlet, Chesapeake Bay Bridge-Tunnel.

White-winged Scoter, Surf Scoter, Black Scoter Abundant in migration, common from mid-October to mid-April on coast and in Chesapeake Bay; rare elsewhere. Assateague, coastal jetties, Eastern Neck, Point Lookout.

Ruddy Duck Common on coastal plain, uncommon to rare elsewhere from October to April; rare in summer. Rivers, lakes, and impoundments. Potomac (at Four Mile Run and Hunting Creek), Bombay Hook, Chincoteague.

Hooded Merganser Fairly common to uncommon throughout region (except Allegheny plateau), November to April; rare in summer. Lakes, rivers, sheltered bays. Chincoteague, Stumpy Lake, Potomac River above Sycamore Landing, Elliott Island.

Common Merganser Fairly common but local from November to April on coastal plain and in piedmont. Rivers and lakes. Bombay Hook (Shearness Pool), Roaches Run, Potomac (Wilson Bridge, Little Falls, Sycamore Landing), Lake Anna.

Red-breasted Merganser Common November to April in salt water, uncommon to rare elsewhere, rare but regular in summer near coast.

Sinepuxent Bay, Assateague, Chesapeake Bay Bridge-Tunnel, Craney Island.

Turkey Vulture Common everywhere all year, except uncommon in mountains in winter and rare on coastal islands. Open country and upland deciduous woods. Georgetown Reservoir, National Zoo, Patuxent River Park.

Black Vulture Shares range with Turkey Vulture but less common; rare to absent in mountains. Georgetown Reservoir, National Zoo, Patuxent River Park.

Goshawk Rare throughout region from October to April, in conifers and woodland edge. See Chapter 35.

Sharp-skinned Hawk Present all year, but rare in summer, uncommon in winter. Mainly in deciduous woods and woodland edge. Common to abundant in migration. See Chapter 35.

Cooper's Hawk Uncommon all year through most of region, uncommon to rare winter visitor on coastal plain. Deciduous woods and woodland edge. See Chapter 35.

Red-tailed Hawk Common all year through most of region, from September to April on coastal plain, in open country, woodland edge, deciduous woods. See Chapter 35.

Red-shouldered Hawk Common all year on coastal plain (less so in northeast), uncommon all year in piedmont and in winter farther west (where rare in summer). Bottomland deciduous woods and edges. C&O Canal, Jug Bay, Myrtle Grove. See Chapter 35. Note: Immatures often mistaken for Broad-winged Hawks.

Broad-winged Hawk Uncommon in summer (rare on coastal plain), common spring migrant, in deciduous woods. Abundant fall migrant. See Chapter 35. Any sighting from November to March overwhelmingly unlikely.

Rough-legged Hawk Rare to uncommon, locally and irregularly, mostly in northern half of region, from December to March. Open country, both marshes and farmland. Bombay Hook, Elliott Island, Deal Island, Dulles Airport. See Chapter 35.

Golden Eagle Rare throughout region from mid-October to mid-April. Open country, lakes and rivers. Highland County, Virginia, Blackwater. See Chapter 35.

Bald Eagle Uncommon and local resident, mostly on coastal plain. Dyke Marsh, Pohick Bay, Blackwater, Bombay Hook. See Chapter 35.

Northern Harrier Common on Delmarva from mid-August to April, uncommon from May to mid-August; uncommon elsewhere from September to April, rare rest of year. Marshes and fields; all Delmarva refuges. See Chapter 35.

Osprey Common from April to September on coastal plain; elsewhere uncommon in migration, rare in summer. Coastal bays, Chesapeake Bay, lower Potomac, Assateague, Hooper Island, Point Lookout. See Chapter 35.

Peregrine Rare throughout region from mid-September to mid-May. Birds seen in summer (and some in winter) are likely to be products of the Peregrine release program conducted by Cornell University. See Chapter 35.

Merlin Rare from late October to early April very close to coast, even more so inland. Fairly common coastal migrant, April and from mid-September to late October. See Chapter 35.

American Kestrel Common throughout region, especially on coastal plain, from September to April, uncommon for rest of year in open country, mostly in cultivated farmland. See Chapter 35.

Ruffed Grouse Uncommon all year in mountains, northern Virginia piedmont and, very locally, on northern Virginia coastal plain. Deciduous and coniferous woodland and edge. Washington County, Highland County, Shenandoah National Park.

Common Bobwhite Common all year throughout region, less so at higher elevations. Open country with good cover; fallow fields and rough meadows, hedgerows and woodland edge. Rock Creek Regional Park, Riverbend Regional Park, Patuxent River Park.

Ring-necked Pheasant. Uncommon and local introduced species, most widespread in northern part of region, in open country with good cover. Bombay Hook, New Design Road, Lucketts, Indian Springs. Note: The Green Pheasant, a Japanese subspecies or sister species, appears to be established in southern Delmarva (Kiptopeke, Brownsville).

Turkey Uncommon and local all year from western coastal plain to Allegheny plateau. Deciduous woods and edges. Riverbend Regional Park, Hughes Hollow and Sycamore Landing Road, Washington County.

King Rail Uncommon to rare, local, and difficult to see, from April to September, in piedmont and on coastal plain. Fresh and brackish marshes. Hughes Hollow, Lilypons, Little Creek, Elliott and Deal islands. Winters in southeast: Back Bay, Pea Island.

Clapper Rail Common from mid-April to mid-October in salt marshes of coastal plain, uncommon to rare for rest of year. Bombay Hook, Assateague, Deal Island, Brownsville.

Virginia Rail Common to uncommon on coastal plain in summer, uncommon in winter; rare elsewhere. Fresh and brackish marshes. Gunpowder Falls State Park, Sandy Point, Elliott Island, Back Bay.

Sora Fairly common on coastal plain from mid-April to mid-May and from mid-August to mid-October, especially in September; rare for rest of year. Less common elsewhere. Fresh and brackish marshes. Miller's Island Road, Sandy Point, Jug Bay, all Delmarva marshes.

Yellow Rail Rare migrant on coastal plain from late March to May and late September to November. Fresh and salt marshes. No known sites where it occurs regularly.

Black Rail Uncommon to rare on coastal plain from late April to mid-October. Fresh and salt marshes. Elliott and Deal islands, Broadkill Marsh, Sandy Point, Miller's Island Road.

Purple Gallinule Rare and irregular summer visitor throughout region from April to August; has nested in all three states. Ponds and fresh marshes with abundant water lilies, spatterdock.

Common Gallinule Uncommon to rare on coastal plain and in piedmont from May to September, rare elsewhere and for rest of year. Fresh marshes; ponds with marshy patches. Bombay Hook, Deal Island, Back Bay.

American Coot Common migrant, uncommon winter visitor from October to early May, more common in southeast; rare in summer. Lakes, rivers, ponds, bays. Georgetown Reservoir, Lake Anna, Deal Island, Back Bay.

American Oystercatcher Common all year on Delmarva coast from Chincoteague south; uncommon to rare on Delaware and Maryland coast and in lower Chesapeake Bay from March to November. Oyster beds, tidal flats, beaches, salt marshes. Chincoteague, Ocean City (Sinepuxent Bay).

Black-necked Stilt Local and uncommon summer resident at Little Creek and Bombay Hook; rare visitor elsewhere near coast from late April to September. Fresh, brackish, and salt marshes. Delaware refuges, Chincoteague, Deal Island.

American Avocet Local and increasingly common near coast, rare elsewhere. Impoundments and salt marshes. Bombay Hook and Little Creek in April and May and from July to October; Chincoteague from August to October; Craney Island from August to February; uncommon to rare for rest of year.

Semipalmated Plover Abundant migrant near coast, uncommon elsewhere in April and May and from mid-July to October; uncommon to rare on coast for rest of year. Tidal flats, freshwater mud flats, beaches, oyster beds. All coastal refuges, Sandy Point.

Wilson's Plover Rare and local, but regular summer resident on coastal islands, from late April to early September. Tidal and sand flats (not ocean beach), often near marsh and dune vegetation. North and south ends of Assateague, Virginia Coast Reserve.

Killdeer Common throughout region all year, less common in winter except on coastal plain; more common in migration. Short-grass pasture and turf, plowed fields, mud flats at pond edges. Roaches Run, Summit Hall Turf Farm, Anacostia Naval Station, Claude Moore Center.

Piping Plover Uncommon and decreasing from mid-March to mid-October on coast and lower Chesapeake Bay, rare in winter; rare migrant on Western Shore and Potomac beaches. Ocean beaches, sand flats, tidal mud flats. Cape Henlopen, Assateague, Virginia coastal islands.

Lesser Golden Plover Rare spring migrant, mid-March to mid-May; rare to uncommon fall migrant, late August to early November, mostly on coastal plain. Fallow fields, mud flats, short-grass pasture and turf. Fields near Bombay Hook, Chincoteague, Summit Hall Turf Farm, Anacostia Naval Station, Kent County.

Black-bellied Plover Common from August to May near coast, uncommon to rare in June and July; uncommon to rare elsewhere in May, August, and September. Tidal flats, grass flats, ocean beaches. Coastal refuges, Cape Henlopen, Ocean City, Baltimore Harbor.

Hudsonian Godwit Rare to locally uncommon fall migrant on coastal plain, regular only at Chincoteague, mid-July to late October. Shallow fresh, brackish, and salt water, from impoundments to rain pools.

Marbled Godwit Rare in spring (May) and rare to locally uncommon in fall and winter, especially August and September. Shares habitat with Hudsonian Godwit. Thousand Acre Marsh, Bombay Hook, Little Creek, Chincoteague (regularly), Back Bay. Some winter in Virginia coastal marshes.

Whimbrel Common to abundant migrant near coast, rare elsewhere on coastal plain; mid-April to May, and July to late September; rare on coast in winter. Ocean beaches and salt marshes. North Assateague, Chincoteague, Virginia Coast Reserve.

Upland Sandpiper Locally uncommon to rare west of coastal plain from April to September; on coastal plain rare in spring, locally uncommon from mid-July to early September. Pastures and hay fields. New Design Road, Lucketts, Garrett County, Del. 9 at U.S. 113.

Greater Yellowlegs, Lesser Yellowlegs Common on coast from April to May and from mid-July to October, uncommon to rare for rest of year; uncommon inland in migration. Marshes, tidal flats, shallow ponds, impoundments. Delmarva refuges, Lilypons, Hunting Creek.

Solitary Sandpiper Fairly common migrant throughout region, less so on coast, from late April to late May, and from late July to mid-October. Pond edges, fresh marshes. Meadowside, Pennyfield Lock, Lilypons.

Willet Abundant summer resident of Delmarva marshes from April to September, rare for rest of year and elsewhere in migration. Salt marshes, ocean beaches, tidal flats. Little Creek, Assateague, Chincoteague, Elliott Island.

Spotted Sandpiper Common throughout region in migration, April-May and July-September, uncommon in summer. Lilypons, C&O Canal, Dyke Marsh, Kenilworth Aquatic Gardens.

Ruddy Turnstone Common to abundant on coast in May, August, September, common in southeast Virginia in winter, rare further north; rare inland in migration. Ocean beaches, jetties, tidal flats, muddy fields. Little Creek, Ocean City, Chincoteague, Locustville, Chesapeake Bay Bridge-Tunnel.

Wilson's Phalarope Nowhere common, but decreases in numbers from east to west. Rare in May and early June, rare to uncommon from late July to October. Fresh and brackish ponds and impoundments, salt marshes. Bombay Hook, Little Creek, Chincoteague, Back Bay, Craney Island.

Northern Phalarope Uncommon well offshore, locally uncommon on coast, rare inland, from May to early June and from August to mid-October. Open ocean, fresh and brackish ponds and impoundments. Bombay Hook and Little Creek.

Red Phalarope Uncommon to rare well offshore, very rare on land throughout region, early April to early May, September to October. Shares habitat with Northern Phalarope.

American Woodcock Uncommon all year, more common in winter on Virginia coast, less common in mountains; common in migration from mid-March to mid-April and from mid-October to mid-December. Clearings in or near bottomland woods. Hughes Hollow and vicinity, Meadowside, Claude Moore Center.

Common Snipe Fairly common in March-April and October-November, common to uncommon in winter on coastal plain, less common elsewhere, especially in highlands. Marshes and wet fields. Summit Hall Turf Farm, Sycamore Landing Road, Dyke Marsh, Blackwater, Chincoteague, Back Bay.

Short-billed Dowitcher Abundant on Delmarva from April to early June and from mid-July to October, uncommon to rare in early summer, rare in winter. Much less common inland on coastal plain, rare elsewhere. Salt and brackish marshes, tidal flats, shallow impoundments. All coastal refuges, Ocean City, north Assateague.

Long-billed Dowitcher Rare on coastal plain and in piedmont, April-May and July-November, most likely in late September and October. Fresh and brackish marshes, ponds, and impoundments, sometimes tidal flats. Delmarva refuges, perhaps Lilypons. (Probably more often reported than seen.)

Red Knot Locally common to abundant migrant on coast from May to early June and from late July to late September; rare for rest of year. Rare in migration elsewhere on coastal plain. Beaches, peat banks, tidal flats; sea walls and jetties, mainly in winter. Chincoteague, Virginia Coast Reserve, Ocean City and Indian River Inlets, Port Mahon.

Sanderling Abundant on coast in April and May and from late July to September, common in winter, uncommon in early summer; rare elsewhere. Coastal beaches and tidal and sand flats. Cape Henlopen, Assateague, Virginia Coast Reserve, Back Bay.

Semipalmated Sandpiper Abundant on coast from late April to early June and from mid-July to October, uncommon in early summer and inland. Mud flats, beaches; less likely to use tidal flats and beaches than fresh and brackish mud flats in fall migration. Coastal refuges, Sandy Point.

Western Sandpiper Rare in spring on coast, irregularly common in August, common to abundant in September-October, uncommon to rare in winter. Uncommon to rare elsewhere in fall migration. Tidal flats, beaches, fresh and brackish mud flats. Coastal refuges, especially Chincoteague.

Least Sandpiper Abundant near coast, uncommon elsewhere, late April to May and mid-July to October; uncommon to rare for rest of year on coast. Mud flats, grassy flats, muddy fields. Delmarva refuges, Summit Hall Turf Farm, Lilypons, Four Mile Run.

White-rumped Sandpiper Locally and irregularly common (spring) to uncommon (fall) on Eastern Shore, rare elsewhere, from May to early June and from August to early November. Muddy fields and flats. Assateague and nearby fields, Delmarva refuges, Elliott Island.

Baird's Sandpiper Very rare in spring, rare from mid-August to late October, mainly on coastal plain. Grass and mud flats, beaches. Coastal refuges, Summit Hall Turf Farm, Anacostia Naval Air Station.

Pectoral Sandpiper Common near coast, uncommon inland, from late March to May and from July to November. Grassy flats, marshes, muddy fields, wet pastures. Delmarva refuges, Lilypons, Summit Hall Turf Farm.

Purple Sandpiper Locally common from November to late May on coastal jetties; rare visitor to Western Shore jetties. Indian River and Ocean City Inlets, Chesapeake Bay Bridge-Tunnel; perhaps Sandy Point, Chesapeake Beach, and Point Lookout.

Dunlin Abundant on Delmarva from late September to late May, rare from July to mid-September; uncommon to rare inland. Tidal flats, marshes, muddy fields, beaches. Delmarva refuges, especially near coast.

Curlew Sandpiper Very rare (accidental in Maryland) on coast in May and from mid-July to October. Mud flats. Bombay Hook, Little Creek, Chincoteague, Craney Island.

Stilt Sandpiper Rare to locally uncommon in spring, uncommon to locally common in fall on Delmarva; rare inland. April-May and late July to late October. Coastal refuges, Craney Island.

Buff-breasted Sandpiper Rare to irregularly and locally uncommon, mostly near coast, from mid-August to mid-October. Grassy flats, pastures, and turf. Chincoteague, Summit Hall Turf Farm.

Ruff Rare, mostly near coast, from late March to mid-May and from July to mid-October. Mud flats, shallow impoundments, rain pools, marshes. Bombay Hook, Little Creek, Chincoteague. Often with yellowlegs.

Pomarine Jaeger Rare, usually well offshore, from late April to May and from September to December. Sometimes seen from Chesapeake Bay Bridge-Tunnel and from coastal beaches.

Parasitic Jaeger Uncommon to rare, usually well offshore, from late April to mid-June and from late August to December. Sometimes seen from Chesapeake Bay Bridge-Tunnel and from coastal beaches.

Great Skua Rare well offshore from December to May.

Glaucous Gull, Iceland Gull Rare from November to May, on coastal plain and offshore, usually among Herring Gulls. Beaches; sand and mud flats in lagoons, bays, impoundments, and rivers; landfills. Back River Sewage Treatment Plant, Sandy Point, Ocean City, Salisbury landfill, Hunting Towers.

Great Black-backed Gull Common year-round on coast (nests with Herring Gulls) and from September to April inland on coastal plain; rare in piedmont landfills. Roaches Run, Hunting Towers, Tidal Basin and East Potomac Park, Baltimore Harbor.

Lesser Black-backed Gull Rare but increasing on coastal plain and in eastern piedmont from September to April; some summer records. See gull listings above for habitats and sites.

Herring Gull Common to abundant year-round on coast and from mid-September to mid-May inland on coastal plain; locally common from mid-November to April in piedmont. See gull listings above for habitats and sites.

Ring-billed Gull Abundant on coastal plain, locally common to abundant in piedmont, uncommon elsewhere from mid-August to early May. Nonbreeders uncommon on coast in summer. The common urban gull in winter, seen in small city parks, shopping malls, flying around city and suburban streets. The Mall, East Potomac Park, Roaches Run, Montgomery County landfill, all other gull sites.

Black-headed Gull Rare visitor, November-May, usually with Bonaparte's or Ring-billed Gulls. Back River Sewage Treatment Plant, Indian River Inlet, Ocean City.

Laughing Gull Abundant near coast and in Chesapeake Bay, April-November, rare in winter mainly near mouth of Chesapeake Bay; common along rivers of coastal plain in late summer and fall. Nests in salt marshes near coast. Mud flats, beaches, marshes, pilings. Ocean City, Chincoteague, Sandy Point; in late summer, Back River Sewage Treatment Plant, Hunting Towers.

Franklin's Gull Very rare visitor, with records from May to November, most in May, August, September, usually with Laughing Gulls. Back River, Sandy Point, Hunting Towers.

Bonaparte's Gull Common in March and April, uncommon from mid-October to November on coastal plain; less common elsewhere. Irregularly common to uncommon in winter, mostly in southeast Virginia. Inlets, harbors, rivers. Back River, Indian River Inlet, Ocean City, Chesapeake Bay Bridge-Tunnel, Craney Island.

Little Gull Rare visitor to coastal plain, with records from August to early June, most from December to April. Usually with Bonaparte's Gulls, at sites listed above; sometimes common at Little Creek in April.

Black-legged Kittiwake Fairly common well offshore from late October to late March, rarely seen from land. Possible at Ocean City Inlet and Chesapeake Bay Bridge-Tunnel, especially in strong easterly winds.

Gull-billed Tern Summer resident on Delmarva coast from May to early September; uncommon in Delaware and Maryland, fairly common in Virginia, especially on uninhabited coastal islands. Rare on shores of Chesapeake Bay. Ocean beaches and marshes of coastal islands. Coastal refuges, especially Chincoteague; Virginia Coast Reserve.

Forster's Tern Common from April to November along coast and Chesapeake Bay, nesting on marsh islands; rare to irregularly common in winter in southeast Virginia. Fairly common in late summer and fall along rivers of coastal plain, rare elsewhere. Delmarva refuges and marshes; Hunting Towers, Miller's Island Road, Point Lookout.

Common Tern Common from April to October along coast and Chesapeake Bay, nesting on sand and marsh islands; uncommon on rest of coastal plain, April-May and late August-September, rare elsewhere. Most common within a mile of coast, throughout its length. Port Mahon, Ocean City, Chincoteague.

Roseate Tern Very rare along coast from April to September, with most records in May. Ocean beaches, Chesapeake Bay Bridge-Tunnel.

Least Tern Common from late April to late September, especially late July to early August, on coastal plain. Ocean, bay, rivers; nesting on beaches, sandbars, spoil piles, flat roof tops. Coastal refuges, Craney Island.

Royal Tern Common from late April to October on coast and Chesapeake Bay; rare in winter in extreme southeast. Nests on coastal islands; gathers in large flocks in late summer and fall; a few wander up tidal rivers in post-breeding period. Cape Henlopen, Chincoteague.

Sandwich Tern Uncommon late April to late September on Virginia coastal islands, rare north of Chincoteague. Sometimes in flocks of Royal Terns at Chincoteague, usually from late July to early September; Virginia Coast Reserve, Chesapeake Bay Bridge-Tunnel.

Caspian Tern Uncommon to locally common, April-May and, especially, August-October; rare to locally uncommon in summer on coastal plain; rare migrant elsewhere. A rare nester on Virginia coastal islands. Chincoteague, Baltimore County (Miller's Island Road), Hunting Creek, Hog Island.

Black Tern Uncommon to rare in May, uncommon to locally common from July to September along coast; rare migrant inland. Marshes, rivers, bays, ocean. Chincoteague, Little Creek.

Black Skimmer Common from mid-April to mid-November along coast and lower Chesapeake Bay; uncommon to rare along rivers and upper bay mainly in late summer and fall; rare in winter in extreme southeast. Nests on coastal islands. Marshes, tidal flats, beaches. Chincoteague, Ocean City, Port Mahon, Sandy Point.

Razorbill Rare well offshore, even more rare along coast, from November to March.

Dovekie Rare offshore and along coast from mid-November to February.

Common Puffin Rare and irregular well offshore, accidental on coast, from January to March.

Rock Dove Common to abundant all year throughout region. City parks, farmyards, bridges.

Mourning Dove Common all year throughout region (except in highlands) in woodland edges, hedgerows, fields, gardens.

Common Ground Dove Very rare visitor, with records from late April to early November. Beaches and sand flats. Most sightings in southeast Virginia and Maryland's Western Shore.

Yellow-billed Cuckoo Common from late April to October throughout region in deciduous woods and woodland edges. C&O Canal,

Meadowside, Seneca Creek State Park, Mason Neck, Huntley Meadows.

Black-billed Cuckoo Uncommon in migration, from May to early June and mid-August to mid-October, throughout region; uncommon in mountains, rare in piedmont from June to mid-August. Deciduous woods and woodland edge. Garrett County parks, Washington County along C&O Canal, Highland County, Shenandoah National Park.

Barn Owl Uncommon all year, decreasing in abundance from east to west. Resident pair under Theodore Roosevelt Bridge across Potomac; also eastern Baltimore County, Bombay Hook. See Chapter 36.

Screech Owl Common throughout region all year. See Chapter 36.

Great Horned Owl Common throughout region all year. See Chapter 36.

Snowy Owl Rare and irregular throughout region from November to March. See Chapter 36.

Barred Owl Locally common throughout region all year. See Chapter 36.

Long-eared Owl Rare all year except on coastal plain, where present only from mid-November to mid-May. See Chapter 36.

Short-eared Owl Local and uncommon from late October to early April, rare in summer on coastal plain and in northern piedmont; rare from November to April farther west. See Chapter 36.

Saw-whet Owl Rare throughout region from mid-October to mid-March; rare and local in summer in Garrett County and Highland County. See Chapter 36.

Chuck-will's-widow Common on Delmarva, uncommon and local on Maryland Western Shore, from late April to mid-September. Pine woods. Assawoman, road to Ocean City Airport, Elliott Island Road, Chincoteague.

Whip-poor-will Common to uncommon throughout region from April to September. Hedgerows and woodlots. Mason Neck, Loudoun County around Dulles Airport, Blairs Valley, Blackwater, road to Ocean City Airport.

Common Nighthawk Locally common throughout region from May to September; abundant from mid-August to early September. Nests on flat city roof tops, migrates in flocks. District of Columbia and suburban centers; Potomac River in May; Bull Run Regional Park (Fairfax County, Virginia) in late August.

Chimney Swift Common throughout region from mid-April to mid-October. In August and September gathers in huge flocks to roost in chimneys and hollow trees. Urban and suburban skies. Recent roost chimneys: Arlington Hospital, 1701 North George Mason Drive, Arlington; and Metro Bus Terminal at Wisconsin Avenue and Jennifer Street, NW, Washington.

Ruby-throated Hummingbird Fairly common throughout region from late April to September. Bottomland deciduous woods, gardens, flowering hedgerows and edges. Mason Neck, Mattaponi Creek, C&O Canal, Blackwater.

Belted Kingfisher Uncommon to common all year throughout region, most common in piedmont. Ponds, creeks, rivers, lakes. C&O Canal, Lilypons, Algonkian Regional Park (Sugarland Run).

Common Flicker Common all year throughout region, especially near coast in fall and winter. Deciduous bottomland woods, woodland edge, open country. C&O Canal, nearby Virginia parks.

Pileated Woodpecker Uncommon to locally common throughout region all year. Deciduous woods and pine stands. Glover-Archbold Park, C&O Canal, Great Falls Park (Virginia), Jug Bay, Meadowside.

Red-bellied Woodpecker Common all year throughout region except in highlands. Deciduous woods and woodland edge. C&O Canal, Hughes Hollow, Seneca Creek, Glencarlyn, Huntley Meadows, Oxon Hill, other local parks.

Red-headed Woodpecker Uncommon and local throughout region all year in deciduous woods. Hughes Hollow, Sycamore Landing Road, C&O Canal, Mason Neck, Myrtle Grove, Paul Friend Road in Garrett County.

Yellow-bellied Sapsucker Fairly common throughout region in April and October, uncommon in winter; rare in summer in Garrett County and western Highland County. Deciduous woods, woodland edge, pine woods, boreal bogs. C&O Canal, Great Falls Park (Virginia), other local parks.

Hairy Woodpecker Uncommon throughout region all year in deciduous woods. C&O Canal, Great Falls Park (Virginia), Jug Bay, other riverside parks.

Downy Woodpecker Common throughout region all year in deciduous woods, woodland edge, hedgerows. All local parks.

Red-cockaded Woodpecker Rare and local all year in southern Virginia; accidental in Maryland. See Chapter 32.

Eastern Kingbird Common throughout region from late April to September. Woodland edge, hedgerows, open country. Claude Moore Center, Meadowside, Seneca Creek State Park, Hughes Hollow, Huntley Meadows.

Western Kingbird Rare in fall, mostly in September and October, very close to coast. A few inland records; sightings as late as January, one or two in May. Bushes, hedgerows, telephone wires in open country and along dune lines.

Great Crested Flycatcher Common throughout region from late April to September. Deciduous woods, pines, woodland edge. Seneca Creek State Park, Sycamore Landing Road, Meadowside, Riverbend, Dranesville Park, Jug Bay.

Eastern Phoebe Common throughout region from March to October, uncommon in winter except in highlands. Cliff faces by streams, small bridges, eaves and rafters. Glencarlyn, C&O Canal west of Pennyfield Lock, Meadowside.

Yellow-bellied Flycatcher Rare throughout region from early May to early June and from late August to early October, somewhat more likely in upland deciduous woods, conifers, and swamps. Nests on Mount Rogers in far southwest Virginia.

Acadian Flycatcher Common from late April to mid-September throughout region, generally below 3,500 feet. Deciduous woods, often near streams. C&O Canal, Riverbend, Jug Bay, Mason Neck.

Willow Flycatcher Uncommon and local west of Chesapeake Bay from early May to early October. Nests in open marshes and bogs with scattered willows and alders. Hughes Hollow, Dyke Marsh, Blairs Valley, Cranesville Swamp, Big Meadows.

Alder Flycatcher Rare and local nester in western highlands. Arrival and departure dates and abundance of migrants not separated from those of Willow Flycatcher. Nests in alders in boreal bogs usually broken up by young conifers. Cranesville Swamp, Herrington Manor; perhaps western Highland County.

Least Flycatcher Rare to uncommon throughout region in migration from late April to late May and from late August to late September; uncommon in summer, generally above 2,500 feet. Typically nests in open deciduous woods. Swallow Falls, Locust Spring, Shenandoah National Park.

Eastern Wood Pewee Common throughout region from late April to late October. Deciduous woods and woodland edge. Rock Creek, C&O Canal, Claude Moore Center, Huntley Meadows, Jug Bay.

Olive-sided Flycatcher Rare throughout region, and in decreasing numbers from west to east, in May and early June and from mid-August to early October. Woodland edges near ponds and swamps, tall snags. Indian Springs, Summit Hall Turf Farm.

Horned Lark Common all year on coastal plain and in piedmont, uncommon elsewhere. Bare fields; grass and sand flats among coastal dunes. New Design Road, Lucketts, Chincoteague, Cape Henlopen.

Tree Swallow Common to abundant in migration, from April to early May and from late August to October; locally common to rare in summer (from east to west). Ponds, marshes. Hughes Hollow, Lilypons, Blairs Valley, Chincoteague.

Bank Swallow Common in migration on coastal plain from mid-April to mid-May and from mid-July to early September; uncommon elsewhere; locally common at breeding colonies. Sand banks near water. Lilypons, Mason Neck, Jug Bay, Bombay Hook.

Rough-winged Swallow Fairly common throughout region from late March to early September. Sandy banks, culverts, bridges. Riley's Lock (mouth of Seneca Creek), Lilypons, Mason Neck, Blackwater.

Barn Swallow Common throughout region, abundant on coastal plain, from April to September. Barns, bridges, house eaves. Riley's Lock, Claude Moore Center, Meadowside, Jug Bay.

Cliff Swallow Rare in migration on coastal plain from late April to late May and from early July to late September; elsewhere locally common from late April to early September. Barns, bridges, dams. Brighton and Rocky Gorge Dams on Patuxent River, Blairs Valley.

Purple Martin Locally common throughout region from late March to September. Martin houses are deserted for huge communal roosts in August. Claude Moore Center, Hughes Hollow, Meadowside, Bombay Hook, Chincoteague.

Blue Jay Common all year throughout region, becoming abundant during migration in late April and May and in October. Hard to avoid except in entirely treeless areas.

Northern Raven Local and uncommon all year around Appalachian ridges. Point of Rocks (where U.S. 15 crosses the Potomac); Shenandoah National Park; Highland, Washington, and Garrett counties; Dan's Rock.

Common Crow Common all year throughout region, including all of metropolitan Washington, abundant from late November to late March.

Fish Crow Uncommon to common inland, common to abundant along coast. Nests around Washington Cathedral and Georgetown University. Not separable from Common Crow by location or habitat. Often raids nesting colonies of water birds, as at Cape Henlopen, Chincoteague, on coastal islands.

Black-capped Chickadee Common all year west of Blairs Valley in Maryland and Shenandoah Valley in Virginia, increasingly uncommon on ridges to the east. Rare and irregular winter visitor in northern piedmont and on northwest coastal plain except in major invasion years. Black-capped x Carolina Chickadee hybrids occur throughout ridge-and-valley province. Deciduous woods, conifers, woodland edge. Shenandoah National Park; Highland, Washington, and Garrett counties.

Carolina Chickadee Common all year throughout region from Blairs Valley and Shenandoah Valley east, uncommon to rare in rest of ridge-and-valley province. Deciduous woods and woodland edge, pines. Glover-Archbold Park, Glencarlyn, Oxon Hill Children's Farm, and any other local wooded park.

Tufted Titmouse Common all year in most of region; rare on coastal islands, uncommon to rare in western highlands. Deciduous woods, woodland edge. All local wooded parks.

White-breasted Nuthatch Uncommon all year on coastal plain, more uncommon near coast, and on Allegheny plateau; common elsewhere. Large trees in deciduous woods. Mount Vernon, Dranesville Park, Glover-Archbold Park, Meadowside, Jug Bay.

Red-breasted Nuthatch Irregularly rare to common throughout region from September to early May, and in mountains all summer. Conifers. Gude's Nursery, National Arboretum, Sandy Point.

Brown-headed Nuthatch Locally common all year on Delmarva and in Southside Virginia in loblolly pines. Assawoman, Blackwater, Chincoteague, Seashore State Park, Hog Island.

Brown Creeper Common in April and October, uncommon to common in winter throughout region, more common in piedmont; rare to uncommon in summer, mostly in highlands. Deciduous woods, especially bottomland woods. C&O Canal, Riverbend (winter), Washington County (summer).

House Wren Locally common throughout region from mid-April to October; rare on coastal plain and in piedmont in winter. Thickets, hedgerows, garden shrubbery, bottomland woods. Sycamore Landing, Claude Moore Center, Meadowside.

Winter Wren Uncommon throughout region from October to April; local and uncommon in highlands in summer. Brush piles, fallen logs, tangles in deciduous woods (winter), coniferous woods, swamps and streamsides (summer). Great Falls Park (Virginia), Blackwater, Bombay Hook (winter), Highland County, Shenandoah National Park, Cranesville Swamp (summer).

Bewick's Wren Rare and rapidly disappearing, in highlands from April to early October. Very few recent winter records, most from southeast and mountains. Thickets, brush piles, abandoned buildings near clearings. Hanging Rock Road (western Washington County), Dan's Rock, Shenandoah National Park.

Carolina Wren Common all year, in decreasing numbers from east to west, throughout region. Bottomland woods, brush piles and tangles near wooded swamps and streams. Dyke Marsh, C&O Canal, Riverbend, Jug Bay.

Marsh Wren (Long-billed Marsh Wren) Locally common on

coastal plain and in piedmont from mid-April to mid-October; uncommon to rare in winter, mostly on Delmarva. Salt and fresh marshes, in fairly extensive patches of tall coarse grass. Hughes Hollow, Lilypons, Dyke Marsh, Jug Bay, Elliott Island, Bombay Hook.

Sedge Wren (Short-billed Marsh Wren) Rare to uncommon and local on Delmarva from May to mid-September, more widespread in southeast marshes in winter. Rare at any time west of Chesapeake Bay. Broom sedge marshes with scattered marsh elder bushes; damp grassy meadows. Elliott and Deal islands; sometimes Port Mahon, Broadkill Marsh, Saxis, and Point Lookout.

Northern Mockingbird Common all year throughout region except in highlands. Residential city and suburban streets, gardens, hedgerows. Metropolitan Washington, Oxon Hill Children's Farm, National Park Service Nursery, Claude Moore Center, Meadowside, National Arboretum.

Gray Catbird Common throughout region from late April to early October; rare in winter to uncommon on coastal plain. Hedgerows and gardens, bottomland woods and woodland edge. Hughes Hollow, Seneca Creek, Jug Bay, Huntley Meadows.

Brown Thrasher Common throughout region from April to mid-October; rare in winter, rare to uncommon on coastal plain. Hedgerows, tangles, and thickets in outer suburbs, open country. Meadowside, Hughes Hollow, Claude Moore Center.

American Robin Abundant in migration; common all year on coastal plain (except in north) and in summer farther west; uncommon in winter on northern coastal plain and in piedmont, irregular elsewhere. Gardens, woodland edge, open woods, lawns and fields. Suburban Washington and all local parks; in winter, Gude's Nursery, Jug Bay.

Wood Thrush Common throughout region from late April to mid-October. Near forest floor in damp deciduous woods. Potomac Overlook and Dranesville Parks, C&O Canal, Meadowside, Jug Bay, and all wooded local parks.

Hermit Thrush Common throughout region in migration, in April and from October to early November; fairly common in winter on coastal plain and in piedmont, uncommon to rare farther west. Conifers and deciduous woodland. Rare in summer at Locust Spring in Highland County, and at Herrington Manor and Swallow Falls in Garrett County.

Swainson's Thrush Common throughout region in migration in May, September, and October. Woodland, especially along coasts, rivers, ridges. Mason Neck, Potomac Overlook, C&O Canal, Jug Bay, and all wooded local parks.

Gray-cheeked Thrush Uncommon throughout region in migration in May, September, October. Habitats and sites as for Swainson's Thrush, but much less common.

Veery Common in highlands in migration, from late April to late May and from late August to September, uncommon farther east; locally common in summer in Washington, D.C., and in the mountains. Deciduous woods near streams, conifers, bogs. Battery Kemble, Glover-Archbold, and Rock Creek Parks, Shenandoah National Park, Garrett County.

Eastern Bluebird Uncommon to locally common throughout region all year. Pastures, fields, woodland edges and clearings. Hughes Hollow, Claude Moore Center, Algonkian Park, Merkle.

Blue-gray Gnatcatcher Common throughout region from the end of March to late September; rare in winter in southeast. Open deciduous woods. C&O Canal, Mason Neck, Jug Bay.

Golden-crowned Kinglet Common in migration throughout region; common to uncommon in winter on coastal plain and in piedmont, uncommon farther west, from early October to mid-April. Rare and local in summer in highlands. Conifers and boreal bogs in summer; conifers and deciduous woods and thickets in migration and winter. Locust Spring, Cranesville Swamp (summer), Gude's Nursery, National Arboretum, Sandy Point, Blackwater, Chincoteague (winter), riverside parks.

Ruby-crowned Kinglet Common throughout region in migration from late March to early May and from late September to November, less common in winter than Golden-crowned Kinglet except in southeast Virginia. Thickets, bottomland woods, pines. Meadowside, Potomac Overlook, Claude Moore Center, riverside parks.

Water Pipit Common on coastal plain, especially in southeast, from October to April; uncommon and irregular in rest of region, chiefly in migration from mid-March to April and from October to early November. Plowed and harvested fields, mud flats. Fields near Point Lookout, Kiptopeke (winter), New Design Road (migration).

Cedar Waxwing Common but irregular all year west of piedmont, and from late August to May in piedmont and on coastal plain, where rare in summer. Woodland edge, clearings, hedgerows, gardens and orchards, wherever there are small fruits and berries. Gude's Nursery, National Arboretum (the cherry grove), Indian Springs.

Northern Shrike Very rare throughout region, with records from late October to early March. Woodland edge, hedgerows by fields, marshes.

Loggerhead Shrike Uncommon and decreasing, throughout region all year. Open country, with hedgerows, woodland edge. Sharpsburg and vicinity; northern Loudoun County; in winter, fields near Bombay Hook.

European Starling Abundant throughout region all year.

White-eyed Vireo Common on coastal plain and in piedmont from mid-April to mid-October; uncommon to locally common farther west, mostly in lowlands. Thickets and tangles on woodland edge, hedgerows. Seneca Creek, Meadowside, Hughes Hollow, Claude Moore Center, Jug Bay.

Yellow-throated Vireo Common in piedmont, uncommon to locally common elsewhere from mid-April to mid-October. Crowns of tall deciduous trees beside streams, roads, woodland edge. Violet's Lock, Riley's Lock, Algonkian Park, Great Falls Park (Virginia).

Solitary Vireo Uncommon on coastal plain and in piedmont in migration, from early April to early May and from late September to October; common in highlands from early April to October. In conifers and mixed woods (summer); deciduous and mixed woods (migration). Shenandoah National Park; Highland, Washington, and Garrett counties; riverside parks in migration.

Red-eyed Vireo Abundant throughout region from mid-April to October. Deciduous woods. All wooded local parks.

Philadelphia Vireo Rare throughout region in May, a little more common in September. Woodland edge, along streams, fields, roads, clearings. C&O Canal, Shenandoah National Park, Kiptopeke (fall).

Warbling Vireo Uncommon to locally common in piedmont and in lowlands farther west from late April to September, rare transient elsewhere. Mature deciduous trees overhanging water. C&O Canal, especially from Violet's Lock to Sycamore Landing and in Washington County.

Black-and-White Warbler Common throughout region from early April to mid-October, less common in summer in the south; some winter records. Deciduous and mixed woods. Mason Neck, Great Falls Park (Virginia), Shenandoah National Park, Pocomoke Swamp, all local parks in migration.

Prothonotary Warbler Locally common on coastal plain and in piedmont from mid-April to mid-September, rare elsewhere. Bottomland woods and swamps. C&O Canal, especially from Fletcher's Boat House to Carderock; Myrtle Grove, Pocomoke Swamp, Dismal Swamp.

Swainson's Warbler Locally common in Southside Virginia; rare and local on Delmarva, mid-April to early September; rare visitor elsewhere. Canebrakes and catbriar tangles in cypress swamps and pine woods; swampy understory in bottomland woods, rhododendron thickets. Dismal Swamp, Pocomoke Swamp and Pocomoke State Forest.

Worm-eating Warbler Rare on southeast coastal plain, uncommon north and west and in piedmont, common on slopes of western ridges, from late April to late September. Hillsides in deciduous woods with scattered rhododendrons, often above swamps and streams. Pocomoke Swamp, Dismal Swamp, Great Falls Park (Virginia), Mason Neck, Shenandoah National Park, Highland and Washington counties.

Golden-winged Warbler Uncommon to rare on coastal plain and in piedmont from end of April to mid-May and from mid-August to mid-September; uncommon and local in western mountains from late April to mid-September. Woodland edge by overgrown fields, clearings, streams. Highland, Washington, and Garrett counties, Dan's Rock; in migration, any local park, especially C&O Canal.

Blue-winged Warbler Uncommon to rare on coastal plain and in piedmont from late April to early May and from late August to mid-September. Local and uncommon in ridge-and-valley province from late April to mid-September. Overgrown clearings and fields with young trees, woodland edge. Along back roads off Md. 77 near Foxville in Frederick County; in migration, C&O Canal, Algonkian Park.

Golden-winged x Blue-winged Warbler Hybrids Rare; "Brewster's" type much more often seen than "Lawrence's" type. Sometimes near Foxville (see above); occasionally near Potomac in migration.

Tennessee Warbler Rare on coastal plain, rare to uncommon in piedmont, uncommon in mountains in May; somewhat more common in each province from the end of August to mid-October. Deciduous woods and woodland edge. Riverside parks, Shenandoah National Park.

Orange-crowned Warbler Rare throughout region in May and October; a few winter on Delmarva. Thickets, hedgerows, woodland edge.

Nashville Warbler Rare on coastal plain, rare to uncommon in piedmont, uncommon in mountains in first half of May and from early September to mid-October. Rare and local in summer in Highland and Garrett counties. Boreal bogs, woodland edge and scrub. Locust Spring, Cranesville Swamp (summer), local parks.

Northern Parula Warbler Common throughout region from mid-April to mid-October. Bottomland woods, close to water. C&O Canal, Great Falls Park (Virginia), Riverbend, Mason Neck, Jug Bay, Pocomoke Swamp, Dismal Swamp.

Yellow Warbler Common on Delmarva, uncommon to common in rest of region, increasing in numbers from east to west, from mid-April to mid-September; most common in first half of May. Hedgerows, thickets, willows and alders, near water, marshes, and wet meadows. Hughes Hollow, Lilypons, Blairs Valley, all Delmarva refuges.

Magnolia Warbler Uncommon on coastal plain and in piedmont, common farther west from end of April to late May and from late August to mid-October; common in western highlands in summer. Conifers near water in summer; deciduous and mixed woods in migration. Locust Spring, Herrington Manor, Swallow Falls (summer), riverside parks.

Cape May Warbler Uncommon on coastal plain and in piedmont and common farther west from the end of April to late May; common throughout region from September to mid-October. Conifers and deciduous trees along woodland edge and in open forest. Local parks.

Black-throated Blue Warbler Common throughout region from late April to late May and from September to mid-October. Common in western highlands in summer. Mixed woodlands with dense understory; also woodland edge and hedgerows in migration. Shenandoah National Park, Locust Spring, Herrington Manor, Swallow Falls, local parks.

Yellow-rumped Warbler Common throughout region in migration, abundant in winter on Delmarva, uncommon elsewhere, October to mid-May. Thickets of wax myrtle, red cedar, poison ivy in winter; woodland edge and hedgerows in migration. All Delmarva refuges, local parks.

Black-throated Green Warbler Uncommon on coastal plain, common elsewhere from mid-April to mid-May and from September to mid-October. Locally common nester in Dismal Swamp from end of March to early July and in mountains from mid-April to October. Shenandoah National Park, Ramsey's Draft, Highland County, Garrett County parks, riverside parks.

Cerulean Warbler Rare and local on coastal plain, locally common elsewhere from late April to early September. Open deciduous woods with tall trees near streams; woodland edge. C&O Canal, Great Falls Park (Virginia), Shenandoah National Park, Highland and Washington counties, Dan's Mountain State Park.

Blackburnian Warbler Rare on coastal plain, uncommon farther west in first three weeks of May and from late August to mid-October; uncommon in summer in western highlands. Mixed woodland with tall trees. Shenandoah National Park, Locust Spring, western Washington County, Garrett County, C&O Canal, Great Falls Park (Virginia).

Yellow-throated Warbler Common on coastal plain, locally common to uncommon in piedmont, locally uncommon to rare in western lowlands. Deciduous bottomland woods with tall sycamores, cypress, mature pines. C&O Canal, especially west of Riley's Lock, Myrtle Grove, Jug Bay, Pocomoke Swamp, Dismal Swamp.

Chestnut-sided Warbler Uncommon to rare on coastal plain, common farther west from end of April to late May and from late August to late September; common in western highlands in summer. Woodland edge. Shenandoah National Park, Highland and Garrett counties, riverside parks.

Bay-breasted Warbler Rare to uncommon on coastal plain, uncommon elsewhere from early to late May; somewhat more common from end of August to mid-October. Deciduous woods and woodland edge. Parks in Fairfax, Loudoun, and Montgomery counties.

Blackpoll Warbler Common throughout region from May to early June, somewhat less common from mid-September to late October; a few summer records. Deciduous woods, woodland edge. Local parks.

Pine Warbler Abundant on coastal plain, common in piedmont, locally common to rare farther west from early March to late October. Uncommon to rare in southeast, rare and irregular elsewhere in winter. Pine woods and woodland edge. Huntley Meadows, National Arboretum, Seneca Creek State Park, Sandy Point.

Prairie Warbler Common throughout region except in highlands, from mid-April to late September; a few sometimes linger into December. Overgrown fields with scattered junipers, hedgerows, woodland edge. Jug Bay, Claude Moore Center, Huntley Meadows, Seneca Creek State Park.

Palm Warbler Uncommon throughout region from early April to early May and west of coastal plain from early September to October. Common to abundant on coastal plain, mainly close to coast, from mid-September to October, sometimes much later in southeast Virginia. Rare throughout region in winter. Woodland edge and scrub near water, muddy fields, grassy flats, dunes. Riverside parks, coastal refuges.

Ovenbird Common throughout region from mid-April to mid-October, abundant in migration. Upland deciduous woods and pines, on forest floor. Dranesville Park, Great Falls Park (Virginia), C&O Canal, Jug Bay, Sugarloaf Mountain.

Northern Waterthrush Uncommon throughout region from late April to late May and from early August to early October; nests in Garrett County. Woodland swamps, bogs, streams. Swallow Falls, Cranesville Swamp, riverside parks, Meadowside, Mason Neck.

Louisiana Waterthrush Common throughout region from end of March to late September. Bottomland forest streams. C&O Canal, Great Falls Park (Virginia), Jug Bay, Myrtle Grove, Pocomoke Swamp.

Kentucky Warbler Common on coastal plain, locally common in piedmont, uncommon farther west, from end of April to early September. Moist bottomland forest with dense understory. Great Falls Park (Virginia), C&O Canal, Jug Bay, Mason Neck, Myrtle Grove, Pocomoke Swamp.

Connecticut Warbler Very rare throughout region in May, rare from September to mid-October. Damp woodlands and woodland edge in brush, tangles; tall weeds.

Mourning Warbler Rare throughout region from early May to early June and from September to late October; rare in summer in western highlands. Dense brush and briar tangles by roadsides, bogs, woodland edge. Locust Spring, Backbone Mountain in Garrett County, perhaps Dan's Rock in Allegany County, Washington County (in migration).

Common Yellowthroat Abundant on coastal plain, common elsewhere mid-April to late October, rare in winter. Thickets, tangles, and cattail stands in and around marshes, wet meadows. Hughes Hollow, Dyke Marsh, Jug Bay, Meadowside, Kenilworth Aquatic Gardens.

Yellow-breasted Chat Common throughout region except southeast, where uncommon, from late April to late October. Rare on coastal plain and very rare in piedmont in winter. Hedgerows and tangles in cutover forest, abandoned fields, overgrown pastures. Hughes Hollow, Seneca Creek State Park, Meadowside, Claude Moore Center, Washington County, Jug Bay.

Hooded Warbler Common throughout region except in highlands, from late April to mid-September. Swampy bottomland woods; in mountains, forested slopes, usually near streams. Great Falls Park (Virginia), Myrtle Grove, Jug Bay, Pocomoke Swamp, Dismal Swamp.

Wilson's Warbler Rare on coastal plain and in southern piedmont, uncommon elsewhere from early to late May and from late August to late September. Hedgerows and thickets near streams and wet meadows. Hughes Hollow, Lilypons, Washington County.

Canada Warbler Rare on coastal plain, uncommon to common in piedmont, and common farther west, from early to late May and from mid-August to late September; common in highlands in summer. Woodland stream and swamp edges in summer; clearings and thickets in migration. Shenandoah National Park, Locust Spring, Swallow Falls, Meadowside, Great Falls Park (Virginia), other riverside parks.

American Redstart Common throughout region from late April to early October, though local in west. Open deciduous woods with second-growth trees or well-grown understory, especially in swampy areas. C&O Canal, Potomac Overlook, Claude Moore Center, Jug Bay, Mason Neck.

House Sparrow Common throughout region all year, near people.

Bobolink Common throughout region from early to late May and from late August to late September; locally common in Highland and Garrett counties in summer. Fields of alfalfa, clover, and hay in spring and summer, reed marshes in fall. Highland County south of Bluegrass, Garrett County south of Oakland, alfalfa fields near Lucketts, New Design Road, western Montgomery County in spring, Bombay Hook and Little Creek in fall.

Eastern Meadowlark Common throughout region all year in meadows, fields, and pastures. More likely along country roads than in refuges and parks. Claude Moore Center, Lucketts, New Design Road.

Yellow-headed Blackbird Rare and irregular, mostly on Delmarva, from September to April. Harvested fields, pastures, and marshes; usually a single bird in huge flocks of Red-winged Blackbirds, grackles, and cowbirds.

Red-winged Blackbird Common throughout region all year; abundant on coastal plain, irregular elsewhere in winter. Fresh and brackish marshes, fields, pastures, salt marshes, woodlots. Dyke Marsh, Hughes Hollow, Lilypons, Delmarva.

Orchard Oriole Common on coastal plain and in piedmont, common to uncommon in lowlands farther west, from May to August. Scattered shade trees in open country, orchards, farmyards. Claude Moore Center, Seneca Creek State Park, Meadowside, Huntley Meadows, Pennyfield Lock, Riley's Lock, Lilypons, Gunpowder Falls State Park.

Northern (Baltimore) Oriole Common in northern piedmont and lowlands farther west from late April to September; uncommon on coastal plain, common in southern piedmont from late April to late May, common throughout from mid-August to September. Uncommon to rare in winter, often at feeders. Woodland edge, shade trees in open country and near houses, often near water. Fletcher's Boat House, C&O Canal, Meadowside, Algonkian Park, Jug Bay, Lilypons.

Rusty Blackbird Uncommon throughout region from mid-October to late April, somewhat more common before mid-November and after mid-March. Swampy woods. Dyke Marsh, Seneca Marsh (above Riley's Lock), Hughes Hollow, Sycamore Landing Road.

Brewer's Blackbird Rare throughout region from October to April; most records from coastal plain and western Virginia valleys. In harvested fields, farmyards, pastures, usually in flocks with other blackbirds. Bombay Hook and vicinity, Highland County.

Boat-tailed Grackle Common all year on Virginia coast and, locally, in lower Chesapeake Bay. Common in summer but less common in winter on Maryland and Delaware coast. Small breeding colony at Point Lookout. Salt marshes. Coastal refuges, Assateague, Virginia Coast Reserve, Point Lookout.

Common Grackle Common throughout region except in mountains, abundant in winter on coastal plain, irregularly abundant elsewhere. Fields, swampy woods, conifers. All local parks and farmland.

Brown-headed Cowbird Common throughout region all year. Woodland edge, woods, harvested fields. All local parks and farmland.

Western Tanager Very rare, with most records from coastal plain, from October to May.

Scarlet Tanager Common throughout region from late April to early October, in deciduous woods. C&O Canal, Great Falls Park (Virginia), Riverbend, Jug Bay, Lilypons, Sugarloaf Mountain.

Summer Tanager Fairly common on southern coastal plain and in southern piedmont, uncommon and local elsewhere, from late April to late September. Open mixed woodland of pine, oak, and hickory. Great Falls Park (Virginia), Jug Bay, Sugarloaf Mountain, Blackwater, Elliott Island Road, Pocomoke Swamp. (Much more likely at Delmarva sites.)

Northern Cardinal Common to abundant throughout region all year. Urban and suburban residential areas, bottomland deciduous woods, woodland edge, hedgerows. Metropolitan Washington, local parks.

Rose-breasted Grosbeak Rare to uncommon on coastal plain; uncommon in piedmont, uncommon to common farther west, from late April to late May, and from late August to late October. Locally common in highlands in summer. Woodland edge with large deciduous trees and tall shrubs. Shenandoah National Park, Highland County, Garrett County parks, C&O Canal, Great Falls Park (Virginia).

Black-headed Grosbeak Very rare visitor throughout region with records from October to May, most of them at feeders.

Blue Grosbeak Fairly common on coastal plain and in piedmont, uncommon in lowlands farther west, from May to early October. Woodland edge and hedgerows in farmland. Sandy Point, Jug Bay, Point Lookout, Elliott Island Road, farmland around Pocomoke Swamp, Blairs Valley, W&OD Trail.

Indigo Bunting Common on coastal plain, abundant elsewhere, except in mountains, from late April to late October. Woodland edge, scattered trees in pastures, fields, clearings. Hughes Hollow, Seneca Creek State Park, Meadowside, Jug Bay, Merkle.

Painted Bunting Very rare, with scattered records from August to May, mostly on coastal plain and at feeders.

Dickcissel Rare and irregular throughout region from May to September; in winter, rare but regular in southeast Virginia, elsewhere occasionally reported at feeders. Alfalfa fields. In last decade fewer than one pair a year reported on territory in Montgomery, Howard, Frederick, and Loudoun counties combined.

Evening Grosbeak Irregularly abundant to rare throughout region from late October to mid-May. Mostly seen at feeders with sunflower seeds, sometimes in box elders. Feeding stations in Rock Creek Park, Meadowside, Riverbend.

Purple Finch Common to uncommon throughout region from October to early May, more common from late March to early May. Uncommon to rare in summer in western highlands. Mixed coniferous and deciduous woods. Locust Spring, Herrington Manor, Gude's Nursery, C&O Canal (especially Violet's Lock to Riley's Lock), Great Falls Park (Virginia), Mason Neck, Jug Bay, National Aboretum.

House Finch Common and rapidly increasing throughout region from mid-October to early May; uncommon to rare but expanding throughout region in summer. Urban and suburban areas. Metropolitan Washington; feeders at nature centers.

Pine Grosbeak Very rare and irregular in most of region from November to March; more regular in western mountains. Coniferous forest edge, especially roadsides.

Common Redpoll Rare and irregular in northern half of region from December to mid-April. Weedy fields, birches, alders, coastal dunes, feeders.

Pine Siskin Irregularly rare to common throughout region, mid-October to mid-May. Conifers, weeds, alders, woodland edge, feeders. Often with goldfinches. Gude's Nursery, National Aboretum, feeders at nature centers.

American Goldfinch Common throughout region all year; abundant from early April to early May and from mid-October to mid-November. Weedy fields, hedgerows, tangles on woodland edge; feeders. C&O Canal, Hughes Hollow, Meadowside, Claude Moore Center, Jug Bay, Huntley Meadows.

Red Crossbill Irregular and rare to uncommon in most of region; apparently a permanent resident on Shenandoah Mountain. Usually seen and heard in flight over stands of conifers.

White-winged Crossbill Rare and very irregular throughout region from November to May. Conifers. More often in residential areas than Red Crossbill.

Rufous-sided Towhee Common throughout region; from November to March more common on southeast coastal plain, much less common in northern piedmont and western valleys, absent from highlands. Thickety woodland edge and hedgerows. Seneca Creek State Park, Meadowside, Claude Moore Center, Riverbend, Huntley Meadows, Jug Bay.

Savannah Sparrow Common in winter along coast, uncommon to rare inland; common throughout region from mid-March to mid-May and from mid-September to early November. Rare in summer in northern piedmont and western highlands. Wet meadows, grassy flats next to fresh or tidal marshes. Ipswich race in sandy coastal dunes. Delmarva refuges in winter; Jug Bay, Sandy Point in migration; Highland and Garrett counties in summer.

Grasshopper Sparrow Uncommon to locally common throughout region from mid-April to late October. Hay fields and old pastures. Lucketts, Claude Moore Center, Seneca Creek State Park, New Design Road.

Henslow's Sparrow Local and rare to uncommon throughout region from mid-April to late October. Weedy meadows, predominantly broom sedge, often at marsh edges. Elliott Island Road, Saxis Marsh, Broadkill Marsh, possibly Claude Moore Center.

Sharp-tailed Sparrow Locally common on coast and Chesapeake Bay, in southern Delmarva in winter, in more northern marshes in summer. Salt and fresh marshes. Port Mahon, Assateague and Chincoteague, Deal Island, Saxis, Point Lookout.

Seaside Sparrow Common to abundant in Delmarva marshes from late April to early November; uncommon to rare in winter, more numerous in Virginia. Salt marsh. Port Mahon, Elliott Island, Assateague and Chincoteague, Deal Island.

Vesper Sparrow Uncommon to common throughout region from early March to early May and from late September to early November; rare on coastal plain and in southern piedmont in summer; uncommon to locally common elsewhere; rare in winter. Upland pastures and fields. Lucketts, New Design Road.

Lark Sparrow. Rare visitor along coast, with most records in August and September, a few in May, and others from October to April. Even rarer in highlands and piedmont. Grassy areas by coastal dunes; pastures.

Dark-eyed Junco Common to abundant throughout region from October to April; common in mountains in summer. Conifers and deciduous woods, along roads and clearings; urban and suburban residential areas, hedgerows, and field edges in winter. Shenandoah National Park, Highland County, metropolitan Washington and local parks, especially nature centers with feeders.

American Tree Sparrow Uncommon to rare throughout region from early November to late March; more common north of Washington, irregular south of it. Weedy fields near thickets and woods. Fields off River Road, Meadowside, Sandy Point, Bombay Hook, Brandywine.

Chipping Sparrow Common throughout region from late March to early November; rare in winter, sometimes uncommon in southeast

Virginia. Suburban parks and gardens, shaded lawns and pastures, grassy clearings. Fort Hunt, Belle Haven Picnic Area, Montrose Park, Jug Bay, Meadowside (April and May only).

Clay-colored Sparrow Rare visitor, with almost all records along coast, from September to November. Grassy areas.

Field Sparrow Common throughout region all year; more common on coastal plain in winter. Weedy fields, thickets, hedgerows, woodland edge. Hughes Hollow, Meadowside, Claude Moore Center, Jug Bay, Huntley Meadows.

Harris' Sparrow Rare visitor throughout region except for Virginia coastal plain, with records from October to March. Brush piles, hedgerows, weedy fields. Often with White-throated and White-crowned Sparrows.

White-crowned Sparrow Uncommon east of mountains, common in western valleys from early October to early May. Multiflora and other hedgerows, thickets, weedy fields. Hedgerows around fields off River Road (Isaac Walton League property on Willard Road), Blackwater Visitor Center, Shenandoah Valley.

White-throated Sparrow Common to abundant throughout region from October to late May. Residential areas, bottomland woods and woodland edge, feeders, all local parks.

Fox Sparrow Fairly common throughout region from late February to March, uncommon in November and in southeast Virginia in winter; uncommon to rare in rest of region in winter. Forest floor in mixed woods and woodland edge near thickets and brush piles. C&O Canal, Jug Bay, local wooded parks; Norfolk area parks in winter.

Lincoln's Sparrow Rare throughout region in April and May, from late September to early November; rare in southeast Virginia in winter. Brush piles and thickets at edges of weedy fields and marshy areas.

Swamp Sparrow Uncommon to abundant throughout region in migration, increasing in numbers from northwest to southeast; common to abundant on coastal plain and in southern piedmont in winter, rare to uncommon in northern piedmont and western valleys. Uncommon and local in summer in western highlands and Delmarva. Marshes with rank vegetation, weedy fields, hedgerows. Hughes Hollow, Dyke Marsh, Jug Bay, Sandy Point, Bombay Hook (all year), Locust Spring, Cranesville Swamp (summer).

Song Sparrow Common throughout region except in mountains all year, abundant on coastal plain and in piedmont in winter. Hedgerows, thickets, brush piles, weedy fields, swamps, shrubbery. Residential areas, Meadowside, Hughes Hollow, Oxon Hill Children's Farm, National Aboretum.

Lapland Longspur Rare near coast, rare and irregular inland in northern third of region from late October to April, usually seen December-February. Grassy mud flats, dunes, harvested fields, turf. Cape Henlopen, Assateague; more rarely Sandy Point and Summit Hall Turf Farm.

Snow Bunting Uncommon near coast, rare and increasingly irregular from east to west, from end of October to March. Dunes, sand and mud flats, harvested fields. Cape Henlopen, Assateague, Sandy Point (November).

RARITIES AND ACCIDENTALS

The following species have been recorded in the region since 1950, but with such infrequency that even very active birders should not expect to see them in five years or more of intensive and varied field work. Several have been seen only once. Species listed only as hypothetical on both the Maryland and Virginia checklists have not been included.

Sightings of birds listed below or described on the preceding pages as rare, or not mentioned at all, deserve good documentation, including photographs when possible, a prompt effort to notify a maximum number of other birders, and a report to the state records committee with a copy to the regional editor of *American Birds.*

Yellow-nosed Albatross	Mew Gull	Varied Thrush
Western Grebe	Sabine's Gull	Northern Wheatear
White-tailed Tropicbird	Arctic Tern	Bachman's Warbler
Black-capped Petrel	Sooty Tern	Black-throated Gray Warbler
Brown Booby	Bridled Tern	Kirtland's Warbler
American White Pelican	White-winged Black Tern[1]	Lazuli Bunting
Magnificent Frigatebird	Common Murre	Hoary Redpoll
American Flamingo	Thick-billed Murre	Green-tailed Towhee
Ross's Goose	Groove-billed Ani	Lark Bunting
White-cheeked Pintail	Rufous Hummingbird	Baird's Sparrow
Sandhill Crane	Gray Kingbird	LeConte's Sparrow
Limpkin	Scissor-tailed Flycatcher	Bachman's Sparrow[2]
Mountain Plover	Ash-throated Flycatcher	Black-throated Sparrow
Long-billed Curlew	Say's Phoebe	Smith's Longspur
Long-tailed Jaeger	Western Wood Pewee	Chestnut-collared Longspur
South Polar Skua	Boreal Chickadee	
Thayer's Gull	Sage Thrasher	

[1] Multiple occurrences at Little Creek and Chincoteague only.
[2] Formerly rare breeder in Virginia and Maryland, now accidental.

Washington and the Suburbs

The city of Washington's abundance of wooded parks and open and sheltered waters means for the hurried or car-less birder that there is no need to go beyond the city limits to see an impressive variety of birds. In recent years diligent field observers have shown that some 180 species can be found in a year of single-minded searching if no key habitats are neglected.

If you want to compile your own District of Columbia bird list, remember that the District limits include the waters of the Potomac up to the high tide line on the Virginia shore from a little above Chain Bridge to just below the Wilson Bridge (though the line there angles sharply north toward the Maryland shore). Columbia Island, including the marina above Rochambeau Bridge, is also part of the District.

Most of the areas described here are parkland, unlikely to be developed in the foreseeable future. (The probable exceptions are the Catholic University property and Fort Lincoln.) They can nearly all be reached by public transportation combined with a short walk. Nonetheless, a car is a real convenience, particularly in the areas close to the Potomac and Anacostia rivers.

A free, official city map and a Washington/Virginia transportation map available from Metro for $1 will be helpful supplements for the determined explorer.

NORTHWEST

1. **Roosevelt Island,** especially the south end around Roosevelt Bridge for wintering finches and the paths across the marsh and along the ridges for migrants. The marsh may have transient rails and shorebirds, as well as herons and egrets in late summer. Night herons fly over at dusk. Scope the south tip from the Virginia shore for gulls; look overhead for hawks and eagles.

2. **The overlooks along the George Washington Parkway** in Virginia, north of Key Bridge, are good spots from which to scan the river for ducks and gulls. Watch for migrating swifts, swallows, and nighthawks, as well as accipiters and buteos, especially in September and October.

3. **Fletcher's Boat House,** along the C&O Canal at the junction of Reservoir Road and Canal Road. The edges of the parking lot are prime habitat for warblers and orioles. For Barred Owls and Prothonotary Warblers check the sides of the railroad track and

the woods along the towpath north to the District Line. About one-quarter mile north of Chain Bridge, turn left down a dirt track to a marshy area with several ponds attractive to wintering waterfowl and sparrows.

4. **Battery Kemble Park.** The area around the Chain Bridge Road entrance can be excellent in migration. Follow the path to MacArthur Boulevard. Veeries nest here.

5. **Georgetown Reservoir,** especially October to December, for ducks, coot, gulls, Fish Crows, and Black and Turkey Vultures. This is the most reliable spot in the District to see Canvasbacks.

6. **Glover-Archbold Park,** mainly in migration. Warblers may be at every level including the highest tree tops. The underbrush along the creek is best after the sun is high enough to reach it; look for thrushes, especially nesting Veeries. Somewhere there is a resident Screech Owl.

7. **Rock Creek Park.** Ask the advice of the rangers at the Nature Center; one or two are interested in birds and can point you to good birding areas. Ross Drive is especially good in migration. Louisiana Waterthrushes and Veeries nest along most of the streams.

8. **The National Zoo,** for the Black-crowned Night Herons that roost over the eagle cages, and for Black and Turkey Vultures, which raid the dinners of the carnivores in open pens. Take advantage of the opportunity to study waterfowl field marks on the captive birds in the duck ponds.

9. **Montrose and Dumbarton Oaks parks,** the latter behind the Dumbarton Oaks estate, both off R Street in Georgetown, are excellent for woodland migrants.

NORTHEAST

10. **The National Aboretum,** especially the conifer groves on Hickey Hill for a variety of owls, and the area close to the Anacostia River behind the holly groves. Check the river for grebes, ducks, and gulls. Look for hawks and finches in fall and winter.

11. **Fort Lincoln.** Enter through the apartment complex on South Dakota Avenue. The extensive brushy area behind the hill is good for wintering sparrows and hawks, nesting Blue Grosbeak, Yellow-breasted Chat, and Grasshopper Sparrow. Follow the dirt roads on foot; they may be too muddy to drive on. (This area is under development.)

12. **Catholic University.** The woods south of the Taylor Street-

Hawaii Avenue intersection are excellent in migration. Follow the paths. The barren field northeast of the intersection is good in migration and in winter, especially the brushy ravine on the north side, where Lincoln's Sparrows appear in October. Check the pines for owls, the snags for hawks. Park at the Seven-Eleven store.

13. **Kenilworth Aquatic Gardens,** for herons and other marsh birds. Check the gardens; then keep right from the parking lot and follow the service road down to the cove to look for herons, ducks, and shorebirds. Ask the ranger there where else you can go safely.

14. **Lake Kingman.** Park in the Kennedy Stadium lot and cross the lake (really a stretch of the Anacostia River) on the foot bridges. Good in winter for ducks, gulls, hawks, and sparrows.

SOUTHEAST

15. **Fort Dupont Park.** A good variety of habitats has produced all kinds of land bird migrants. This area is well worth exploring if you live nearby.

16. **Anacostia River Park,** along the south bank west of Pennsylvania Avenue. The river itself has grebes and ducks in winter, and the bushes along the bank serve as a migrant trap in season.

SOUTHWEST

17. **Tidal Basin and East Potomac Park.** Excellent in migration for loons, grebes, diving ducks, and gulls, usually easy to observe from your car. Look in the Washington Channel or among the Ring-billed Gulls on the golf course for Lesser Black-backed Gulls.

18. **Anacostia Naval Air Station.** Enter through the north gate, where the guard on duty usually lets birders in. Do not peer in at the President's helicopter; above all, do not take pictures near it. Look over grassy expanses and around rain pools for shorebirds, especially in September and October. Golden Plover, Baird's and Buff-breasted Sandpipers have all occurred here fairly regularly.

19. **Blue Plains Sewage Treatment Plant.** Sometimes accessible to the public; try weekends before 4:00 P.M. Exit from I-295 for the Naval Research Laboratory and continue south to Blue Plains. Inside the gate keep left, and watch out for trucks. Check the round tanks for gulls and go on to the mouth of Oxon Run.

Follow the shore west and north to a large concrete dock, the best vantage point for Goose Island. Scan the shore in summer for shorebirds, rails, gallinules, and bitterns. The flats and pilings are excellent at low tide for cormorants, gulls, terns, and skimmers in late summer and fall.

20. **The Mouth of Four Mile Run.** One of the best spots in the District for waterfowl, herons, and shorebirds, this area is just south of National Airport in Virginia and just east of the parkway along the river. Park 0.3 mile south in the Washington Sailing Marina and walk back along the bicycle path to a little knoll just south of the bridge over the creek. Take care not to flush the birds below you on the flats. Come only near low tide, in late afternoon for the best light. Earlier in the day, look from the marina picnic area. Bring a scope.

As in any large city, the less-used Washington parks are not always safe to wander around in alone. This is especially true in the warmer months and in the northeast and southeast sections. While very few birders have ever been threatened, it just makes sense to carry with you nothing you cannot afford to lose, to leave nothing of value visible in a locked car, to keep your binoculars as inconspicuous as possible, and to stay alert for suspect behavior. Bird with a companion if you can, but do not let the lack of one keep you indoors. If you have qualms, keep to the areas along the Potomac or west of Rock Creek Park.

5 In and around Alexandria

Among the most thoroughly explored birding areas around Washington is the stretch between Shirley Highway, I-395, and the Potomac River north of Mount Vernon. Despite its urban character, Alexandria contains a diversity of habitats that make for interesting birding all year long.

The best-known spots are along the Potomac, all accessible from the George Washington Parkway:

Roaches Run is a tidal lagoon on the west side of the parkway just north of National Airport; it can only be reached if you are southbound. Best birded in morning light, it is worth checking from fall to spring for gulls, dabbling ducks, all three merganser species, Great Blue Herons, Black-crowned Night Herons, and Pied-billed Grebes.

The **old National Park Service nursery** runs along the river south of the Washington Sailing Marina. It is very good for migrant passerines and wintering hawks and sparrows, and a likely place to look for shrikes and owls. Park in the "Additional Parking" lot on the south side of the marina entrance road. Enter the nursery by way of the gate barring the service road south.

From the marina you can also walk back to the mouth of Four Mile Run, properly within the District of Columbia (see page 46).

The **mouth of Hunting Creek** is best viewed from below Hunting Towers Apartments, east of the parkway just after it goes over the beltway. (You must make this left turn from the right lane.) Turn right into and through the first parking lot for the apartments and drive down to the firm open ground by the cove. The pilings on the left are renowned for their high-tide populations of terns, especially from July to September, and gulls (including occasional Glaucous, Iceland, Lesser Black-backed, and Franklin's); assorted herons turn up along the shoreline and Double-crested Cormorants, Greater and Lesser Scaup, and Ruddy Ducks may be farther out in the river. There are also pilings and flats in the creek just west of the parkway, and a pullout on that side from which to check them. Look for Pintail and Green-winged Teal in winter.

By following the road that runs along the north side of the apartments and under the beltway and by looping east on Green Street and south on South Lee Street you can reach **Jones Point,** the land beyond the cove, as well as an excellent overlook of the river around Wilson Bridge. The woods are rewarding in migration, the swamp shelters breeding Willow Flycatchers, and the far side of the river is often full of wintering ducks.

Dyke Marsh lies south of Belle Haven Picnic Area, east of the parkway just below Hunting Creek. After checking for waterfowl in the Potomac from the picnic grounds (in season), walk around the woods at the south end, cross the paved road that goes out to the Belle Haven Marina and follow the gravel road that leads eventually out to the marsh. Breeding birds include Canada Goose, sometimes Common Gallinule, Least Bittern, Willow Flycatcher, Marsh Wren, Yellow Warbler, and Yellowthroat. In autumn and winter look for hawks, waterfowl, shrikes, and sparrows; both spring and fall are good for rails and all kinds of land birds. In the swampy woods west and south of the marsh, you may find Great Horned Owls, Fox Sparrows, and Rusty Blackbirds. The woods are most easily reached from the bicycle path along the parkway, which will take you to a pleasant bridge from which you can inspect another part of the marsh.

The eastern side of **Fort Hunt Park** and the woods around the **parking lots for Mount Vernon,** on both sides of the parkway, can be stupendous in migration for woodland species—flycatchers, thrushes, warblers, and tanagers. The latter area has resident Great Horned and Barred Owls and White-breasted Nuthatches; and nesting warblers include Hooded, Black-and-white, Kentucky, and Oven-

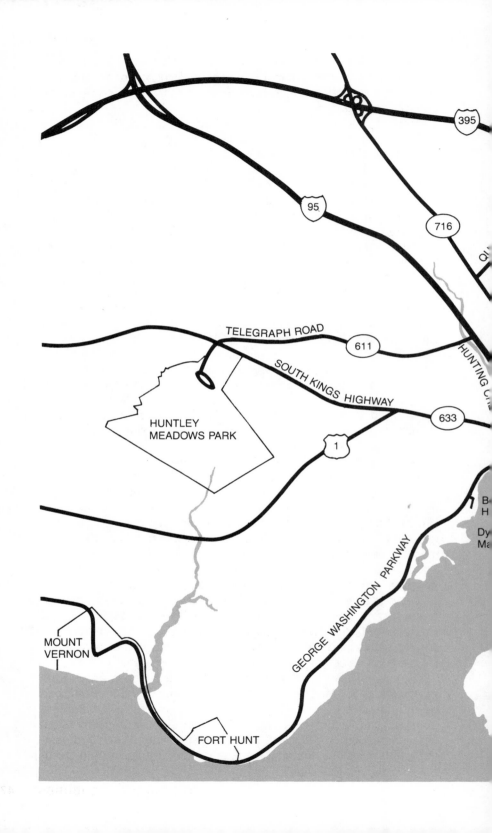

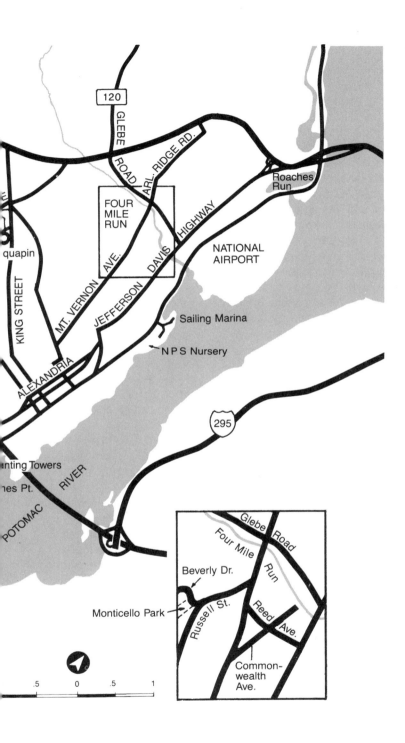

ROACHES RUN TO MOUNT VERNON

bird. Look for Bald Eagles along the Potomac from the parkway overlooks north from Mount Vernon to Dyke Marsh.

Away from the river four other spots are recommended:

To visit **Four Mile Run upstream,** leave I-395 on Arlington Ridge Road or Glebe Road East. Where these two roads intersect, the former becomes Mount Vernon Avenue and crosses Four Mile Run. Take this avenue over the bridge, turn left into a parking lot on the south side of the creek, and bird from the bank. At low tide the flats can be a good place to study gulls, especially in late winter and early spring. They attract more than their share of Lesser Black-backed Gulls, in particular. In migration, check the flats for shorebirds; a half-dozen species are often present, sometimes such uncommon ones as Wilson's Phalarope and White-rumped Sandpiper. Either follow the path downstream or continue on Mount Vernon Avenue to Reed Avenue (a link to U.S. 1), go left, and again left into Commonwealth Avenue, which will take you back to Four Mile Run.

Monticello Park is a postage-stamp area with tall tulip trees, oaks, and a little stream, reached by taking Russell Road, the third street on the right south of Four Mile Run, running off at an angle from Mount Vernon Avenue. After five short blocks on Russell Road, turn right on Beverly Drive. In 100 yards or so, where Beverly Drive bends sharply right, you will see the park on your left. It is a favorite spot for warblers in the spring. What is so entrancing for birders is the opportunity to see the birds bathing as close as one's binoculars will focus. The variety of species is extraordinary.

Chinquapin Park is 1.0 mile from I-395; take the exit for King Street East, drive through the major intersection with Braddock Road and Quaker Lane, and continue to T. C. Williams High School on the right. Just beyond the school go right onto Chinquapin Drive, a loop road, and park anywhere along it. Nearby is a swampy wood. Bird the edge for migrants, and then take any trail away from the road and you will come to fields and woods of Virginia pine, the latter especially good for Red-breasted Nuthatches, Golden-crowned and Ruby-crowned Kinglets, Pine Warblers, Pine Siskins and other irregular pine-loving visitors, as well as a considerable assortment of migrants.

Huntley Meadows is a Fairfax County park on the south side of South Kings Highway, Va. 633, where it ends at the junction with Telegraph Road, Va. 611. Take Exit 2 south from the beltway and drive 3.4 miles; turn left, crossing into the park entrance. The park is open from dawn to dusk, but the entrance gate is open only from 8:30 A.M. to 5:00 P.M. Among the species to look for are Red-tailed, Red-shouldered, and Cooper's Hawks; Wild Turkey; Woodcock (displaying at dusk from March to early May); Whip-poor-will; all the local woodpeckers including Redheaded; Prothonotary, Pine, and Prairie Warblers; Yellow-breasted Chat; and Summer Tanager. A park bird list and a trail map are available.

A few miles south of Alexandria two other areas, not often explored by birders, are worth a visit.

Pohick Bay Park is still the most dependable place close to Washington to see Bald Eagles. Take I-95 south from the junction with I-395 about 7 miles to the exit (mile 0.0) for Lorton, Road 642. Signposts for the park are conspicuous at every turn. At the T-junction with Road 642 go left; at 0.8 mile turn right on Road 748, which merges with U.S. 1 south at 1.0 mile. At 1.9 miles turn left on Road 242. The entrance to the park is on the left at 5.2 miles. Drive down to the boat-launching ramp and scan Pohick Bay from there. Check the shoreline, woods, and all soaring birds. A fee is collected in the busy season except from Northern Virginia residents.

Mason Neck National Wildlife Refuge is 2.2 miles farther along Road 242; turn left when you leave the park. Established and managed specifically to protect nesting Bald Eagles, it is entirely closed to the public from December 1 to March 31, and most of the refuge is inaccessible all year. From April through November you may fork right at the refuge sign onto High Point Road, unpaved and poorly maintained, and drive to the parking area at 0.7 mile for Woodmarsh Trail. The trail can be rewarding for passerines in migration and for breeding birds typical of deciduous bottomland forest. Look for Barred and Great Horned Owls, Woodcock, Green Heron, Wood Duck, and Kentucky Warbler, as well as the eagles, of course.

Six Nearby Virginia Parks 6

The parks in Arlington County and northern Fairfax County are pleasant enough for hiking in winter, but the birdlife is rarely exciting: plenty of ducks in the river, woodpeckers and chickadees in the woods, perhaps a Barred Owl or even a Wild Turkey and assorted winter finches and sparrows.

In migration they come into their own, particularly in the spring, when there are not only songbirds overhead but a splendor of wild-flowers underfoot.

The most remote of the parks described here is about 18 miles from Key Bridge and only 8 miles beyond the Washington Beltway, I-495 (though one of the others extends far into Loudoun County).

Glencarlyn Park, along with **Long Branch Nature Center,** which has been carved out of it, lies on the southwest edge of Arlington County. Access is possible from dawn to dusk into Glencarlyn, and,

UPRIVER FROM THE BELTWAY

MARYLAND

FALLS ROAD

Pennyfield Lock Rd.

POTOMAC

RIVER ROAD

Violets Lock Rd.

112

Rileys Lock Rd.

RIVER ROAD

Summit
Hall Turf Farm

Sycamore
Landing Rd.

Hughes
Hollow

Hunting
Quarter Rd.

Algonkian Park

POTOMAC RIVER

190

1268

603

603

602

637

637

625

640

641

641

642

659

653

Washington and   Old

7

STERLING

Dominion Regional Park

Claude Moore Center

28

DULLES
INTERNATIONAL
AIRPORT

Dranesville

OLD   GEORGETOWN   PIKE

193

606

RESTON

VIRGINIA

189

Great
Falls
Park

MACARTHUR BLVD.

Dranesville
Park

738

495

123

VIENNA

1.5   0   .5   1

from 8:00 A.M. on, into the parking lot of Long Branch. You can walk from one into the other as you please.

Approach them both from Washington via Arlington Boulevard, U.S. 50, by taking an exit right for Carlin Springs Road, 1.7 miles west of Glebe Road, Va. 120. At the foot of the exit ramp, turn right at the T-junction. At 0.3 mile a left turn on Fourth Street takes you to another T-junction with Harrison Street (at 0.7 mile), which borders Glencarlyn Park, with entrance roads both left and right, leading down to parking areas at the bottom of the hill.

You will reach the nature center by continuing on Carlin Springs Road past the Northern Virginia Doctors Hospital to the first left turn beyond, which appears to be a driveway for the Medical Center, just 0.7 mile from the foot of the U.S. 50 ramp. Follow the driveway back to the nature-center parking lot; check the ponds on the way in.

From the path to the nature center take the trail uphill to the left. It curves right, up to an overgrown meadow on the ridgeline and down again behind the center. Scan the scrub in the meadow and trees around the edge. Then take the paved trail along Long Branch, through the Glencarlyn parking area, across the bridge over Four Mile Run to the bicycle trail that runs under the power line. Climb up to the path along the ridge beside the trail and follow it left to its end, then right as far as a cluster of tall, dead trees up the hill across the ditch beside you. This very short walk can be so rich in birds that it may take you most of a morning.

The nature center, like the others mentioned below, can provide you with a trail map, a bird list, and good advice from the birders on the staff. It is open 10:00 A.M. to 5:00 P.M. Tuesday to Saturday, and 1:00 P.M. to 5:00 P.M. Sunday.

Potomac Overlook Park, run by the Northern Virginia Park Authority, is also in Arlington, off Military Road. Go 0.8 mile from its junction with Lee Highway, U.S. 29-211, or 1.5 mile from its intersection with Glebe Road, Va. 120, and turn onto Marcey Road at the sign for the park.

The park's 95 acres, high above the Potomac, are laced with more than two miles of trails that connect with other trails through adjacent parkland. The main habitats include deciduous woods, woodland edge, fields, and streambeds. Up to twenty-five species of warblers have been recorded in migration as well as virtually all the thrushes, vireos, cuckoos, orioles, and tanagers that are found in the region.

In April and May more than fifty species of flowers may be in bloom, and a wildflower list is available at the nature center, open the same hours as Long Branch.

Dranesville District Park is just outside the beltway on Va. 193, Georgetown Pike. Turn in at the second entrance 0.7 mile downhill from the beltway exit for Great Falls, and park in the lot beside Scott Run.

This is a Fairfax County Park with no facilities or visible staff or official bird list. Breeding and winter bird surveys have been conducted here since 1971, with results published in *American Birds.*

The census plot is in quite uniform upland hickory-oak woods and the record shows that only the most common deciduous forest birds breed and winter regularly in this park. The interesting area in migration is along Scott Run, where there are dense thickets, tall trees overhanging a stream, steep slopes, and, down by the Potomac, a rocky gorge lined with hemlocks. If you feel like climbing to the heights above the gorge, keep to the trails close to the river for a maximum of bird life.

It would be a pity to ignore the flowers, though, especially since there is a fine little pamphlet called *A Habitat Guide to Spring Wildflowers of Dranesville District Park.* You can buy it for a dollar at the Interpretive Center at Riverbend Park (see below).

The booklet provides you with a map of the park showing the trails and the six habitats, a species list for each habitat, and an overall checklist indicating blooming time and abundance. It is invaluable for all the parks in the area.

Great Falls Park, a national park, is 4.3 miles up Georgetown Pike from I-495; turn right at the light onto the entrance road. It is the only park with a year-round entrance fee, which you can avoid by arriving before 8:00 A.M., though you also miss receiving a handy little map with all the trails.

Make a U-turn to the right just beyond the tollbooth and park at the end of the road. In migration, birds are likely to be in all the trees along the edges of the lawns, roads, and parking lots, but the most productive area is the woodland behind the rest rooms, close to the old Potowmack Canal and the river. Cerulean, Hooded, and Kentucky Warblers are among the nesting species, and in recent years a Swainson's Warbler has been setting up territory every spring. Look for Acadian Flycatchers, Yellow-throated and White-eyed Vireos, and Summer Tanagers.

It is worthwhile to follow the service road that goes toward the south end of the park and to loop west from it on the Swamp Trail.

North of the visitor center take the trail up to the dam above the falls. From November to April Ring-necked Ducks are regular; Bufflehead, Common Goldeneye, Common and Hooded Mergansers are often present, and are sometimes joined by other species. You may find loons, grebes, and gulls above the dam. This end of the park is good for Warbling Vireo and Prothonotary and Yellow-throated Warblers.

Throughout the park look for Brown Creepers, Winter Wrens, and both kinglets in winter, Pileated Woodpeckers, and Eastern Bluebirds all year.

Riverbend Park, another Fairfax County Park, is only a mile upstream from the dam along the river trail, but it is 5 miles by road. Go back to Va. 193 and turn right (mile 0.0). At 0.3 mile turn right again on Riverbend Road and follow the signs to the park, forking right on Jeffery Road at 2.3 miles.

After 3.2 miles the entrance sign gives you a choice: the road straight ahead goes to the Interpretive Center, while a right turn takes you to a visitor center, rental boats, a boat ramp, and fine views over the river. There is a fee charged on summer weekends except to Fairfax County residents. Look for Ring-billed and Bonaparte's Gulls and Common Merganser in March and April; later in the spring it is a splendid vantage point to watch migrating swallows, swifts, and nighthawks.

You can join the trail along the river here, but you may do better to go back to the road to the Interpretive Center, open 9:00 A.M. to 5:00 P.M. on weekdays, 1:00 P.M. to 5:00 P.M. on weekends, and closed altogether in January and February. The park grounds are open from dawn to dusk.

There is much variety of habitat in this park, including overgrown fields and brush; it is the best of the six to look for Wild Turkeys and sparrows. Although you can assume that the birds you may see are very similar to those elsewhere along the river, records here are incomplete and your reported sightings would be welcome.

Still under development (in 1982), the **Washington and Old Dominion Railroad Regional Park,** known for short as the W&OD Trail, is 100 feet wide and nearly 45 miles long, most of it lying south of Va. 7 and roughly parallel to it. This old railroad bed extends from I-395 in Shirlington in Arlington County to Purcellville in Loudoun County. By the end of 1981 the trail was open from Lee Highway, U.S. 29-211, in Arlington for 27 miles to the U.S. 15 bypass east of Leesburg, and a trail guide for the entire route was available.

Much of it goes through residential districts and is heavily used as a bicycle and jogging trail and a neighborhood footpath, but west of Vienna there are fine stretches for birds, wildflowers, and scenery. In Fairfax County, try the two miles from Vienna to Difficult Run. The trail runs beside Piney Branch and crosses it several times, passing through bottomland forest and open fields. You can park in Vienna at the library on the corner of Va. 123 (Maple Avenue) and Center Street.

Farther west, sample the trail from Ashburn to Tuscarora Creek, some five miles of coniferous and deciduous woods, orchards, pastures, ponds, and creeks. For points of access, east to west, take Va. 7 into Loudoun County and turn left (south) on Road 641, Ashburn Road, or on Road 659, or on Road 653. Each crosses the trail in two miles or less.

Among the breeding species to look for are Black Vulture, Willow Flycatcher, Yellow-breasted Chat, Summer Tanager, Blue Grosbeak, and Grasshopper Sparrow.

7 The Towpath from Carderock to Seneca

While birding can be rewarding in almost any patch of woods or hedgerow in the month of May, the great good fortune of Washington area birders is that they live along one of the continent's major flyways, the Potomac River. Moreover, the towpath of the C&O Canal offers a unique topography that makes birding along the river conspicuously better on the Maryland side west of Washington than elsewhere. The special configuration of a strip of great trees with an often dense understory sandwiched between the broad, swift river and the placid ribbon of the canal seems to pull in birds from the skies for food and rest with extraordinary effectiveness, and the towpath blesses us all with a stumble-proof route for humans who need to be looking in all directions but down and straight ahead.

Any stretch of the canal from the Washington Beltway (I-495) west is prime habitat year-round for Barred Owls, Hairy, Downy, Red-headed, Red-bellied and Pileated Woodpeckers, and White-breasted Nuthatches, joined by Common Flickers, Yellow-bellied Sapsuckers, Brown Creepers, and Rusty Blackbirds in the cooler months. In early spring Wood Ducks move in to nest high in the sycamores, and Eastern Phoebes set up territories on bridges and cliff faces. Pied-billed Grebes, Green Herons, and Yellow-crowned Night Herons start nesting in April and May, mostly west of Great Falls.

The diversity of land birds that arrive to breed along the river is mouth-watering: Yellow-billed Cuckoos; Chimney Swifts; Ruby-throated Hummingbirds; Belted Kingfishers; Great Crested and Acadian Flycatchers; Eastern Wood Pewees; Rough-winged and Barn Swallows; Wood Thrushes and Eastern Bluebirds; Blue-gray Gnatcatchers; White-eyed, Yellow-throated, Warbling, and Red-eyed Vireos; Black-and-white, Prothonotary, Parula, Yellow, Cerulean, Yellow-throated, and Kentucky Warblers; Louisiana Waterthrushes; Yellow-throats; American Redstarts; Northern and Orchard Orioles; Scarlet and Summer Tanagers. These and a dozen unnamed permanent residents range from uncommon and local in their canal-side distribution to abundant and widespread.

It is, however, the concentration of transient species that brings out birders in droves from late April to late May. Some species come through early, some late, and often a species is here and gone in less than a week. Swallows and flycatchers, thrushes and kinglets, vireos and warblers all speed through to the north, offering the local birder only a few days a year to observe them in spring plumage and hear them singing. (They return more silently, often in drab and puzzling plumage, from August to October.) While birding in May is rarely dull, there is no doubt that activity slows steadily to a nadir in midafternoon. You are likely to see and hear twice as many birds between dawn and 9:00 A.M. as all the rest of the day.

The locations that follow are only points of access to the canal, but they have been birders' landmarks for decades. If you walk west from each, the morning sun will be at your back.

Carderock Picnic Area. Take the first beltway exit north of the Potomac River (marked Exit 41, Carderock and Great Falls), and proceed 1.0 mile west of I-495. There is good birding here on weekdays, but this location is too populated on weekends except perhaps at dawn. Use the left-hand parking lot to bird the edges of the picnic area; use the rightmost lot to reach the canal towpath (20 yards away). Walk west 0.5 mile to the bridge over the canal; just beyond, go left through Marsden Tract Campsite I, and take the loop trail at the far end down to the river and clockwise back to the towpath. There are nesting Yellow-throated and Parula Warblers at eye level. You will find an hour or two of fine before-work birding—or more if you continue west to the next area.

Old Angler's Inn. This area is 2.8 miles west of I-495 (same exit) on MacArthur Boulevard. (Go left at end of the parkway.) Park on the left and walk downhill to the towpath. Look for Cerulean Warblers right there. Walk west on the towpath, making detours down trails toward the river for birds and wildflowers. Look for ducks, hawks, gulls, and sandpipers on or over Widewater, the stretch where the canal expands into a lake. At the second lock west of Widewater, cross the canal, and walk back on the park road. Worm-eating Warblers sometimes nest on south-facing slopes; migrant thrushes are likely.

Great Falls Park. Go 5.1 miles west of I-495 (same exit). Bird here weekdays only. (There are *mobs* on weekends.) Look for ducks in season from the overlook just in front. Orioles like the parking lot edges. Birding can be good east and west along the towpath, and east along the trails through the woods on the north side of the canal.

Pennyfield Lock. Take the River Road exit (Exit 39) west from I-495, 3.3 miles to the traffic light in Potomac. Continue 5.1 miles to Pennyfield Lock Road. Turn left and drive 0.9 mile to the parking area by the gate at the end of the road. Cross the canal at the lock just east, and walk west at least 1.5 miles to Blockhouse Point, where the towpath angles sharply right and the river is immediately adjacent.

This stretch can be wonderful in migration—experts can find more than twenty warbler species in a peak morning; novices may find a dozen. The edges of the ponds of the waterfowl sanctuary are noted for shorebirds, bitterns, water-thrushes, and Prothonotary Warblers. A mile west of the lock, there is a pipeline cut down to the river. Bird the edges of the cut, and, beyond it, look for Scarlet and Summer Tanagers, Northern Orioles, and Cerulean Warblers on the far bank of the canal. Look out over the river from Blockhouse Point in mid-May for hundreds of swifts, nighthawks, and swallows streaming up the flyway. If the ground is not too wet, come back along the river's edge.

Violet's Lock. Turn left off River Road onto poorly marked Violet's Lock Road, 7.6 miles west of the Potomac traffic light. Check the playing fields on the right for "grasspipers," and bird the rich scrub north of the parking lot by the lock before crossing to the towpath. Take your scope and scan the river just west of here above Seneca Rapids. From autumn to spring, loons, grebes, ducks, and gulls ride the water near the Virginia shore. Orioles, finches, and sparrows are often especially good here, and warblers and vireos can be abundant. (By the towpath it is 2.5 miles from Pennyfield Lock to Violet's Lock.)

Seneca. River Road meets a T-junction 0.3 mile west of Violet's Lock Road and continues to the left. After 0.7 mile (8.6 miles west of the Potomac traffic light) go left, just before a flat bridge, on Riley's Lock Road through the settlement of Seneca, and park by the lock house in the lot at the end of the road. Cross the aqueduct, below which swallows nest. The next 1.5 miles west can equal Pennyfield in birding delights. Take the spur road that leads off right behind the marshy pond, good for coots, gallinules, and Blue-winged Teal.

You can follow an obscure trail, marvelous for warblers, upstream along the north side of the canal for a half-mile or so. The towpath side of the pond has Yellow-throated and Warbling Vireos, Prothonotary and Yellow Warblers, and Northern Orioles. Westward along the canal look for waterthrushes, Acadian Flycatchers, thrushes, Yellow-crowned Night Herons and, a mile farther, Yellow-throated Warblers.

After spring migration is over, come back in June and July to enjoy the breeding birds and their young. At the first inkling of autumn it pays to start patrolling the towpath again for the trickle of fall migrants that swells to a flood by mid-September and subsides gradually through October.

The Piedmont

From Hughes Hollow to the Turf Farm 8

Less than two miles beyond Seneca, Maryland, you will find an entirely different combination of habitats, and thus quite a different assortment of birds from the ones mentioned in the previous chapter. From Hughes Hollow west to the Summit Hall Turf Farm, the species birders look for include Yellow-crowned Night Herons, Least Bitterns, Wild Turkeys, Golden Plovers, Buff-breasted Sandpipers, Red-headed Woodpeckers, Willow Flycatchers, Marsh Wrens, Kentucky and Prairie Warblers, Yellow-breasted Chats, Blue Grosbeaks, and a wide variety of sparrows.

This territory begins some 10.7 miles out River Road from the traffic light in Potomac, or 2.8 miles west of the junction with Md. 112. Just after passing a big, unpainted farmhouse on the left, turn left on Hunting Quarter Road (an easy road to overshoot).

Hughes Hollow is the birder's name for the part of McKee-Beshers Wildlife Management Area that is accessible from Hunting Quarter Road. At the first bend, at the bottom of the hill, a chained-off road runs out to the left. Known to some as the Hunter's Path, this muddy track, together with the adjacent swampy woods, is one of the best sections of Hughes Hollow for Kentucky Warblers and an assortment of migrant warblers. It probably does not pay to walk out into the fields beyond.

It is worthwhile in May to drive along Hunting Quarter Road very slowly with your head out the window for warbler song and your eyes on the road shoulders looking for Woodcocks, which may with luck be seen at any time of day. Green Herons, Broad-winged and Red-shouldered Hawks, Yellow-billed Cuckoos, Rusty Blackbirds, and Purple Finches are all to be expected in their respective seasons.

The middle section of Hughes Hollow is marked by another chained-off road and a small parking lot, 0.6 mile from the beginning of Hunting Quarter Road. It is identified, clumsily, as the part "where the drive-through barn is." The road goes all the way to the river, mostly through fields where Yellow-breasted Chats and Grasshopper Sparrows breed and Vesper Sparrows visit in migration. Transient ducks are likely to be found in rain pools in the fields. In the wet woods between the fields look for Eastern Bluebirds and Red-headed Woodpeckers; more isolated trees are favored by Eastern Kingbirds, Indigo Buntings, and Blue Grosbeaks.

As you continue down Hunting Quarter Road, the swamp on your left becomes a large impoundment favored by Coots, Wood Ducks, hunting Ospreys, roosting night herons of both species, and all kinds of swallows. Park at the next chained-off road, 0.2 mile farther along, where there is a large parking lot, and walk out on the dyke straight ahead. There are three impoundments in all, a huge one on the left and two smaller ones on the right. The first is mostly open water; the second is an overgrown marsh with a rich breeding population of Least Bitterns, Willow Flycatchers, Marsh Wrens, White-eyed Vireos, Yellowthroats, and Red-winged Blackbirds. The more water-loving species are decreasing as the vegetation matures but it is still an exciting area for both eyes and ears for much of the year. Immature Purple Gallinules once appeared in late summer there.

Beyond the impoundments there is a vast area of mixed habitats: fields planted for wildlife, hedgerows, a growing stand of pines, swampy woods, and brushy tangles. A whole spring day can be spent exploring it for migrants and for summer residents setting up territories; in autumn, sparrows pour in from the north to join the resident species, and at any time of year it is important to search the sky for hawks and the edges of the fields for Wild Turkeys, present but always elusive. A March-to-May evening visit to the nearest fields may reward you with displaying Woodcocks, and Barred Owl calls will keep you company.

Hughes Hollow is always likely to be muddy and frequently insect-plagued, and the fields and woods are webbed with poison ivy and catbrier and drenched in morning dew, but it is all worth it, especially for the novice birder or western visitor. (Note: the impoundment area is more quickly reached by continuing down River Road 1.6 miles beyond Hunting Quarter Road to Hughes Road and turning left. In 100 yards you will be at the west end of Hunting Quarter Road, and another 100 yards east will take you to the parking lot.)

Sycamore Landing Road goes left from River Road to the C&O Canal 0.25 mile beyond Hughes Road, 12.7 miles from the Potomac traffic light. It is marked by a sign to Maddux Island. A slow drive along it may yield any of the species Hughes Hollow has to offer, but it is most renowned for the swampy stretch south of a small bridge, 0.4 mile from the corner, where Yellow-crowned Night Herons like to hunt. You may not coincide with them very often but they are seen there every spring and summer by many observers.

At the end of the road a footbridge takes you over the canal to the towpath. Right there a Warbling Vireo has its nest, and a hike upriver to your right will lead you past a colony of House Wrens and abundant habitat for woodpeckers and Barred Owls.

Summit Hall Turf Farm can be reached from the towpath by crossing over a well-beaten dryish patch in the canal bed soon after the turf-farm fields can be seen through the trees. The direct way to reach it is from River Road a mile beyond Sycamore Landing Road. A small sign and a well-barred gate make conspicuous the driveway on the left. Park carefully wherever you think the "No Parking" signs do not apply, preferably back a bit along River Road. Crawl under or climb over the gate and head down the drive, birding all the way. The marshes en route can be alive with ducks and herons, but you must sneak up on them. Warblers, flycatchers (including an occasional migrant Olive-sided), and sparrows may line your path, and Red-shouldered Hawks and Barred Owls live in the woods to the left.

At the end of the driveway the turf stretches out before you all the way to the canal, far to your left and even farther to your right. With the major proviso that *you must keep to the roads,* avoiding both grass and deturfed areas, the place is yours. This splendid expanse is a magnet for shorebirds, especially in wet years when there are plenty of both grassy and muddy rain pools. Both yellowlegs species and Pectoral Sandpipers are common, all the "peep" are frequent visitors, Golden Plovers and Buff-breasted Sandpipers are reasonably hoped for, and a Ruff was found at least once. Snipe, Killdeer, Horned Larks, and Savannah Sparrows overwinter; Water Pipits and Lapland Longspurs are sometimes present in early spring, but late summer and autumn are the best seasons.

The left, or eastern, end is more accessible because of roads across the turf, and the swamp along the north edge has been known to catch waves of warblers. The woods east of the driveway are actually part of McKee-Beshers and you will notice the trail that leads into the sanctuary. This area is very good for migrant thrushes as well as Wild Turkeys and Red-headed Woodpeckers, but it is easy to get lost in (though rarely for long).

A pleasant 3-mile circuit can be made by going clockwise around the east end of the turf farm to the crossover to the towpath, walking left (downriver) to the Sycamore Landing bridge, up Sycamore Landing Road, and left again on River Road back to your car.

Rockville and Gaithersburg

Aside from the area between the Potomac and River Road, Montgomery County has a number of other good sites for birding. Occasionally one of them produces a real rarity and becomes a point of pilgrimage, but in general they simply provide easy access to a variety of attractive habitats.

The locations described below are all near I-270 and can be reached from the Md. 28 exit in Rockville or the Md. 124 exit in Gaithersburg.

Rock Creek Regional Park was developed in the 1970s around

ROCKVILLE AND GAITHERSBURG

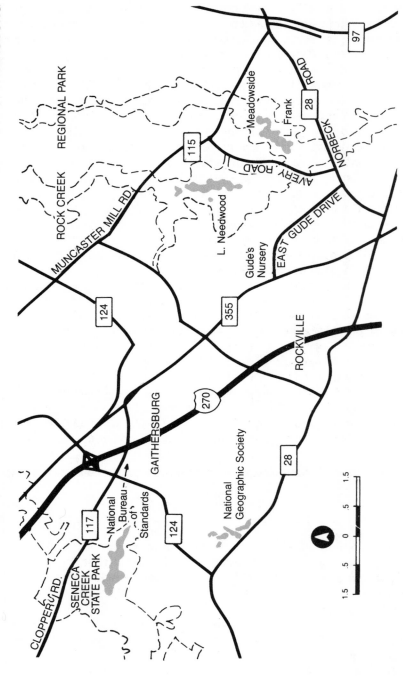

two man-made lakes, Needwood and Frank, constructed for flood control of the Rock Creek drainage. Its 1,000+ acres contain upland fields, stands of pine, deciduous woods, swamps, and streams. The section around Lake Frank and Meadowside Nature Center is managed for fishing, hiking, and nature study.

From I-270 drive east on Md. 28 1.7 miles to Avery Road, turn left, and continue 0.8 mile to the unmarked parking lot on the left. Walk another 0.1 mile along the road to the trail on the right, with the sign "Hiking Path to Lake Bernard Frank," which will take you to the south end of the lake.

Alternatively, continue on Md. 28 another 2.6 miles to Md. 115, Muncaster Mill Road (0.2 mile from the junction of Md. 28 and Md. 97). Go north on Md. 115 for 1.5 miles to Meadowside Lane, the entrance road to the nature center and to the Smith Environmental Education Center.

A trail map, a bird list, and staff birders to answer your questions are available at Meadowside, but the center is not open at all on Mondays, before 1:00 P.M. on Sundays, or before 9:00 A.M. the rest of the week. Various feeders, both close to the building and in front of nearby blinds, offer good opportunities to study and photograph resident species and winter finches and sparrows.

Trails of special interest to birders are the Rocky Ridge and Backbone Trails behind the center, which provide good eye-level views into the tree tops for migrants; the Meadow and Sleepy Hollow Trails (the latter with some rough, often wet walking), which have mixed field, hedgerow, and deciduous woodland habitats and are particularly good for thrushes; and the Big Pines and Lakeside Trails, which allow you to circumnavigate Lake Frank and the marsh upstream. Owls favor the vicinity of the old graveyard along Walnut Grove Trail, and migrant warblers the clearing around the covered bridge. Bobwhites and Red-shouldered Hawks are among the residents, while Acadian Flycatchers, Brown Thrashers, White-eyed Vireos, Yellowthroats, Yellow-breasted Chats, and Indigo Buntings may be conspicuous in summer. Lake Frank attracts Green Herons and Spotted and Solitary Sandpipers in spring and summer, Snowy Egrets in early fall, and any water bird from loons to Oldsquaw in migration.

Gude's Nursery is on East Gude Drive, which curves north and west from Md. 28 to Md. 355. From I-270 go east on Md. 28 for 1.3 miles, turn left on East Gude Drive, and drive 1.6 miles to the nursery entrance on the right. (At this point you are 0.5 mile east of Md. 355.)

Only a small part of the property is still being actively managed as a nursery, and its days may be numbered. While it lasts, birders are welcome to roam freely through the grounds. The many varieties and sizes of conifer and the tangles of catbrier and honeysuckle provide abundant cover and food for winter finches, hawks, and owls. It has proved a prime location for Barn, Great Horned, Long-eared, and Saw-whet Owls. Red-tailed, Sharp-shinned, and Cooper's Hawks are regularly present. Cedar Waxwings love the holly berries and Red-breasted Nuthatches winter in the pines; Red and White-winged Crossbills and Common Redpolls are likely to be at Gude's if they are around at all. Some days, even in winter, you will find nothing around of more interest than a Robin or a Blue Jay.

Seneca Creek State Park comprises several discontinuous areas totaling 6,600 acres, mostly along Seneca Creek and its tributaries, with a stretch of managed hunting land between River Road and the C&O Canal. Much of the park is yet to be developed, but the upper section around Clopper Lake has many visitor facilities including a good trail system.

To reach this section from I-270, take the Md. 124 exit and go west 0.5 mile. At Md. 117, Clopper Road, turn right and drive 1.5 miles to the park entrance, which appears suddenly on the left. Park in the lot for the visitor center. If the gate is not open, birders often park along the shoulder of the road a little farther north and bird along the power line or the gas pipeline that cross Clopper Road.

You can pick up a trail map and a bird list in the visitor center; documented reports of additional species or of nesting species will be welcomed by the staff. For your first visit it is a good idea to call in advance, ask about opening hours, and try to join a conducted bird walk. Inquire about access to the locked nature study area, designed and maintained by birders for birders. The telephone number is (301) 924-2127.

The recommended birders' route is as follows: take Great Seneca Trail from the northeast corner of the parking lot, with a short cut along the jeep trail under the power line (Prairie and Kentucky Warblers and Yellow-breasted Chat), as far as the bluff over the creek. Then go back to the Chickadee picnic area and work the fields behind the rest rooms (Grasshopper Sparrow and Eastern Meadowlark). Turn right on the main park road and then left to the Overlook, from which you can scan the lake for herons, waterfowl, and shorebirds (Pied-billed Grebe, Common Merganser, and diving ducks in early winter; Green Heron, Wood Duck, and Spotted Sandpiper in summer). Look for Red-headed Woodpeckers behind the Overlook.

Continue down the main road to the picnic pavilions; there may be lots of birds en route. Prairie Warblers and Orchard Orioles are present near the pavilions in breeding season, Cedar Waxwings in winter. Then take Mink Hollow Trail, which starts behind the rest rooms; in migration this is an outstanding route for thrushes, vireos, and warblers. After a mile go right on a jeep trail, cross the meadow diagonally to an old farm road, with hedgerows excellent for field birds. In fall look for raptors overhead and check the trees at the top of the hill for passerine migrants.

Return via the jeep trail to a road over the dam. Turn right on the north side of the lake on the Lakeshore Trail and follow it as far as the Boat Center. Walk through the Pine Plantation north of it, turn right on the main road and left through the Cardinal picnic area, good for Pine Warblers, Yellow-breasted Chats, and Turkeys. From the northeast corner go around the guardrail, turn left on an old road and right on the red-blazed Old Pond Trail, which leads back to the visitor center.

Two other lakes in the vicinity attract many waterfowl from November to March, but both are open only on weekdays. Continue west on Md. 124 about 0.2 mile beyond Clopper Road, turn left into the entrance for the **National Bureau of Standards,** and drive to the lake. Then continue on Md. 124 for 2.1 miles. At Md. 28 turn left and drive 1.0 mile to the entrance for the **National Geographic Society.** The lake is just ahead. Geese and ducks appear to travel freely between the two lakes, often stopping on the golf course of the Washingtonian Country Club nearby. Recent rarities have included a White-fronted Goose and a (blue) Snow Goose.

You can also reach the National Geographic Society by taking Md. 28 west from I-270 for 4.2 miles.

Southern Frederick County, Maryland 10

There is hardly a better area to bird west of the Chesapeake Bay than southern Frederick County in Maryland. The wooded slopes around Sugarloaf Mountain, the fish ponds of Lilypons, the upland fields and pastures off New Design Road, and the back roads and trails along the Monacacy and Potomac rivers provide a remarkable diversity of habitat. On a fine day in May it is not hard to find 100 species in the course of twelve hours or so, if you reach the foot of Sugarloaf Mountain early enough to hear the Great Horned Owls, Screech Owls, and Whip-poor-wills.

Leave I-270 at the Clarksburg exit (mile 0.0), drive 0.5 mile northeast to Md. 355 and turn left. At 1.5 miles go left again on Comus Road and follow it to the foot of **Sugarloaf Mountain** at 7.1 miles, listening for night birds the last 2 miles or so. Park at the circle and bird on foot the edges of the property, officially named The Stronghold. There is a large grove of conifers just inside the entrance and along the last leg of Comus Road just beyond the circle.

All the migrant thrushes and many species of warblers show up here and along Sugarloaf Mountain Road, which runs northeast from

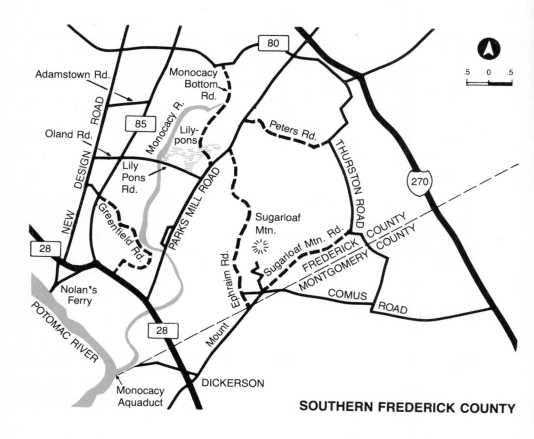

SOUTHERN FREDERICK COUNTY

the circle. This stretch has been known to produce migrants in spectacular numbers and variety on gray days when the ceiling is so low that the mountain itself is invisible.

As soon as the gates are open (before the place is overrun with tourists), drive up the mountain as far as the first overlook and bird the lower slopes, looking especially for Summer Tanagers and Worm-eating Warblers. Hawk-watching from the summit, spring or fall, can be quite good, but the climb is steep and anything but solitary.

Comus Road runs along the left side of The Stronghold past a pond to the west and ends at Mount Ephraim Road (0.4 mile), a narrow, unpaved road that is excellent for woodland birding. If you follow it north (right) to its end on Park Mills Road, 3.8 miles from the circle, you will be just 1.0 mile north of Lily Pons Road.

A longer but equally interesting route from Sugarloaf Mountain (mile 0.0) to Lilypons (the name of the place is one word, the name of the road is two) is via Sugarloaf Mountain Road to Thurston Road at

2.5 miles and Thurston Road north to Peters Road at 5.0 miles. Make a hairpin turn left on Peters Road, which is unpaved and pretty, following a stream through a narrow valley, with a good chance for ducks, kingfishers, orioles, and sparrows. At 8.3 miles you will have climbed out of the valley to intercept Park Mills Road, where you turn left toward Lilypons.

If you take this route or Mount Ephraim Road slowly, you should have no trouble at all, but neither is well maintained. If you are more comfortable on broad, paved surfaces, leave Sugarloaf via the southwest on a road that soon becomes Mount Ephraim Road and reaches Md. 28 on the north side of Dickerson at 2.8 miles. (In May, look for Bobolinks in the alfalfa fields.) Go north on Md. 28 to the junction with Md. 85 at 6.5 miles and continue north on Md. 85 to Lily Pons Road at 10.2 miles. Turn right and, after crossing the Monocacy River, park near the entrance at 11.5 miles.

Lilypons Water Gardens, named after the opera singer, who came to its opening, is an extensive network of dyked ponds where water lilies and goldfish are raised. Water levels and maintenance of the ponds fluctuate constantly: some are full, attracting ducks in migration; some are drained, pulling in Water Pipits and a great assortment of shorebirds; and others provide enough reedy cover to entice a regular breeding population of Least Bitterns, Marsh Wrens, and King Rails. Green Herons, Red-winged Blackbirds, swallows of all kinds, Belted Kingfishers, Ospreys, Black and Turkey Vultures, and Red-tailed and Red-shouldered Hawks are plentiful in season. Ibis, egrets, and herons often show up in late summer, wandering inland from coastal breeding colonies. Almost any land bird that likes freshwater marshes and bottomland woods may be found along Bennett Creek, which runs along the north side of the property and joins the Monocacy River on the west.

The direct route from Washington to Lilypons is to take the Urbana-Buckeystown exit (mile 0.0) from I-270, heading west on Md. 80 for 1.7 miles to Park Mills Road. Turn left and follow Park Mills Road (past Peters Road at 3.7 miles and Mount Ephraim Road at 4.3 miles) to Monocacy Bottom Road at 5.0 miles where you can turn right or continue another 0.3 mile to Lily Pons Road.

Monocacy Bottom Road is narrow and unpaved but has two or three spots to park before it fords Bennett Creek. (Leave the gates on either side unobstructed.) It gives you the best access to the woodland edge, the creek, and the less-maintained ponds, where you are most likely to find marsh birds, families of Wood Ducks, and surprises, which included, one famous spring, a Limpkin!

Lily Pons Road has wide, paved shoulders for parking. The entrance road to the sales office is 0.6 mile from Park Mills Road, but birders are asked not to use the tiny parking lot for customers, and the limited hours that the gate is open are restricting anyway. (The area is open to birders on foot at all hours.) As Lily Pons Road approaches the bridge over the Monocacy, it gives you an excellent view over all the ponds on the south side of the property—you can check for water levels and the location of shorebirds or ducks before you set out on foot. It is a long way from Lily Pons Road to the ponds beyond Monocacy Bottom Road, and you may want to cover the area in two stages.

Don't go to Lilypons when the air is hot, heavy, and still; it is an exceptionally miserable heat trap. Otherwise it is almost always interesting, at least from March to November.

West of Lilypons, Md. 85, which runs north to Frederick, is a heavily traveled road with no shoulders to park on. Parallel to it and less than a mile to the west lies **New Design Road,** a wide, quiet farm road, renowned for its nesting Upland Sandpipers (hard to see, but easiest at dawn), Ring-necked Pheasants, Grasshopper and Vesper Sparrows, Horned Larks and occasional Dickcissels, its migrating Water Pipits and its wintering Rough-legged Hawks and Short-eared Owls. The birdiest part of New Design Road is the 3.7-mile stretch from Adamstown Road south to Md. 28.

Oland Road, the westward extension of Lily Pons Road to New Design Road, is bordered on the south by a pasture where the sandpipers, pipits, and sparrows are often most easily visible.

South of Md. 28, New Design Road becomes Water Plant Road, which leads to **Nolan's Ferry Recreation Area,** a picnic spot between the C&O Canal (here dry-to-damp) and the Potomac. Though best in the morning, it can be good all day in migration for birds on the river flyway: hawks, ducks, gulls, swifts, swallows, and nighthawks, as well as woodland species along the towpath, especially flycatchers, tanagers, and orioles, and the resident Barred Owls and woodpeckers.

You can also reach the canal by taking Mouth of Monocacy Road off Md. 28 0.3 mile north of Mount Ephraim Road and 2.5 miles south of the end of Md. 85. Follow the signs to Monocacy Aqueduct, a handsome bridge of white granite. These two points of access to the canal are 2.4 miles apart.

If you have time you should explore the 3.3-mile loop made by Greenfield Road, heading east from Md. 85 a mile south from Lily Pons Road. It goes south along the Monocacy, past long-abandoned fishponds, through woods and fields, returning to Md. 28 0.6 mile below its junction with Md. 85.

Among the more accessible and rewarding areas in the northern Virginia piedmont are several locations in Loudoun County. The sites described below can be combined into a long morning or a short day of pleasant open-country birding at almost any time of year.

Starting from the intersection of the Washington Beltway (I-495) and Va. 193, drive west on Va. 193 for 9.6 miles until it merges with Va. 7 at Dranesville. Continue west on Va. 7 for 3.0 miles and turn right on Road 637 at the sign for **Algonkian Regional Park.**

This small park, 2.2 miles down the road on the banks of the Potomac, is clearly managed primarily for golfers, swimmers, picnickers, and boaters, and is apt to be crowded with all of them in pleasant weather, especially on summer weekends. From January to March you may have it to yourself all day, but the rest of the year it is advisable to arrive close to dawn and plan to spend no more than a couple of hours there.

Unless you are a resident of northern Virginia with a Park Authority sticker, be sure to arrive before 9:00 A.M. on weekends from April to September or you will have to pay a stiff fee, and it frankly is not worth it from a birding viewpoint, especially that late in the morning.

The best birding is along the river; drive straight ahead to the parking lot above the boat-launching area. The Potomac itself should be scanned for loons, grebes, geese, diving ducks, and mergansers in the colder months; it serves as a highway for migrating nighthawks, swifts, and swallows in spring and fall.

A walk downstream will take you to the mouth of Sugarland Run, which may shelter teal, Wood Ducks, Pied-billed Grebes, and other waterfowl avoiding the strong river current. An abundance of dead trees around the creek is especially attractive to woodpeckers, including Red-headed Woodpeckers. In the early morning, the driving range just north of the creek is sometimes visited by Yellow-crowned Night Herons, which nest somewhere in the vicinity.

In wet summers the meadow to the right of the boat ramp may have rain pools attractive to shorebirds such as yellowlegs and Pectoral Sandpipers, and they once lured a much-admired Northern Phalarope. Migrating flocks of Water Pipits have also turned up here.

The picnic area upriver and the strip of trees along the road to the pro shop and park office are good for Northern and Orchard Orioles, Scarlet Tanagers, tree-top warblers, and perhaps Yellow-throated Vireos. The marshy area on the far side of that strip of trees has turned up Common Snipe in season, and is, incidentally, of particular interest to botanists for the freshwater meadow plants and wild-flowers that grow there.

The edge of the golf course away from the river has nesting Prairie Warblers and Yellow-breasted Chats and migrating Blue-winged and Golden-winged Warblers. It is best birded from the sewer line along the park border.

Red-shouldered Hawks and Barred Owls are resident around the park, and so are Eastern Bluebirds, thanks to plenty of bluebird boxes, but the last are most likely to be seen close to dawn or dusk.

When you run out of birds or peace at Algonkian, go back to Va. 7, cross it, and continue on Road 637 for 1.2 miles to the entrance (on the left) to **Claude Moore Conservation Education Center,** owned by the National Wildlife Federation. This is a gem of a wildlife area run by birders for birders and anyone else who enjoys nature study. Thoughtfully managed habitats include ponds, cattail marsh, mead-ows, scrub, pine woods, and deciduous forest.

Go into the little wooden building by the parking lot, pick up a trail guide and a bird list, and study the chart of all species sighted, week-by-week, as well as the list of the most recent sightings. If you can manage a weekday visit, try to be there some Monday morning at 7:15 A.M. for the bird walk the center manager conducts year-round.

Trails are still being developed, but the Overlook, Pine Woods, and Bluebird Trails are clearly marked and easy to follow. (The Bluebird Trail is off limits March-August.) You can ask the naturalist for other suggestions or the location of specific species.

In 1979 and 1980 nesting Henslow's Sparrows were the star attrac-tion, but the center bird list includes more than 160 species—60 of them breeding there. The ponds have attracted Horned Grebes, Whistling Swans, Common Goldeneyes, and Hooded Mergansers; the raptor list is substantial, and nesting birds include Woodcock, Pine and Prairie Warblers, both orioles, Blue Grosbeaks, and Grasshopper Sparrows.

Even if you find nothing particularly unusual, the diverse habitats should make for a solid day-list or simply a satisfying experience, and you will have the singular pleasure of birding an area run by people who understand and share your interest. (Your pleasure will be enhanced if you wear waterproof footgear and protect yourself against ticks.)

Next, head west on Va. 7 for 10 miles and take the Leesburg bypass on U.S. 15. Take your mileage at the intersection. Just beyond the point where Bypass 15 and Business 15 merge, you might stop at a marshy area next to the road, which often has migrating shorebirds.

The next road to the right leads to the smallest of all our national cemeteries, **Ball's Bluff,** worth a short visit both in its own right and for its little network of birdy riverside trails.

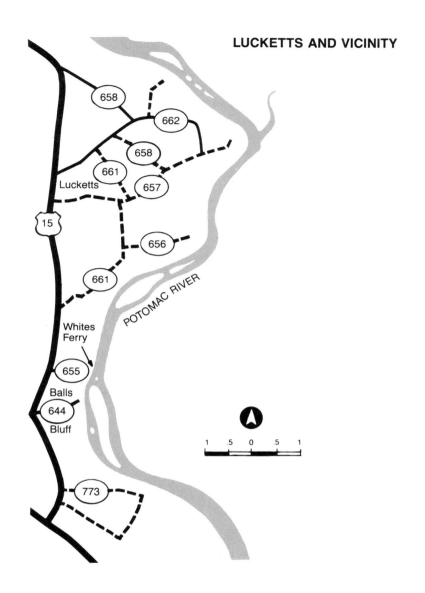

At 3.6 miles you will pass the road to White's Ferry (which you may take to western Montgomery County, Maryland); then you will cross Limestone Branch and come (at 5.0 miles) to Road 661 on the right, marked by a group of mailboxes. Turn here and slow to a crawl. You are entering a section of farmland, behind the village of **Lucketts,** laced by almost untraveled gravel roads where you can stop virtually at will if you just pull over far enough to allow another car to pass. Please do not trespass anywhere.

The area is especially good for Vesper and Grasshopper Sparrows, soaring hawks and vultures, Water Pipits and Horned Larks, Bobolinks in May, and, once in a while, a Loggerhead Shrike or a Dickcissel. The lush pastures with scattered rocky out-croppings should be scrutinized for Upland Sandpipers. (You may just see a head above the grass.) Farm ponds, hedgerows, and a few patches of deciduous woods all are worth checking, and the occasional little streams can produce anything from a Louisiana Waterthrush to a Yellow-crowned Night Heron.

A right turn onto Road 656, 2.2 miles from U.S. 15, will lead to a dead end at a farm after going through bottomland pastures and fields. Try to keep out of the way of farm trucks.

Road 661 ends at a T-junction with Road 657, where a left turn will take you back to U.S. 15 and a right turn will eventually (in 3.0 miles) lead to another dead end. Go all the way to the end, then retrace your route to the first right turn onto Road 662. After 2.5 miles turn right again onto Road 658, which ends at U.S. 15 after 2.0 more miles. (The last half-mile or so of Road 658 has been the best area to see Upland Sandpipers, but keep your expectations low.)

Similar habitat and back roads lie on the other side of U.S. 15 and on the south side of Va. 7 between Sterling and Leesburg, and you should explore them for yourself, preferably armed with a county map. Try the W&OD Trail, described on page 55.

Finally, if you have a particular interest in finding Whip-poor-wills on a summer's night or Rough-legged Hawks on a winter's day, you may want to take Va. 606, which begins on Va. 7 2.3 miles southeast of the junction with Va. 193 and runs past Reston west through the north end of Dulles Airport. The airport is especially good for the hawks and any road north and west of it is likely for Whip-poor-wills. (They are all over the county, but hard to hear in more populated areas.)

12 Lake Anna

In a triangle, the corners of which are marked by Charlottesville, Richmond, and Fredericksburg, Virginia, lies long, man-made, and many-armed Lake Anna, warmed by the discharge of the cooling canal of a nuclear power plant and enormously attractive to waterfowl. It is an especially rewarding area to explore in late fall and early spring.

Essentially, the route that follows begins at the west end of the lake

LAKE ANNA

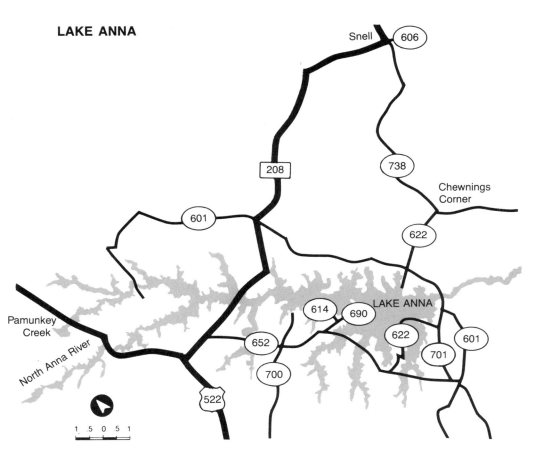

and runs east along the south side, with several detours north to fingers and bays along the lake shore.

To reach the starting point take I-95 south to Va. 3 in Fredericksburg. Go west 12.6 miles on Va. 3, fork left onto Va. 20, and follow that 13.6 miles to U.S. 522. Take your mileage at this intersection. Head south on U.S. 522 and in 8.8 miles make your first stop where the highway crosses unmarked Pamunkey Creek. This initial drive from Fredericksburg is an attractive route past rolling piedmont farms; you should be on the alert for raptors all the way.

Pamunkey Creek can be good for gulls, ducks, and shorebirds in season, especially in the cove west of the highway. You can park in the old roadbed.

You cross the North Anna River next, then at 14.7 miles turn left on Va. 208, which crosses the lake itself. You can scan the water briefly from your car on the shoulder or park (with permission) at a campground on the northwest side of the highway. Look for loons, diving ducks, and mergansers.

Make a U-turn at the far end of the bridge (18.1 miles), retrace your path, and turn left on Road 652 (21.3 miles). The next left, at 24.6 miles, is Road 700. This will take you to the nuclear plant and North Anna Visitor Center (closed Saturdays), which you may find instructive. On the coldest days of winter, the stops to the west of this point often are mostly frozen over, but all stops to the east are open. Clearly, the warming effect of waters flowing out of the plant through the cooling canal is substantial.

Turn left from Road 652 again, 1.9 miles east of Road 700, onto Road 614 and explore all its side roads unless marked by "No Trespassing" signs. Road 614 itself turns left and ends at a birdy cove; its extension, Road 690, turns into Road 1201 and ends at Duerson Point, with excellent views in three directions and consistently more birds than any other spot on the lake.

Wintering birds include numerous Pied-billed Grebes, Coots, American Wigeon, Greater and Lesser Scaup, Bufflehead, Common Goldeneye, and Hooded Mergansers. The records show that plenty of puddle ducks, Canvasbacks, Redheads, Ring-necked Ducks, plus Common Loons, Horned Grebes, Double-crested Cormorants, gulls, and terns have turned up here as well, and a variety of sparrows can be flushed out of the brush.

Return to Road 652 and check the next two creek crossings as you continue east. Both can be rewarding for loons, diving ducks, and gulls, but they require cautious stopping.

Turn left on Road 622 3.3 miles east of Road 614. Look for Red-shouldered Hawks and check the edges of the road for land birds. Where the highway turns right, keep straight on the road into the development called Jerdone Landing. The marked nature area looks good for land birds, and you can survey a cove from the boat-launching ramp at the west end of the road.

Continuing on Road 622 you will cross a long causeway with the main dam of the lake on the left. You can bird from your car or park at either end. In addition to all kinds of ducks, look for loons, Horned and Pied-billed Grebes, and Bonaparte's Gulls, and hope for a repeat of such rarities as Rough-legged Hawks and Snow Buntings. In the warmer months, especially in autumn, egrets, terns, and shorebirds are all possibilities.

The most direct route back to Washington is as follows: Road 622 at the east end of the causeway (mile 0.0) to Road 701, then left on Road 701 at 0.7 mile and left again on Road 601 at 1.5 miles. Go right on Road 622 at 4.1 miles and left on Road 738 at 7.0 miles to Snell at 16.1 miles. In Snell turn right on Road 606, which will take you to I-95 in 5.0 more miles.

Most of the field work around the lake has been done from fall to spring, with the greatest numbers of birds showing up from November to March. Because the lake is so new (it was first filled in 1972), the habitat is still changing, with marshes and reed beds forming around the edges and likely flats for shorebirds developing here and there, especially at the west end.

Lake Anna will repay exploration at any time of year, including the day after a hurricane! Included among its most exotic visitors are Sooty Shearwaters, Brown Pelicans, and Sooty and Bridled Terns.

Ridges, Valleys, and the Allegheny Plateau

In early May the variety of birds is so rich and the weather typically so perfect that most Washington birders have no need to go far from home to find all the woodland species anyone could ask for. Later in the month the first sticky day may bring with it a distraction of midges along the canal, a reminder of the drawbacks of a Washington summer, and a stimulus to head for the nearest hill.

From mid-May to the end of June the Shenandoah National Park, less than 70 miles from the Washington Beltway, offers the opportunity to study northern migrants, high-country summer visitors, and permanent residents hard to find closer to home. Not only that, but the park has a recently compiled bird list that is available at the Big Meadows Visitors Center, where a sighting log is kept up to date by both staff and transient observers. Since the published bird list is based on an all-too-thin set of records, a copy of your day's list on any visit would be enthusiastically welcomed, especially if you included numbers and locations for all but the commonest species.

Because of the park's immense popularity you will want to be in its boundaries and birding as close to dawn as you can—luckily the radio-toting multitudes are not early risers on the whole, but day hikers may be.

By the time you get to Warrenton you should decide how you will spend the morning, especially if you are making the trip on a weekend. For migrants, including raptors, take U.S. 211 toward Thornton Gap. For nesting warblers and vireos, stay on U.S. 29 to Orange and there turn southeast on Va. 230, which joins U.S. 33 at Stanardsville. U.S. 33 takes you west to the park entrance at Swift Run Gap.

If you choose the former route in May and start birding as soon as you leave Sperryville, pulling off wherever you can find a spot, you should be able to see and hear over forty species before you reach Skyline Drive.

Turn south on the drive and stop at every overlook and picnic area that catches your eye. The most widespread species near the road will be Chestnut-sided Warblers, Rose-breasted Grosbeaks, and Dark-eyed Juncos. Ravens are likely at any stop, Solitary Vireos probable anywhere above 2,500 feet. Philadelphia Vireos and Bay-breasted Warblers are among the regular spring migrants.

The figures after place names in this chapter are mileages based on the mileposts along the Skyline Drive.

At both ends of **Mary's Rock tunnel** (32.4), look and listen for Winter Wrens and Eastern Phoebes; at **Hemlock Springs Overlook,** walk along the shoulder checking the hemlocks for Black-throated Blue and Black-throated Green Warblers, as well as winter finches—Pine Siskins can linger late when they are around at all.

Take note of the parking area for White Oak Canyon Trail and a third of a mile further along turn left into the unmarked parking area for **Limberlost Trail** (42.9), a mile-long loop that yields Solitary Vireos, Blackburnian Warblers, and Veeries as nesters, plus unpredictable transients.

If you take a sharp left just beyond the bulletin board you will link up with a bridle path that runs through an old orchard and second-growth woodland. Here you might find Ruffed Grouse if you are the first on the trail for the day.

Grouse are the park's star attraction for lowland birders, but the difficulty of finding them is enough to spoil your day unless you set your expectations very low. The only strategy to follow is to enjoy any bird you may find in the habitat that grouse like—scrubby cutover land with a mixture of open ground and small trees with low branches.

The next stop is the parking area for the **upper Hawksbill Mountain Trail** (46.7). The mile-long trail to the summit is good for migrants and the brush across the drive holds nesting Woodcock and grouse in the low hemlocks. The trail up the north side of Hawksbill is shorter, steeper, but good for Canada Warblers.

By now, if you have been birding systematically, it is likely to be lunchtime just when you find yourself at Big Meadows Wayside (51.3 miles), where you can buy lunch if you like and stop in at the visitor center for bird news.

Save birding at **Big Meadows** for the afternoon; the open-country birds there are likely to be visible at any hour and the area is enough off the beaten path that you may have it to yourself.

Head across to the east side of Skyline Drive and work around the edge of the meadow, pushing back into the brush wherever it opens up enough. You are as likely to see not only grouse but Wild Turkeys here as anywhere, but the easy species will be Field and Song Sparrows, Eastern Bluebirds and Yellowthroats. Irregular nesters have included Prairie Warblers, Least and Willow Flycatchers, Blue Grosbeaks, and Vesper Sparrows. Migrant Common Snipe are out in the boggy center of the meadow.

At this point you have reached the end of both this route and the alternate one coming up from the south, described below.

If you approach the park from Swift Run Gap, at the toll booth you will be 2.8 miles south of the **South River Picnic Area** (62.9 miles), the trail head for the best walk for breeding birds in the park. Since it is also a popular trail for hikers, get there as soon after sunrise as you can.

With plenty of birds, this 3.5-mile loop can take you most of the morning. Your route, the falls trail, will take you downhill 1.0 mile to an overlook across from the top of South River Falls, then up to the left on a trail that connects with the South River Fire Road, which deposits you on Skyline Drive just north of the picnic grounds. (You can continue down to the foot of the falls for the view, but it is steep down and steep up; don't say you weren't warned!)

The particular charm of this walk is a result of the steep slope across which the trail runs, allowing good views into the forest canopy. The number of breeding species is remarkable: Louisiana Waterthrush; Ovenbird; American Redstart; Black-and-white, Blackburnian, Hooded, Worm-eating, Black-throated Blue, Black-throated Green, Parula and Cerulean Warblers (the last mostly on the fire road); Red-eyed, Yellow-throated, and Solitary Vireos; Wood Thrushes; Veeries; and Scarlet Tanagers.

Up the drive, milepost 61 marks one of the best areas for Ruffed Grouse; see what else you can find there. The next good stop is at **Booten's Gap** (55.3). The parking area is beside the Appalachian Trail, which meets Laurel Prong Trail 0.5 mile to the north. Turning right on Laurel Prong, you should find several pairs of nesting Canada Warblers in the first mile.

The entire stretch from **Milam Gap** (53.0) to **Tanner's Ridge Overlook** (51.7) is excellent birding, easily accessible because of the Appalachian Trail, which runs west of and parallel to Skyline Drive here. Grouse are always possible, and this may be the best area in the park for migrants, even better in fall than spring.

Big Meadows lies just ahead.

While the focus so far has been on spring and early summer, the park can be just as rewarding in the fall. Land-bird migrants stick to the ridges and peaks, and hawk-watching can be excellent. The rule is to look on the side of the ridge the wind is coming from. (Don't look for hawks on calm days!)

The best all-wind hawk-watching spot is **Hawksbill,** which offers a 360-degree view. For westerly winds **Mary's Rock,** up a 1.8 mile trail above Panorama at Thornton Gap, and **Stony Man,** a mile walk up Stony Man Nature Trail close to Skyland Lodge, are prime spots, and The Point Overlook (55.8) can provide superb viewing from your car.

Big Meadows attracts harriers and falcons irregularly and in small numbers. On a cold day you can scan it comfortably from inside the Visitor Center, but you should not expect a sure reward. Later in the season Snow Buntings may drop in, and winter finches may be found in the spruces north of the center.

Finally, a word on chickadees. Most you see in the park will be Carolinas, a handful will be unequivocal Black-caps, and the rest will have features of both. Reputable birders check every field mark with great care and still leave many chickadees unidentified.

Almost anyone with wanderlust is pulled toward the mountains in October, and you may want to explore Highland County in western Virginia for the first time while the foliage is at its most beautiful and the migrants are slipping south along the ridges.

The resident Ruffed Grouse, Common Ravens, Black-capped Chickadees, and Red Crossbills may be seen at any time, though, and midwinter and early June are even more inviting. From December to February or March, Golden Eagles are always present, and the nesting species of early summer include Winter Wrens, Hermit Thrushes, Golden-winged and Mourning Warblers, Bobolinks, and Rose-breasted Grosbeaks.

The most direct route from the Washington Beltway, I-495, is via I-66 and I-81, a swift, dull 2.5 hours to Staunton. From I-81 drive west on U.S. 250 about 22 miles, and, in spring, stop along the road for the next mile or two to listen and look for Golden-winged Warblers.

At 24.9 miles **Ramsey's Draft Picnic Ground** is a good spot to look for Black-capped Chickadees, breeding Winter Wrens, and Black-throated Green and Parula Warblers, either next to the road or along the hiker's trail.

The highway to the west becomes a very steep, winding road with many switchbacks. Exactly 1.9 miles west of the picnic-ground turn-off, as the road climbs Shenandoah Mountain it curves sharply left. Park at the curve on the broad gravel shoulder on the right. An hour or so after sunrise at any time of year, Red Crossbills come to collect grit at this curve after their first meal of the day. They are quite tame, and you can usually get out of your car and watch them scratching around on the opposite shoulder. Some may be in the pines on either side of the road. They cannot be relied upon at other times of the day.

Continue 0.1 mile to the crest of the mountain and the county line, Highland County to the west, Augusta County to the east. Park in the lot for the **Confederate Breastworks,** if you like, and walk up the trail, which is steep for the first half-mile and then level. The first hikers of the day may find turkeys and grouse, while Dark-eyed Juncos, Pine Warblers, and Red Crossbills are among the nesting species.

Red Crossbills may, in fact, be found all along this ridge, north from U.S. 250 to U.S. 33 in Rockingham County. If you did not see them on the eastern slope, look for them on the western slope, just before the sign "Highland FFA Welcomes You."

From the crest of the mountain, drive 2.9 miles and turn left on

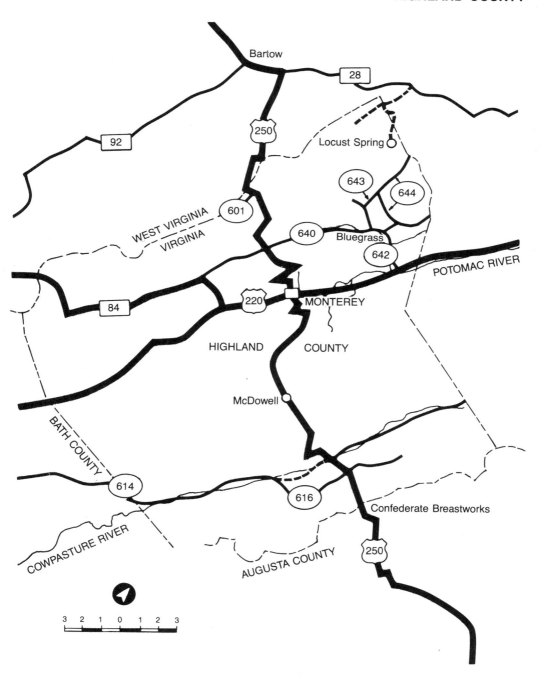

Bartow

28

92

250

Locust Spring

643

644

601

WEST VIRGINIA

VIRGINIA

640

Bluegrass

642

POTOMAC RIVER

84

220

MONTEREY

HIGHLAND   COUNTY

McDowell

BATH COUNTY

614

616

Confederate Breastworks

250

COWPASTURE RIVER

AUGUSTA COUNTY

3 2 1 0 1 2 3

Road 616. A delightful loop of 7.1 miles returns to U.S. 250 via Road 614, turning right at the T-junction immediately after crossing the Cowpasture River on a small right-angle bridge, rejoining the highway less than 2 miles west of Road 616. The lack of traffic makes it easy to stop to bird wherever you like, but the most unusual species to a piedmont birder is likely to be a Black-capped Chickadee.

The next ridge you climb is **Bullpasture Mountain.** Stop on the eastern slope wherever you can park off the road to listen and look for the nesting species: Yellow-throated and Solitary Vireos, and Kentucky, Cerulean, Golden-winged, Worm-eating, Parula, and perhaps Nashville Warblers.

In the valley on the far side is the village of **McDowell,** a good spot for Eastern Bluebirds, which nest in the fenceposts; from there to the top of **Jack Mountain,** the next ridge, Golden-winged Warblers and Cedar Waxwings are common. At the crest, a road runs south about 6 miles to **Sounding Knob,** an especially good area for Ruffed Grouse, Black-throated Green and Chestnut-sided Warblers, and Rose-breasted Grosbeaks.

In the next valley, 9 miles (without detours) from the county line, is **Monterey,** the county seat, a little town with a motel and a couple of restaurants. If you want a map of Highland County, ask the way to the office of the Highway Department.

Take a right at the flashing light onto U.S. 220. From this intersection, drive 5.4 miles to a trout hatchery on the right, worth checking for Wood Ducks, Green Herons, and other migrant water birds. If you are here in March, look for Brewer's Blackbirds in the fields en route. At 6.4 miles turn sharp left on Road 642, which runs beside the South Branch of the Potomac River. A Warbling Vireo nests on the corner.

The circuit described below is the route to take if you are looking for Golden Eagles in the winter. (Note: for the protection of the eagles do not mention them to residents of the area.) After 1.2 miles on Road 642, the ridge called the **Devil's Backbone** rises ahead on your right. The eagles often use it as a roost and circle above it. At 2.4 miles take Road 640, the first right in the village of **Bluegrass,** and at 3.9 miles go left on Road 644, or continue 2.0 miles to the state line and retrace your steps. Check all the snags and flying raptors. (Incidentally, the roads around Bluegrass are excellent in summer for Cliff Swallows and Savannah and Vesper Sparrows.)

At 5.5 miles (9.5 if you went to the state line) turn left on Road 643 (or continue a bit on Road 644 and come back), and at 6.5 miles turn left again on Road 642. At the next junction, at 7.4 miles, turn right on Road 640 and drive at least the 6.3 miles to U.S. 250, about 5 miles west of Monterey. (This is a likely stretch to look for Bobolinks in June.) If you have not seen an eagle yet, continue south 4.3 miles, turn left on Va. 84, left again after 2.4 miles onto U.S. 220, and return to Monterey.

Other raptors that winter in the county include Red-tailed, Red-shouldered, and Rough-legged Hawks, American Kestrels, and once, at least, a Bald Eagle.

If you come in early summer, go west on U.S. 250 from the intersection with Road 640, crossing into West Virginia at the crest of Alleghany Mountain. Along the first half-mile from the intersection look for Bobolinks and Cliff Swallows, then for Golden-winged Warblers in appropriate habitat. At 3.4 miles the edges of the stream and the old beaver ponds can be rewarding, and at 6.3 miles Road 601 south makes an interesting side trip for sparrows and ravens.

In West Virginia, a left turn at the junction with U.S. 28 (14.7 miles) leads in 2.2 miles to Bartow, where there is a motel suitable as a base for both exploring the bird-rich Cheat Mountains beyond and for birding the northwest corner of Highland County. For the latter pursuit go right, instead, on U.S. 28, and after 6.5 miles turn sharp right on a gravel road at the sign for **Locust Spring Picnic Ground.**

In 0.5 miles the road meets a T-junction. The road right immediately crosses back into Virginia and provides splendid birding as far as you want to go. The road left leads via the first right fork to the picnic ground in 0.6 mile. You are at about 4,000 feet here, and you are in Virginia after going through the open gate.

Nesting birds along the roads and nearby trails include Least Flycatchers; Veeries; Hermit Thrushes; Golden-crowned Kinglets; Solitary Vireos; Mourning, Black-throated Blue, Black-throated Green, Magnolia, Canada, and Blackburnian Warblers; Rose-breasted Grosbeaks; and Purple Finches. Try the path down to the beaver ponds beyond the end of the road into the picnic ground and listen for the Nashville Warbler that has been found on territory here.

On the way back, look for the Alder Flycatcher that may have returned to the southeast corner of the junction of U.S. 250 and U.S. 28.

Note on chickadees: The common species in Highland County is the Black-capped, but Carolinas and Black-capped x Carolina hybrids do occur. Identification cannot be deduced from location alone.

Washington County, Maryland 15

In the heart of Maryland's Ridge and Valley province, Washington County offers a scenic landscape and resident Turkey, Ruffed Grouse, Raven, Black-capped Chickadee, and Loggerhead Shrike.

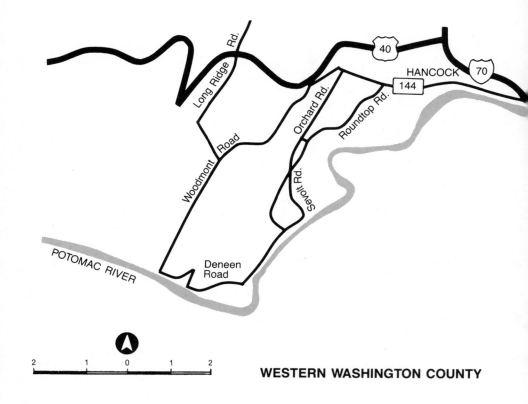

WESTERN WASHINGTON COUNTY

Breeding species include Cliff Swallow, Worm-eating, Golden-winged, and Cerulean Warblers, and a small, declining number of Bewick's Wrens. Migration time, spring or fall, can provide unsurpassed landbirding: try the third week in May just after a day or two of stormy weather, or an autumn day following the passage of a cold front.

From the Washington Beltway, I-495, drive north and west via I-270 and I-70 for 69 miles to the exit for Clear Spring. Enter Md. 68 west at mile 0.0 and get in the left lane. Cross U.S. 40 onto Mill Street, where there is a sign for Indian Springs Wildlife Management Area. At 0.5 mile turn right at the T-junction on Broadfording Road, and at 1.1 miles go left on Blairs Valley Road. At 3.8 miles turn left into the main parking lot for **Blairs Valley Lake.**

Ravens nest on top of the ridge across the lake, and in the spring Turkey and Ruffed Grouse can be heard calling or drumming from the hillsides on both sides of the valley. Barn and Cliff Swallows nest abundantly under the eaves of the barn near the parking lot, more than 100 pairs of Purple Martins flourish in the martin houses, and the numerous bluebird boxes support expanding populations of Tree

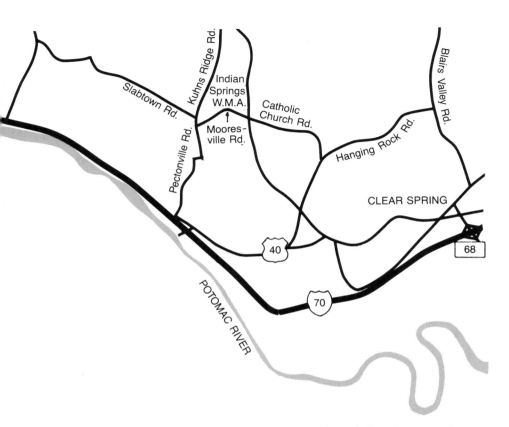

Swallows and Eastern Bluebirds. Rough-winged Swallows and Belted Kingfishers breed on the broken slopes south and west of the dam. Look for American Bitterns, Soras, and Swamp Sparrows in the marsh under the dam.

If you walk around the south end of the lake, you will find a choice of three trails to take you north on the far side of the valley: close to the lake and the creek that feeds it, near the foot of the ridge, and along the slope.

The lake itself attracts migrating loons and diving ducks. Willow Flycatchers, Warbling Vireos, Yellow-throated and Yellow Warblers, Yellow-breasted Chats, Northern and Orchard Orioles, and Blue Grosbeaks breed in the valley in the varied streamside, sycamore, and hedgerow habitats. Driving on up the road, you can park on the left in a lot at 4.0 miles, or turn left on a hunter's access road (4.4 miles) across the valley, or simply park at safe spots along the shoulder.

At the north end of the valley, turn right into a parking area at 5.1 miles. If you are there at dusk, listen for the courting Woodcock across the road. Stay a bit longer and you will be surrounded by calling Whip-poor-wills. Earlier in the day, just retrace your route 2.0 miles and turn right on **Hanging Rock Road** (mile 0.0).

Along this road you have your best chance to find a Bewick's Wren. Stop near any house with a ramshackle outbuilding to listen for the song. (Ask permission to enter private property, of course.) The thickety patches along the road are excellent for transient Mourning Warblers in late May.

Keep left at the fork at 1.6 miles, and, at 3.1 miles turn right across a wooden bridge onto **Catholic Church Road.** At 4.7 miles turn right into the site of the long-vanished church; the cemetery is still to be seen at the back of the lot. This is another good spot for Turkey, Ruffed Grouse, and Raven, as well as nesting Cooper's Hawks. Look in the marshy area downhill from the cemetery for Black-and-white, Golden-winged, and Worm-eating Warblers, Louisiana Waterthrush, and Yellow-breasted Chat. If you walk back up the road as far as a pasture on the right, there will be a stand of white pines on the left that attract Wilson's Warblers in migration.

Continue west; when the road ends at a T-junction, turn right and park in the center of the fork immediately ahead at 5.6 miles. Breeding species in the immediate vicinity include White-eyed Vireo; Black-and-white, Worm-eating, Golden-winged, Prairie, and Kentucky Warblers; and Yellow-breasted Chat.

Continue on the left fork, Mooresville Road, and turn right at 6.2 miles opposite R. Shank's mailbox. Drive into the headquarters of the **Indian Springs Wildlife Management Area** and park in a small lot by the pond on the left. This is often such a birdy area that you could easily spend the rest of the day here.

A well-marked nature trail begins at the left end of the pond and loops around through an open area with pines and alders, and then through the woods on the far side. Cedar Waxwings, Yellow Warblers, and Northern Orioles nest near the pond. Blue-winged Warblers and Northern Waterthrushes pass through in migration and Pine, Cerulean, and Kentucky Warblers nest here; Red-breasted Nuthatches winter in the pines and Rusty Blackbirds visit the swampy woods in early spring. Look for transient Olive-sided Flycatchers in May and early September.

When the nature trail joins a logging road, you can keep left on that and follow a series of tracks at random as far as you like, taking care to avoid getting lost. An especially productive road is the one that runs north just before you get back to the barn near the manager's residence. Check the thickets and woodland edges in the area opposite the parking lot for Mourning Warblers in spring migration.

When you leave, turn right on Mooresville Road. At the T-junction in 0.8 mile turn right on Pectonville Road. You have a choice at the next junction. You can either go straight ahead for a bit on **Kuhn's**

Ridge Road, which can be full of migrant warblers, with nesting Golden-wings in the clear-cut area; or you can turn left on **Slabtown Road** as far as a field that opens up on the left, where Vesper Sparrows breed. The woods en route have Pine Warblers and Ovenbirds. You will find Worm-eating Warblers off both roads.

Turn around and follow Pectonville Road all the way back to U.S. 40, a distance of 2.8 miles. Turn left and drive east about 0.4 mile. Just before the highway crosses the bridge over Licking Creek, turn right on a gravel road, drive 0.3 mile and park on the left just after crossing the railroad tracks. Immediately ahead at the "Boundary Line" sign, take a path on your left that crosses the bed of the C&O Canal and ends on the towpath. Turn left and cross the aqueduct ahead. The next mile offers excellent birding: among the nesting species are Brown Creeper, Warbling Vireo, Cerulean and Parula Warblers, and American Redstart. In May the migrant species are much more likely to be here in late morning than at dawn; look for them on the ridges earlier in the day.

Here, as everywhere else west of Blairs Valley, the common chickadee is the Black-capped, but there are both Carolinas and hybrids around. Listen for the three-note song that the hybrid usually sings.

Then return to U.S. 40 and turn left. In 0.6 mile U.S. 40 merges with I-70; continue west for about 6 miles and take the Hancock exit on Md. 144. Drive 3.4 miles to the far side of town and turn left on Round Top Road (mile 0.0).

At 3.4 miles turn left on Orchard Road and immediately left again on Sevolt Road. (You could go straight on Orchard Road, but Sevolt is the scenic route.) Sevolt Road ends at 5.2 miles, with Orchard Road coming in from the right. Go left on Deneen Road and park at the bend in 0.1 mile. Cross the canal bed on the left and walk east along the towpath.

This stretch is another good spot for Raven, Turkey, and Ruffed Grouse; Brown Creeper; Black-capped Chickadee; Warbling Vireo; Cerulean, Redstart, and Parula Warblers, and occasionally Prothonotary and Yellow-throated Warblers. If you are particularly looking for Ceruleans, here or anywhere, keep in mind that their favored habitat includes an abundance of grapevines.

Continue west 0.9 mile and, after crossing the railroad tracks, pull into an abandoned road on the left. You can walk west either on the towpath or the railroad tracks or the abandoned road. All three converge in about a mile and you can return on an alternate path. The same birds that are listed for the previous stop are found here, too.

Drive on about 2 miles and look for Blackburnian Warblers in the pines and the large oaks, especially around the sharp left turn. In another mile where Deneen Road ends at a T-junction, turn right and

SHARPSBURG AND VICINITY

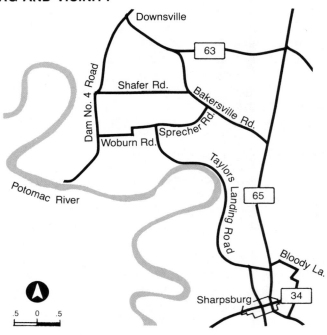

uphill on Woodmont Road. In the pine woods up on the ridge about 2.4 miles from the T-junction you may find both Pine and Blackburnian Warblers.

In another 4.0 miles you will reach U.S. 40 just after crossing Md. 144. A right turn will take you back to I-70 in 3.9 miles.

The best area to find Loggerhead Shrike is well to the east, along some back roads a few miles south of Hagerstown. From I-70, exit south on Md. 65 and drive 4.9 miles. Turn right on Md. 63 and drive 3.9 miles west to Downsville. Go south from there on Dam No. 4 Road and follow it to its end at the Potomac River. Head north again and turn right on Woburn Road, the first road east. The next right, Taylor's Landing Road, will take you south to the village of Sharpsburg.

If you have not yet seen a shrike, go left on Main Street for one block and turn left again, heading north on Md. 65. In about 0.9 mile go right on Bloody Lane, which runs east and south around a section of Antietam Battlefield, becomes Richardson Avenue, and intersects with Md. 34. Bloody Lane has had a nesting pair of shrikes in residence for the past few years.

Md. 34 leads northeast to Boonsboro, where U.S. 40A will take you east to a connection with I-70.

The Allegheny Plateau 16

When the flood of spring transients has slowed to a trickle at the end of May, think seriously about heading for a long weekend in western Maryland where Bewick's Wrens flash in and out of the rocks, Alder Flycatchers sing clear in the swamps, and Saw-whet Owls pipe in the night.

The mountains of Garrett and Allegany counties are so laced with quiet back roads, state parks, wildlife areas, and upland farms that any birder with a drop of explorer blood can find a dozen private birding spots in a few days of investigation; the sites described here are just a few of the essential ornithological landmarks.

The straightforward nonstop route from Washington is I-270 to Frederick, I-70 west to Hancock, U.S. 40 on to Cumberland, and U.S. 48 to Exit 34, from which you take Md. 36 south to Midland. From the junction of I-270 and I-495, the Washington Beltway, to Midland is 140 miles, an easy three-hour drive.

The little town of Midland is bordered to the north by a creek. Immediately after you cross the highway bridge over it, take your first left and cross it again. The second left on this side of the creek is Dan's Rock Road, which will take you to the top of Dan's Mountain (2,895 feet).

At the summit is **Dan's Rock**, a large monolith, and some radio towers. The view from the top of the rock can be stunning on a clear day. June is the best time of year for looking and listening for a Bewick's Wren, a rapidly disappearing species in the East, which likes the mixture of low scrub and rocky open spaces offered on this mountain top. Take your time and (on foot) poke down all the short unpaved roads on the summit; they all lead to a tower or shed and perhaps a brush pile, and the wrens ought to be around one of them, if not on Dan's Rock itself. Keep an eye out for the nesting pair of Ravens that sometimes perform spectacular acrobatics overhead. (Next fall keep in mind that Dan's Rock is perhaps the best hawk-watching site in Maryland.)

On your way down the mountain, stop frequently—especially for Golden-winged Warblers and perhaps Mourning Warblers.

Continue south on Md. 36 and, if you have plenty of time, go left in the village of Lonaconing to **Dan's Mountain State Park**, a pleasant picnic area in a woods with Cerulean Warblers in the tree tops.

At Westernport go right on Md. 135 and follow it 24 miles to Oakland, which is, for birders, the most central town with good motels in Garrett County. To reach the main birding areas go north on U.S. 219 for two blocks and turn left on Green Street, which soon

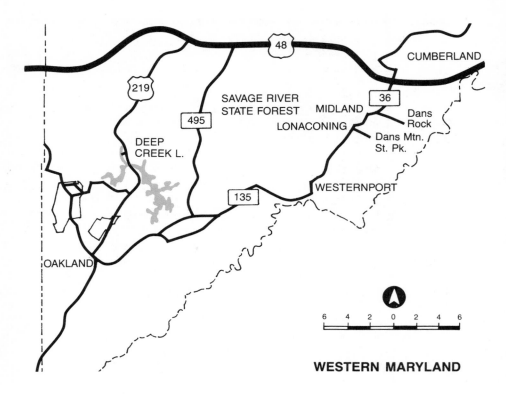

WESTERN MARYLAND

turns into Herrington Manor Road. The road runs northwest 4.2 miles to Herrington Manor State Park and continues another 2.0 miles to a fork. Bear left on Cranesville Road for Cranesville Swamp; bear right on Swallow Falls Road for Swallow Falls State Park.

Try to visit **Herrington Manor** as early in the morning as you can get in; if the entrance gate is closed, bird along the entrance road or poke along the highway. Once inside, work your way around the artificial lake in either direction, not wasting much time in the red-pine plantation but exploring thoroughly the deciduous trees, the alder swamp, and the white-pine forest off to the left of the visitor center. Alder Flycatchers; Veeries; Hermit Thrushes; Golden-winged, Chestnut-sided, Magnolia, and Black-throated Blue Warblers; and Rose-breasted Grosbeaks are among the summer residents; and the chickadees you see and hear will be Black-capped.

The main entrance to **Swallow Falls State Park** is 3.2 miles north; on a holiday weekend especially, it pays to beat the crowd, as some of the most interesting birds are close to the parking lot, in the hemlocks along the river that nonbirders enjoy just as much as you do. Look for Solitary Vireos, Black-throated Green, Blackburnian, Canada, and Magnolia Warblers in the forest and Northern Waterthrushes on and over the river rocks. Beyond the parking lot, Maple Glade Road—unpaved but pleasant—departs northwest past park headquarters and ends at Cranesville Road in 2.5 miles. The narrow road gets little traffic and is especially good for Least Flycatchers. Park carefully and explore the old trails that branch off on either side for a better look at some of the species that like a mixed coniferous-deciduous forest.

At Cranesville Road turn right and drive 2.1 miles. The road eventually descends toward **Cranesville Swamp** and winds along its eastern edge for the next three miles. The first left, beside a little square house, promptly doubles back to the south and into West Virginia. The daring birder who ventures into the bog, either in waders or in clothes to get soaked in, will find that either road gives good access; those who would remain dry-shod will find the un-traveled West Virginia road best for frequent stops and close listening. Make a night visit to hear the Saw-whet Owls, a challenge to sort out from the hundreds of noisy frogs. Come back in the morning to study the songs of Alder and Willow Flycatchers, which both nest in the alders, the former apparently to the south of the square house, after the bog widens out and is broken up with stands of young conifers, the latter mostly to the north where the bog is narrow and open. (Both species have been found around the church 0.1 mile farther up Cranesville Swamp Road). Other inhabitants include Golden-crowned Kinglets, Nashville Warblers, Swamp Sparrows, and many of the species listed under the state parks.

A small bog close to Oakland is reached by taking U.S. 219 north from Md. 135 about 3.5 miles and turning left into the Mount Nebo Wildlife Management Area. (The gravel road is on the south side of the headquarters buildings and looks like a driveway.) Parking is difficult (even for a small car) but possible at the bog, which has at least one pair of Alder Flycatchers, plus Veeries, Golden-winged and Chestnut-sided Warblers, and Swamp Sparrows. The road leads on to a paved road that goes left back to Oakland or right toward Swallow Falls. The road through Mount Nebo can be very muddy; try it only in dry weather.

When bird song dies down in the afternoon, use the time in exploration of habitat. A likely stretch is reached by taking U.S. 219 south of Oakland and then looping back on several of the roads through farmland to the left and right of the highway. The first left, Jasper Riley Road, goes past **Welch Road**, a spur that leads north to a gas well and two small impoundments, good for Wood Ducks and Spotted Sandpipers. Savannah Sparrows and Bobolinks may be on both sides of Welch Road, and in the boggy meadow on the western side, the sharp-eyed may find Upland Sandpipers, while Willow Flycatchers sing beside the little stream.

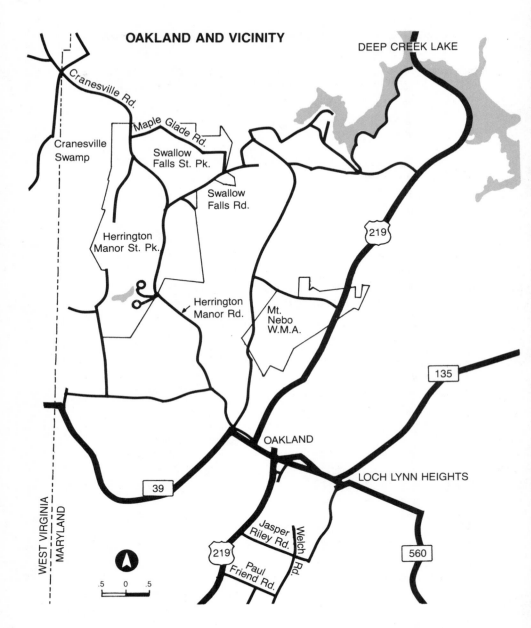

OAKLAND AND VICINITY

DEEP CREEK LAKE

Cranesville Rd.

Cranesville Swamp

Maple Glade Rd.

Swallow Falls St. Pk.

Swallow Falls Rd.

Herrington Manor St. Pk.

Herrington Manor Rd.

Mt. Nebo W.M.A.

219

135

OAKLAND

LOCH LYNN HEIGHTS

39

Jasper Riley Rd.

Welch Rd.

219

Paul Friend Rd.

560

WEST VIRGINIA

MARYLAND

.5   0   .5

If you continue south on U.S. 219, the next left, **Paul Friend Road**, has a small stand of pines 70 yards along on the right. Birding from the road only, look for Red-headed Woodpeckers in the pines.

Try the side roads off Paul Friend Road as well. Several of the farms in this Amish community have feeders that you can see easily from your car, often with interesting visitors.

The Western Shore

The proximity of Baltimore to the Chesapeake Bay provides birders of that city easy access to much-wanted birds that rarely, if ever, turn up close to Washington.

All stops on this tour are on the far side of Baltimore harbor. To reach them you must pay seventy-five cents each way to take either the Harbor Tunnel or the Francis Scott Key Bridge (or squander the equivalent in gasoline by driving all around the Baltimore Beltway, I-695).

If you want to make a full day of it, rise early and head for **Gunpowder Falls State Park**, renowned for resident owls, wintering waterfowl and sparrows, and breeding Least Bitterns, Virginia Rails, Whip-poor-wills, Bald Eagles, and a wide assortment of passerines.

The most direct route is by way of the Harbor Tunnel and I-95 to the Whitemarsh exit, 3.1 miles north of I-695. Go east 1.4 miles to U.S. 40, then north 0.6 mile to Ebenezer Road, Md. 149, and follow it 4.2 miles east to the park; Ebenezer Road becomes Grace's Quarter Road in the village of Chase.

The main entrance to the park, the Hammerman Area, opens at 8:00 A.M. A $3 fee is charged, except from October to April, or weekdays in May and September, or summer Mondays.

An always free section lies farther down the road, which forks soon after the right turn for the marina. Bear right and park 1.3 miles from the park entrance. Walk down the track that forks left from the continuation of the road. In spring and summer, Virginia Rails in the small marsh respond readily to a tape; Yellow-breasted Chats and Orchard Orioles sing around the edges.

The track ends at Dundee Creek, with winter views of Whistling Swans, American Wigeon, and other dabbling and diving ducks. You can walk to the right along the shore to a boat ramp and back 0.1 mile along the road to your car.

The stand of pines on the road above the parking area should be checked for owls, Eastern Bluebirds, and Red-breasted Nuthatches. Any trail can be good for land birds at any season.

The main park is well worth a visit, especially out of season. Park at Picnic Area A and walk down to the marsh, where Virginia Rails and Least Bitterns are present all summer. Then drive down to the boat ramp and check the trees across the creek that serve as a Bald Eagle roost.

The Gunpowder River, overlooked by the beach, is excellent for waterfowl in winter, especially for Common Mergansers. On the far side of the parking lot a trail leads out into yet another marsh.

The center of the park is being allowed to revert from lawn to

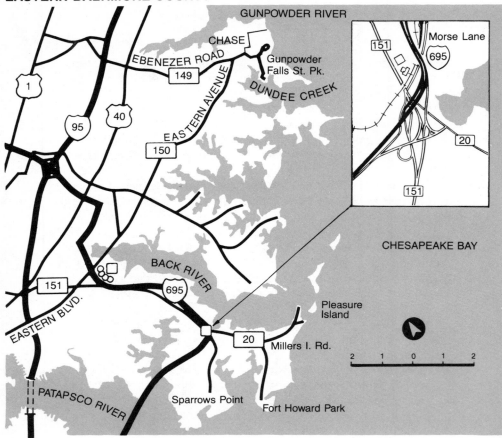

abandoned field. It should be worth checking for sparrows at any season.

On leaving the park, go back 0.5 mile to Md. 150, turn left, and follow it all the way back to Baltimore. (It is variously named Eastern Avenue and Eastern Boulevard.) After about 8 miles, the road crosses the Back River.

At the next light go right onto Diamond Point Road and fork right onto the gravel road next to it. In 0.2 mile, just beyond the blue house, drive into the hard grassy field that goes out to the river's edge. Except at full high tide, extensive mud flats lie before you, very popular with gulls and terns though not much used by shorebirds. In late August and September it is the best location in the region to look for Franklin's Gulls among the thousands of resting Laughing Gulls. The rarest tern species to show up here so far was a pair of Roseates. The light is always good.

Drive back to Eastern Boulevard and cross it straight into the **Back River Sewage Treatment Plant**, perhaps the best birding area in Baltimore. You are welcome to drive or walk anywhere except through the gate in the chain-link fence in the southeast corner (which leads to a private landfill, never open to the public.)

The pine stand near the entrance was famous one winter for a visiting Boreal Chickadee; it is always worth checking for owls, Red-breasted Nuthatches, and migrants.

Leave the Mechanical Screen Building to your right and continue straight ahead up to the round settling tanks. In the fall, look for Franklin's Gulls among the Laughing Gulls, mostly sitting on the grass. In the winter, Ring-billed Gulls fly round and over the tanks; they are sometimes joined by a Black-headed Gull and possibly (and always controversially) by a Mew Gull. In March and April, Bonaparte's Gulls predominate, with occasional Little and Black-headed Gulls among them.

Retrace your route to the first right turn, which will take you downhill past aerators that attract thousands of Starlings and once in a while a Brewer's Blackbird. (The aerators may be replaced soon by more settling tanks.)

At the end of the aerators is a network of square tanks laced by catwalks, a wonderful place for gull photography, especially of Bonaparte's Gulls. Blackbirds and waterfowl are partial to the square tanks as well.

Where the paved road curves left around these tanks, keep straight on the gravel road and drive as far as the entrance to the landfill to check the cattail and mallow marsh on the right for herons, shorebirds, and rails. Keep out of the way of trucks!

Then go back to the corner, turn right, and right again at the next intersection. The road ends at the river, where model-plane enthusiasts may be flying their planes. Make a point of keeping out of their way.

The river is at its best on a winter afternoon when it is half frozen over and the landfill is functioning. Among the thousands of wintering Herring and Great Black-backed Gulls, you may find Glaucous, Iceland, Thayer's, Lesser Black-backed, and all the smaller gulls to be looked for at the round tanks. The mouth of Bread-and-Cheese Creek is on your right and is especially good for ducks, small gulls, and shorebirds.

Explore the north side of the sewage plant as you have time. There are sludge piles and ponds, sparrowy fields, and swampy woods. Blue Grosbeaks are common in summer and a Cooper's Hawk is resident in winter. Red-tailed and Red-shouldered Hawks often circle overhead.

The odorless sludge ponds in the plant are filled, emptied, and

BACK RIVER SEWAGE TREATMENT PLANT

after Jim Stasz

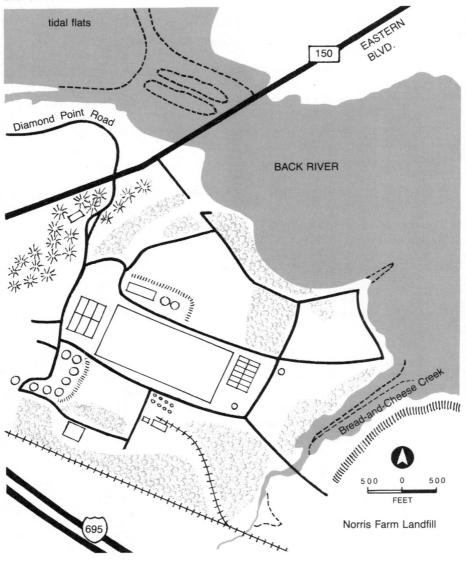

tidal flats

150

EASTERN BLVD.

Diamond Point Road

BACK RIVER

Bread-and-Cheese Creek

500   0   500
FEET

Norris Farm Landfill

695

relocated so unpredictably that no directions to them can be given. In the months of shorebird migration, seek them out for yourself; they can be excellent for Black-bellied and Lesser Golden Plovers, Pectoral, Spotted, and Solitary Sandpipers, both yellowlegs, and all the "peep."

When you leave, turn left and after 0.5 mile head toward Sparrow's Point on I-695, just west of the plant. After 4.8 miles, keep right on Md. 151 south, get in the lane for Edgemere and Fort Howard, and exit at 5.3 miles, keeping in the right lane for Md. 20. At the T-junction at 5.8 miles, turn left on Md. 20, which merges in 0.25 mile with Md. 151 north.

Immediately, just before the railroad overpass, turn right on Morse Lane and park under the second overpass of the beltway. If you are wearing shoes with good traction, walk up the steep, paved slope on the right almost to the top. Look across to the first beltway overpass and the vertically rectangular metal boxes on its side. The most famous (and inaccessible) Barn Owls in Maryland live here, but you can only see into the boxes from high up.

If you don't see the owls, go back to Md. 151, turn right, and stop in 0.1 mile just before the second gate (into DAP, Inc.) after the railroad overpass. Look over to the beltway overpass to your right, and you will see two identical boxes. Sometimes the owls are there instead, but you will probably need a scope to see them.

Make a cautious U-turn and exit onto Md. 20 from the left lane. Continue south about 1.8 miles and turn left on **Miller's Island Road**. Measuring from the turn, after 0.7 mile, note Hertzinger Road on the left. On spring evenings Woodcock use the field west of this road as a display ground, and both Whip-poor-wills and Chuck-will's-widows nest in the adjacent woods. You can pull into Hertzinger Road to watch and listen; then continue on Miller's Island Road.

At 1.0 mile, park carefully on the left (go too far and you're in a swamp). On the right is a vast marsh with nesting King, Virginia, and Black Rails, migrant Soras, Common Gallinules, and American Bitterns, breeding Least Bitterns, Marsh Wrens, and Swamp Sparrows. In the warmer months all the local herons (except Yellow-crowned Night Herons), egrets, and ibis can be seen. Ospreys hunt in summer, Northern Harriers from fall to spring, and wintering Common Snipe fly in and out.

Another good stop is at 1.1 miles on the right; you will see more if you stand on the hood of your car. Rails are not as close to the road here, but the very best spot for Soras is at 1.2 miles.

At 1.4 miles turn right at the White Swan Inn and drive to the end of the road, parking by the Ramona Cafe. Walk with your scope out to the tip of the old road. (Light is good only from noon on.)

Across the channel in front of you is Pleasure Island, which has produced a large shorebird list in late July: Piping Plovers, Red Knots, Whimbrel, Ruddy Turnstones, and Sanderlings are all among the Western Shore rarities. Skimmers may appear in late August, and large rafts of scaup and flocks of Bonaparte's Gulls in spring.

The pilings back to your left are excellent for terns: Forster's are the most common, but there are noteworthy records of Caspian, Royal, and Black Terns as well. All the rarer gulls have been seen here, including a Little Gull in summer, and loons, grebes (sometimes a Red-necked Grebe), and waterfowl are regular winter visitors.

The fields along Md. 20 south of Miller's Island Road should be checked for shorebirds and for Franklin's Gulls among the Laughing Gulls. When **Fort Howard Park**, 2 miles farther south, is open to the public (only from April to October), it is worth a visit in migration, especially for hawk watching. To get a permit to enter, you must call the Edgemere-Sparrow's Point Recreation Council at Area Code 301, 477-8330, Monday to Friday, 11:00 A.M.-4:00 P.M.

The last stop is on the way back to Washington. At the Amoco station on Md. 20, 1.1 miles north of Miller's Island Road, go left on Sparrow's Point Road. Turn left in 1.0 mile on Md. 151, right in 0.3 mile on Wharf Road, bear right in 0.2 mile toward Francis Scott Key Bridge and Dundalk, and immediately park on the shoulder for a quick check of the pond below you on the right. Common Gallinules, King Rails, and Wood Ducks have nested here; wintering ducks include American Wigeon, Shoveler, Gadwall, Hooded Merganser, Bufflehead, and Common Goldeneye. Don't step over the railing or take photographs. At the bottom of the hill, merge onto Bethlehem Boulevard and follow the signs to Francis Scott Key Bridge.

Note: If you want to skip either Gunpowder Falls State Park or Miller's Island Road, the direct route to or from the Back River Sewage Treatment Plant is via Francis Scott Key Bridge and I-695 to Eastern Boulevard, exiting east to the first light. Go right for the plant, left for Diamond Point Road.

18 Baltimore Harbor

In the entire region no better place to study gulls from October to May can be found than Baltimore Harbor, which also offers close-to-home opportunities for watching grebes, cormorants, herons, ducks, and shorebirds, as well as raptors and passerines, all in their appropriate seasons. Rarities that have been found here in the last few years include Red-necked and Eared Grebes, Glaucous, Iceland, Thayer's, Lesser Black-backed, and Black-headed Gulls, and a Snowy Owl.

This tour has both scenic and historical attractions. It is limited to the south side of the harbor, requiring no tunnel or bridge tolls for birders coming from Washington.

The harbor shoreline changes constantly, with abandoned land suddenly being converted to a dock, a terminal, or a factory. Most of

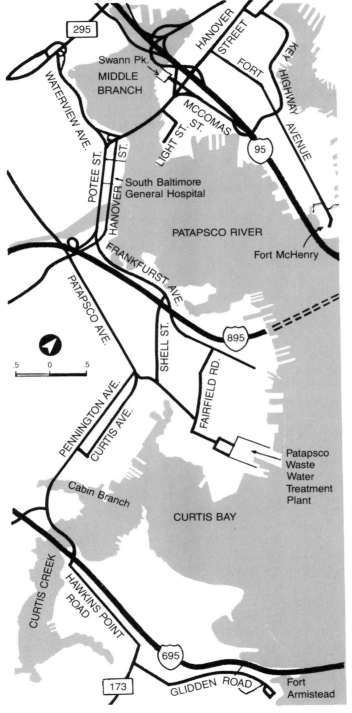

BALTIMORE HARBOR

295

Swann Pk.
MIDDLE BRANCH

WATERVIEW AVE.

HANOVER STREET

FORT

KEY HIGHWAY

MCCOMAS ST.

LIGHT ST.

ST.

95

POTEE ST.

HANOVER ST.

South Baltimore
General Hospital

PATAPSCO RIVER

Fort McHenry

FRANKFURST AVE.

PATAPSCO AVE.

.5   0   .5

895

SHELL ST.

FAIRFIELD RD.

PENNINGTON AVE.

CURTIS AVE.

Cabin Branch

Patapsco
Waste
Water
Treatment
Plant

CURTIS BAY

CURTIS CREEK

HAWKINS POINT ROAD

695

173

GLIDDEN ROAD

Fort
Armistead

the birding areas described here should be accessible for some years to come. If you have time, explore the byways in between on your own.

Take either I-95 or Md. 295, the Washington-Baltimore Expressway, to their shared exit in downtown Baltimore for Hanover Street, Md. 2 south. Stay in the right lane, fork right into the left-turn lane, and turn left across Hanover at the first traffic light onto Cromwell Street.

When Cromwell Street ends in two blocks, turn right on Light Street and drive about a mile to its end at Ferry Bar Park. After looking into the harbor there, bear left around the old warehouse and park in 0.2 mile by an open area on the right. Walk over to the water's edge on the right, taking care not to flush the hundreds of Canvasbacks, Lesser Scaup, and Ruddy Ducks that may be sheltered by the long pier before you. Look for Redheads among them. (This spot may not be worth checking on weekdays, because of human disturbances.)

Go back to Hanover Street and turn right. In 0.7 mile, turn right on West Fort Avenue and follow it about 2 miles to **Fort McHenry National Monument**.

Despite its manicured appearance, Fort McHenry has a good reputation as a migrant trap, with such varied visitors as falcons, Water Pipits, and Upland Sandpipers, as well as passerines hiding in the trees and bushes. There is a resident pair of Ringed Turtle Doves. You may find loons, grebes, and Oldsquaw offshore in winter. At this writing a Lesser Black-backed Gull is passing its fourth winter there, spending most of its time on one of the pilings or along the shore in the cove just to the right of the entrance. (Walk down to the water's edge behind the huge statue of, presumably, Orpheus.)

Now return to Hanover Street, turn left, and, just beyond the second overpass, go right on West McComas Street. It ends just ahead at **Swann Park**, a good stop only in the morning. Cross the open field in front of you with your scope, and scan the harbor and the far shoreline for gulls, shorebirds, and herons.

Back at Hanover Street, turn right and follow it across the bridge over Middle Branch, moving to the left lane. On the far side, the highway divides and becomes Potee Street southbound. Turn left at the second traffic light onto Reedbird Avenue and in one block cross Hanover Street into the grounds of **South Baltimore General Hospital**. The parking lot overlooks the harbor in a good area for loons, gulls, the same ducks you saw near Ferry Bar Park, and, when the reservoirs freeze over, Common Mergansers. Drive up to the north parking lot and little Broening Park just beyond it. A mud flat that emerges across the water at low tide is particularly good for gulls, and you may see Scarlet, the city's resident Peregrine, hunting in the neighborhood.

From the north exit, cross Hanover Street on Cherry Hill Road and turn left on Potee Street again. Continue south 0.6 mile and fork left on Frankfurst Avenue. At 0.8 mile from the fork, make a U-turn via the left-turn lane for Frankchilds Street and go back 0.1 mile. Just beyond the end of the guardrail, park on the shoulder. Walk down the very trashy fisherman's path to a cove in the harbor. Head straight away from the road; don't follow the more conspicuous path to the right.

This cove is perhaps the birdiest in the harbor, with plenty of ducks, plus the possibility of coots and grebes, and gulls and herons standing along the shoreline and on the old wrecks beyond. The light is always good. Don't be deterred from stopping by the seediness of the environs.

Make another U-turn as soon as you can (0.2 mile). When Frankfurst Avenue forks left in 0.5 mile, keep right on Shell Street, which ends at Patapsco Avenue in 0.7 mile.

To reach the promising new **Patapsco Waste Water Treatment Plant**, go left on Patapsco Avenue. In 0.5 mile turn right on Fairfield Road, which becomes Northbridge. Bear left at the stop sign and turn left on Asiatic Avenue at 1.1 mile. Turn right into the plant entrance in 0.1 mile and ask permission to bird. (It has always been granted, so far.) Check the settling tanks and drive down to the harbor where it is easy to scan for water birds.

Return to Patapsco Avenue, keeping in the left lane, and, 0.2 mile after you pass Shell Street, turn left on well-marked Pennington Avenue. In 1.2 miles you cross **Cabin Branch**; if there are birds on the flats on the right or on the pilings on the left, you can park just ahead on the right, where the curb ends. Glaucous, Iceland, Thayer's, and Black-headed Gulls have all turned up here, but a nearby landfill has closed since then.

The road beyond becomes Hawkins Point Road, then Fort Smallwood Road. At 3.5 miles from Cabin Branch, bear right into the left-turn lane for Glidden Road.

Take Glidden Road to its end in 1.5 miles at Fort Armistead, keeping alert for the trucks that hurtle recklessly out of the paint factory entrance road on the right.

Before you reach the fort, stop 1.3 miles from Fort Smallwood Road, park, and walk across to the water under the bridge. Check the pilings and wrecks in the cove for white-winged gulls and cormorants (in memory of the Great Cormorant that was seen here once) and the water for Red-breasted Mergansers and scoters.

Fort Armistead, a small park with good warbler habitat (try the top of the ruins) and a long fishing pier, looks across to Fort Carroll, a harbor island, and Sparrows Point. The gull-filled pilings beyond the paint company dock on the right are best seen from the end of the fishing pier. Bonaparte's Gulls and various terns are often present in spring.

To reach a westbound access point onto the Baltimore Beltway (I-695), return to Fort Smallwood Road and turn right. After 1.7 miles, turn left onto New Ordnance Road, Md. 710, and follow the signs.

If you return instead to your starting point on Hanover Street, an entrance to I-95 is 0.3 mile ahead. If you take it and pass by the first exit for Md. 295 in about a block, you can pull over with complete safety onto the very wide shoulder beyond it and look down into the end of Middle Branch. You may find ducks, gulls, herons, and shorebirds just below you.

19 Sandy Point State Park

Birders who seek the varied pleasures of owling, watching spring and fall hawk flights, finding Black Rails, sorting through gull flocks, building a fat warbler list, scanning for waterfowl, and chasing rarities, should sample Sandy Point State Park. At the west end of the Chesapeake Bay Bridge, it lies but 25 miles from the Washington Beltway (I-495) just off U.S. 50.

You are unlikely to be able to explore all its diverse habitats thoroughly in one day, but just part of a morning can, if you are lucky, provide birding as rewarding as anywhere in Maryland. Ask those who saw a Northern Shrike, a Fulvous Whistling Duck, and a Common Ground Dove one November day, or the ones who viewed a Sabine's Gull before breakfast and had studied a Franklin's Gull and an Iceland Gull by lunch, all on a May morning.

The hours and fees of the park are somewhat unpredictable. The former range from 8:00 A.M. to 5:00 P.M. in winter to twenty-four hours in summer, with a variable expansion in spring and contraction in fall.

The park telephone number is (301) 974-1249.

As you approach Sandy Point, take note of the Sunoco station on the right, at the intersection with Whitehall Road, and then the Shell station on the left, at the intersection with Log Inn Road. (We will come back to these landmarks later.) The approach to the park is by way of an exit to the right at the sign "Oceanic Drive and Sandy Point State Park." The overpass will deposit you on the left side of U.S. 50, at a fork. The left branch takes you to park headquarters, the right one to the tollbooth, which sometimes demands quarters. If you take the first left beyond the tollbooth, you will come to the East Beach parking lot. If you go straight on, you will come to an enormous paved lot on the right serving the marina and the South Beach, and then a

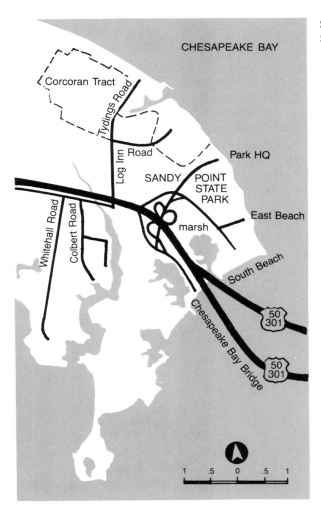

CHESAPEAKE BAY

Corcoran Tract

Tydings Road

Log Inn Road

Park HQ

SANDY POINT STATE PARK

East Beach

marsh

South Beach

Whitehall Road

Colbert Road

Chesapeake Bay Bridge

50 301

50 301

1   .5   0   .5   1

smaller unpaved lot on the left, closed until after the last frost. *Park only in a parking lot at all times of year.*

Across the main road from the East Beach lot, an unpaved road leads to a small picnic area (where you can park in the warmer months) and then to short foot trails, the Pond Trail to the left and the mysteriously named Symbi Trail to the right. Both offer good marsh edge birding, the latter looping back eventually to the picnic area past a large stand of pines much favored by owls, notably Great Horned, Barred, and Long-eared. The marsh has year-round Marsh Wrens and Virginia Rails, and is good for migrant Sora, King and Clapper Rails, and summering Black Rails—it has even been known to shelter at least one Yellow Rail.

When you return to the main road, walk back toward the highway from the tollbooth and take the marked service road on the right, which will take you through excellent sparrow habitat. At the fork, the trail to the left leads to the road to headquarters, which is reliable for Blue Grosbeaks. The right fork goes through a second-growth woods that can be alive with warblers in migration; it ends at the bay beyond a grove of hollies frequented by Cedar Waxwings and Hermit Thrushes. After scanning the bay for waterfowl, gulls, and terns, according to season, walk right along the shore around a cove that borders the small marsh where Black Rails breed regularly. This is easiest at low tide, and occasionally impossible at very high tide. You will find yourself at the East Beach parking lot and picnic area, which can be one of the prime spots for hawk-watching in spring and fall.

Continue south along the beach where stone jetties shelter ducks and gulls and provide habitat for a Purple Sandpiper or two, mostly in November; they are sometimes used by the Snow Buntings that wander the gravel parking lots and the grassier parts of the beach in late fall (often in the company of Lapland Longspurs). The reeds on your right are a dependable spot to look for Tree Sparrows in winter, and they enclose areas that may eventually be developed, if funding permits, into a shorebird sanctuary. Several years ago the reeds were less widespread and the flats they have replaced attracted almost every shorebird on the Maryland list. At present, most are fly-overs, though there is still a lagoon or two they like in the reeds. (The bay shoreline is worth checking, too, of course.)

The man-made hill next on the right is another fine perch for hawk-watching. In spring there are major south-to-north flights up the western shore of the bay, especially of Kestrels, Sharpshins, Ospreys, and Northern Harriers. In autumn, when buteo flights can be spectacular, the movement is east to west, across the bay from Kent Island. In both seasons the best conditions are on a day of light southwest winds three to four days after a strong cold front.

Where the shoreline swings west the beach widens out, becoming a loafing ground for the huge flocks of gulls (up to 10,000 birds) that accumulate here in late April and May. (In winter they prefer offshore ice.) The bathhouse between the south parking lot and the beach provides a good vantage point and windbreak and a rendezvous for the patient birders who scope with remarkable success for Glaucous, Iceland, Lesser Black-backed, and Franklin's Gulls among the hordes of more common species resting on the sand. Bonaparte's Gulls most often occur erratically in March, April, and October, Little Gulls rarely among them, and the only Black-headed Gulls seen so far showed up one January; these species tend to be seen only in flight or on the water.

Least Terns sometimes breed at Sandy Point; all the other tern species (except Sandwich) that breed along the Delmarva coast are regular visitors, as are Black Skimmers.

The jetty at the far corner of the beach by the Bay Bridge is easy to walk on and offers close views of the diving ducks that winter here, especially Canvasback and Greater and Lesser Scaup, and the best chance to see Purple Sandpipers in November. The channel beside the jetty leads into the park harbor; these protected waters can be surveyed first from the jetty, then from a dirt road, and then from the paved parking lot. If you cross the lot and the main road, you can bird your way back to the East Beach lot, working the wood-and-marsh edge on either side of the old mansion. Least Bitterns and Common Gallinules regularly breed in the marsh.

Three spots outside the tollbooth offer prime woodland birding:

(1) Just 0.5 mile from the Shell station, **Log Inn Road** makes a right-angle turn and bends left at 0.8 mile. Park at the bend and take the footpath on the north side of the road, which will lead you to pine stands often popular with Long-eared Owls, and beyond into fine deciduous forest.

(2) The 210-acre **Corcoran Environmental Study Tract** is accessible to any birder who asks permission at park headquarters. The entrance lies 0.7 mile down the road from the Shell station, on the left. (Keep straight on Tydings Road when Log Inn Road turns right.) The tract is fenced in and the gate is locked, but you will be told at headquarters how to get in. Mature pines, tulip poplars, and abandoned fields provide varied habitat for owls and passerines.

(3) For an hour or two of good birding, follow the access road that parallels U.S. 50 on the south, east from the Sunoco station. Take Colbert Road, the first right, and continue straight on for 0.1 mile on gravel beyond the point where the paving goes left. Park by a little log cabin and explore the nature trail across the road and the fields to the east. This sanctuary, owned by the Chesapeake Bay Foundation, is both charming and birdy, especially in migration. Access is unrestricted.

Five Sites South and East of Washington 20

Birders who find themselves closer to the Wilson Bridge than to Rockville have a number of fine nearby areas to explore south and east of Washington.

Among the best and most accessible birding areas within the Washington Beltway is **Oxon Hill Children's Farm**, at the second Maryland exit east of the Wilson Bridge (the first is I-295). Take Exit 3A for Md. 210 south, turn sharp right at the top of the ramp and right

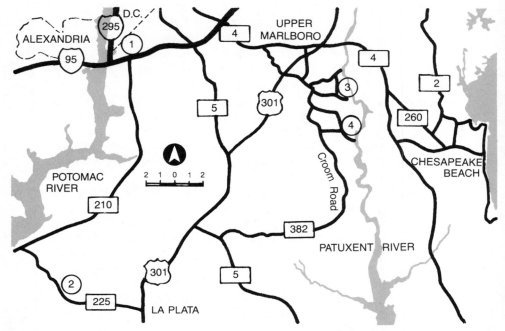

1. Oxon Hill Children's Farm
2. Myrtile Grove Wildlife Management Area
3. Jug Bay Natural Area
4. Merkle Wildlife Management Area

SOUTHERN MARYLAND

again at the first opportunity. This road will take you back over the beltway and deposit you in the Children's Farm parking lot.

The first area to cover, especially near dawn during migration, is the hilltop straight ahead, on the far side of the parking lot from the entrance road (leaving the farm entrance gate to your left). Warblers and other migrants often drop into the tops of the trees on the slopes below and are relatively easy to study. If the ground is soggy, it is best just to work the woods as far as the power line beyond the orchard (in plain sight) and come back along the hedgerow on the other side of the apple trees.

If footing is dry, cross the cleared ground under the power line, plunge into the woods on the left, and walk downhill along the trail you will come to, along a ridgeline. This oak-hickory-beech grove can be birdy or silent, but you are likely to flush a Great Horned Owl, at least, and it is a pleasant route to the open fields below. The fields themselves are usually sterile (though falcons and harriers are probable in winter), but they are intersected by marshy streams with habitat favored by winter sparrows and summer Marsh Wrens, Yellowthroats, and blackbirds.

Ahead and to the left, Oxon Run drains into a good-sized lagoon, the mouth of which is crossed by I-295. The creek sometimes has migrant shorebirds along its edges, and the lagoon harbors coots, grebes, and ducks. Gulls are abundant in the air and on the water, as the Blue Plains Sewage Treatment Plant and the adjacent landfill are just across the way. Flocks should be scanned for rarities, since Glaucous, Iceland, Thayer's, Lesser Black-backed, and Franklin's Gulls have all been reported nearby.

Work your way back to the woodland edge and proceed counterclockwise, birding the slopes until you come to a wire fence, easy enough to climb over since there is no barbed wire. (If you don't climb fences on principle, you will have to return the way you came, and it would probably be better not to take this route in the first place.) On the other side of the field ahead, a dirt road crosses your route. Leftward and uphill, it takes you back through the farm exhibits to the parking lot; rightward and downhill, it converges with a paved road that takes you to bottomland woods, sparrowy thickets, and excellent views of the lagoon. Go downhill and again skirt the woods, working to the left, circling the fields, and exploring any byways that invite you. You are near the river here, and passerines moving up the Potomac flyway can be dense in the trees and bushes. Look for breeding Willow Flycatchers and Blue Grosbeaks. In the colder months this is a prime area for Rusty Blackbirds and Common Snipe.

You will eventually find yourself back at the paved road. Turn right and bird your way uphill and back to your car. (You can, of course, use the paved road downhill as well as up and save some time, though you may miss a few birds. Alternatively, the unpaved road through the lower farm is the shortest cut of all.)

The whole area can be covered quite thoroughly in less than a full morning, and travel time from downtown Washington, Alexandria, and much of Prince George's County is negligible.

Myrtle Grove Wildlife Management Area is further afield but still a half-day outing. Take the same beltway exit, 3A, and follow Md. 210 south 18 miles to Md. 225, where you turn left and go east for 4.9 miles to the Myrtle Grove entrance on the left. Alternatively, go south on U.S. 301 to LaPlata, turn right on Md. 225 and drive 5.8 miles to Myrtle Grove, on the right. It is a good idea to call in advance to find out whether access is currently restricted to certain hours. Call (301) 743-5161.

The entrance road runs for a mile through upland deciduous woods, crisscrossed by trails, to a man-made lake popular with wintering and visiting ducks when filled, and migrant shorebirds when drained, as it sometimes is, unpredictably. Check the hedgerows along the last hundred yards of the road for White-crowned Sparrows and perhaps a Loggerhead Shrike.

A dyke curves around the left side and far end of the lake; walk the road on top of it until it ends in an area of young pines, backed by a tall stand of older pines. If it is not too wet underfoot, a visit to the older trees can yield anything from Pine Warblers to Long-eared Owls to crossbills in season. Otherwise, retrace your steps to a road that runs downhill from the dyke into a deciduous bottomland. All along the dyke be alert for the eye-level birds in the trees growing below its banks.

The road below makes a huge, more-or-less square loop around and through a heavily wooded swamp. Keep right initially, twice, and take a spur road that ends with the debris of some undefinable wooden structures. A plank across the little stream on your right leads up onto a low dyke along a pond where Wood Ducks nest and Yellowthroats haunt the edges.

Go back to the second fork you came to on the way in and turn right. The loop is perhaps a little over a mile long; along it the birds you are most likely to see or hear are Barred Owls; Great Blue Herons; fleets of Wood Ducks; all six of the local woodpecker species, especially Red-headed Woodpeckers; Prothonotary, Yellow-throated, and Hooded Warblers; Louisiana Waterthrushes; Eastern Bluebirds; Red-shouldered Hawks; and Ospreys, as well as an unnamable assortment of migrants. Aside from an occasional quiet fisherman relishing the serenity of the swamp as much as you are, you are likely to have the place to yourself.

Not far from Upper Marlboro, the county seat of Prince George's County, a favorite birders' haunt is a stretch along the west bank of the Patuxent River comprised of the **Jug Bay Natural Area**, a 2,000-acre segment of Patuxent River Park, and the adjacent **Merkle Wildlife Management Area**. A recently published checklist shows 85 nesting species in the park alone, plus 163 others that have been recorded at least five times, mostly since 1979.

A great diversity of habitats, combined with a careful monitoring of public use, make Jug Bay so rewarding that a visit is worth the advance planning that is required. A first-time visitor must make a reservation by calling (301) 627-6074 for a briefing by the staff. Subsequent use requires either a daily permit or an annual permit. The place is geared to handle school groups, and the permit system, requiring a check-in at headquarters, allows individual birders to plan routes that avoid the crowds.

To reach Jug Bay, take U.S. 301 about 1.8 miles south of the intersection with Md. 4, and turn left on Croom Station Road (mile 0.0). At 1.0 mile you will come to a pond on the left, and then a swamp across the road. Park by the bridge at 1.2 miles, well off the road. This is a good spot for Barred and Screech Owls, Blue-winged Teal and Wood Duck, woodpeckers and songbirds, including Prothonotary Warbler.

Continue to a T-junction with Croom Road at 1.7 miles and turn left. Turn left again at 3.3 miles on Croom Airport Road. At dawn or dusk look to the right for the large roost of Black and Turkey Vultures in the tall trees behind the house on the corner. Keep right at the T-junction at 4.7 miles.

If you arrive before 8:00 A.M., the park gate will be closed; continue past the entrance road at 5.3 miles to the end of Croom Airport Road at 6.2 miles, where a field marks the site of the long-defunct airport. The roadsides, the field, and its edges are excellent for such species as Horned Lark, Water Pipit, Eastern Bluebird, Prairie Warbler, Yellow-breasted Chat, Blue Grosbeak, Vesper and Grasshopper Sparrows.

Park and walk down the dirt road to the left, which curves down to the river and Selby's Landing. A chained-off road to the left leads to a canoe-in campsite; explore the trail behind the campsite as well. This whole area is one of the best in the park. The varied habitats have produced breeding Kentucky, Hooded, Pine, and Yellow-throated Warblers, American Redstarts, Yellowthroats, and Summer and. Scarlet Tanagers, plus migrant warblers and all sorts of sparrows.

The entrance road to the park is worth a stop or two. Try the first dip for Louisiana Waterthrushes and owls, and the birdy second trail on the right for Pileated Woodpeckers.

When you check in at headquarters, look for recent rarities on the sighting sheet. You should have your scope with you because of the excellent views from the observation tower over Jug Bay and the Patuxent marshes. Twenty-five species of waterfowl have been recorded here and the list of long-legged waders, including breeding Least Bittern, is extensive. Look for thrushes along the river bank and warblers in the trees at the entrance to Patuxent Village.

Below the headquarters, a nature trail and boardwalk will take you to the edge of the superb rice marsh, out to an observation tower and a photography blind. Depending on the season, look for Marsh and Sedge Wrens, Bobolinks, Rusty Blackbirds, Swamp Sparrows, and the pair of nesting Ospreys. All the rails and both gallinules are on the refuge list. While the variety of shorebirds, gulls, and terns is substantial, relatively few species occur annually, much less regularly. Your best bet for seeing most of them is by canoe, available for rent in the park.

Inland from the marsh a network of hiking trails crisscrosses the woodland from Black Walnut Creek to Swan Point Creek; take them all if you can.

Like most noncoastal areas, Jug Bay is exciting in spring and fall and at its dullest in late summer and late winter. When you run out of birds there, it is time to move on to **Merkle Wildlife Management Area.**

Go back to Croom Road, Md. 382, and turn left (mile 0.0). After 1.1 mile, turn left on St. Thomas Church Road, which becomes Fenno Road at 3.3 miles, and then crosses Mattaponi Creek at 3.6 miles. This creek is regarded as the best area for warblers in Prince George's County. Park by the first bridge and walk downstream (away from the left side of the road) on the left side of the creek. Nesting species include Barred Owl, Ruby-throated Hummingbird, Pileated Woodpecker, Kentucky, Hooded, and Parula Warblers, American Redstart, and Louisiana Waterthrush, supplemented by other species in migration.

The Mattaponi divides Jug Bay from Merkle. At 4.1 miles turn left at the entrance and, at 4.4 miles, go right at the small sign. The area is open 7:00 A.M. to 5:00 P.M. You can drive all its roads for much of the year if you call the manager, at present Tillman Smith, in advance at (301) 888-2214, especially if you plan to come on a weekend. (If you do not call, you may find locked gates barring your way.)

The area is managed for Canada Geese, and 25,000 of them are often present in November and December. Other waterfowl join them, of course, and the open land is much hunted over by raptors. It is a good place to see the Bald Eagles that live nearby, as well as the three breeding buteos; Red-tailed, Red-shouldered, and Broad-winged Hawks. Yellow-throated Warblers nest in the pines, Eastern Bluebirds flourish around their nesting boxes, Blue Grosbeaks and Indigo Buntings summer along the woodland edges, and Grasshopper Sparrows nest in the weeds. There is a nature trail of sorts.

Not far from Jug Bay is **Chesapeake Beach**, a resort community on the Chesapeake Bay. From November to April it is an easy place to see Whistling Swans, Canvasbacks, Greater Scaup, Bufflehead, Common Goldeneyes, and assorted gulls, with loons and scoters passing by in migration. Purple Sandpipers and a Red-necked Grebe have been recorded there but cannot be expected.

Go east on Md. 4 about 6.5 miles from U.S. 301 and turn left on Md. 260, which ends in Chesapeake Beach at 15.2 miles. The four-lane divided highway all the way attests to the heavy traffic in summer, when birds are replaced by people.

Ahead and to your right you will see the big beach parking lot and the two long, stone jetties marking the entrance to the little harbor. You can scan the bay and the birds around the jetties from the lot (free parking in winter) and from the parking area for the conspicuously signed Rod 'n' Reel Restaurant 0.3 mile south on Md. 261, the alongshore highway.

Work your way north another 3 miles or so by the closest roads to the bay, poking out the little streets between the houses.

Come in the afternoon unless it is cloudy, and avoid days of easterly winds.

St. Mary's County, at the southern tip of Maryland, is among the most underbirded areas near Washington.

Though Point Lookout lacks the ornithological drawing power of the great concentration points along the coast like Cape May and Kiptopeke, like them it lies at the tip of a rapidly narrowing peninsula. The funneling effect of the Potomac River and Chesapeake Bay pushes land birds in fall migration into the pockets of woodland and scrub in the park at the end of the road. On any sort of westerly wind chances are excellent for hawks in good numbers overhead, while telephone wires along the farm roads invite shrikes and vagrant flycatchers.

From late summer, when herons, gulls, and terns from the nesting islands across the bay come to loaf on the sandbars, pilings, and jetties along both shores, all through the winter and spring, you are likely to have a wealth of fine birding, with everything but pelagics, dabbling ducks, and shorebirds to keep you happy.

It is about a two-hour drive from the Washington Beltway, I-495 (mile 0.0), via Md. 5. At 14.9 miles Md. 5 leaves U.S. 301 in Waldorf, a left turn easy to miss. At 34.4 miles it forks right from Md. 235.

Numerous detours to vantage points along the Potomac are worth making, but none of them are essential except for the winter stop at **St. George Island** to look at the Great Cormorants.

If you take this side trip (best from December to March), do it in the morning when the light is right, or pick a cloudy afternoon. Take Md. 249 (54.7 miles) to the right at Calloway and drive 8.3 miles to the humpbacked bridge to the island. You can park on either side of the road just before the bridge. The cormorants rest on the tall channel markers to the west, usually on the lower crossbars. You will need a spotting scope for an identifying view.

Then go directly down to **Point Lookout**, keeping an eye out for the resident Bald Eagles in the vicinity of the village of Ridge. Stop at the park administrative office (73.4 miles) and ask for two maps, one of the park, the other of St. Mary's County. If the office is closed, you can pick up the maps at the entrance gate to the campground, just ahead on the right.

Be warned that "No Parking" signs and traffic laws are strictly enforced in the park. "Do Not Enter" applies to vehicles; "No Trespassing" applies to you.

At the end of the road, park beside the tiny naval station. You can get good views, at either end of the fence, of the sandbar and pilings

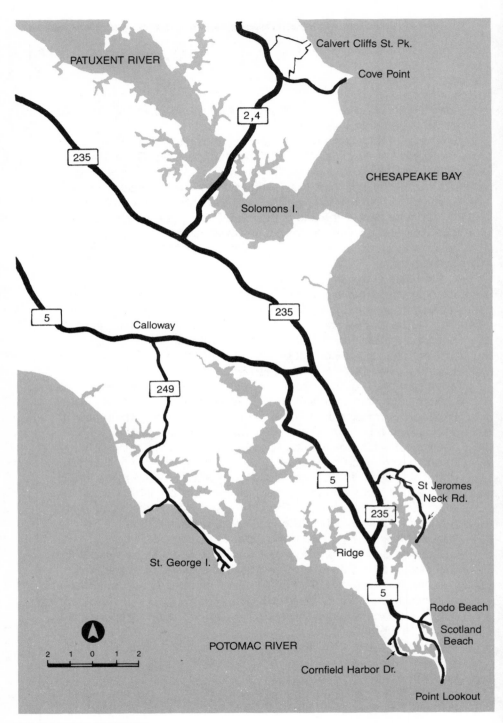

ST MARY'S COUNTY

beyond, favored by gulls, terns, and cormorants. If you did not see a Great Cormorant at St. George Island, you may find one here.

The river and bay, here as elsewhere in this account, may have hundreds of Horned Grebes, Whistling Swans, scaup of both species, Canvasbacks, Buffleheads, Common Goldeneyes, Oldsquaw, all the scoters, and Ruddy Ducks.

Just above the parking area, check the ponds and marsh in season for herons, long-legged shorebirds, Seaside Sparrows, and the only nesting Boat-tailed Grackles on the Western Shore.

You can easily spend the rest of the morning in spring and fall birding all the woods or isolated trees and bushes for land-bird migrants. A walk north along the sea wall to the east leads past a pine stand with resident Great Horned Owls and Pine Warblers to a brushy area that can be alive with sparrows. Above the picnic area to the west the woods are crisscrossed with perfect trails for birding, and the south side of the boat-launching parking lot should be checked as well, especially the cove and marsh in the southwest corner.

Park next at the north end of the fishing area and walk with your scope up the beach to **Tanner's Creek**. Look over the jetty into the bay and inspect the cove, its shoreline and sandbars for herons, swans, ducks, terns, gulls, and perhaps a few shorebirds.

If the camping area is fairly empty, you may find it rewarding to walk to the nature center, bird the north shore of Lake Conoy, and take the hiking trail.

As you leave the park, turn right (mile 0.0) onto Scotland Beach Road and in 0.1 mile left on Rodo Beach Road. The second left (0.6 mile) along this road takes you past a pond that attracts marsh and shorebirds, especially at low tide. At the end of the road (that is, where it makes an acute-angle left turn at 1.2 miles), park and look over the marsh in front of you. It has been known to have rails and both Marsh and Sedge Wrens on the local Christmas count. The path to the right leads to sand dunes with a view of the bay beyond.

The road to the left leads back to Rodo Beach Road. Turn right, then left at the T-junction at 2.2 miles. Scotland Beach provides another view of the bay, glimpses of Tanner's Creek, and a restaurant.

Back on Md. 5, go left 0.8 mile north of the park onto Cornfield Harbor Road, and left again onto **Cornfield Harbor Drive**, marked by cement obelisks at the entrance. Park near the bridge 0.8 mile ahead. In the appropriate season, King Rails and Seaside Sparrows have been seen in the marsh on either side, Redheads have been with Canvasbacks in the creek to the east, and Common, Forster's, and Least Terns on the sandbar to the west. Rafts of cormorants may gather in migration in the river at the end of the road. Woodcock have been found in the woodland edge of Cornfield Harbor Road on the way back to Md. 5.

At the junction of Md. 5 and Md. 235 take Md. 235 to the right. After 2.7 miles, a right turn on **St. Jerome's Neck Road** will lead you eventually back to the bay again after meandering for 4.6 miles through open country largely occupied by Capper's Nursery, likely territory for wire-perching birds and sparrows. Turn right at the T-junction just beyond the nursery, and at the end of the road park on the left in front of the "STOP-Eberly-No Trespassing" signs. Walk out to the bay on your left. At low tide the beach is broad and attractive to migrating shorebirds.

If you continue north on Md. 235, it will eventually rejoin Md. 5, but an alternate route home is Md. 4, 14.2 miles up from St. Jerome's Neck Road. Fork right on Md. 4 (this leg and a new bridge over the Patuxent River may not be on the county map) and drive 2.3 miles. A left turn onto North Patuxent Beach Road just as the high bridge comes in sight will take you down to the banks of the Patuxent, which may be packed with diving ducks from late fall to early spring.

Retrace your steps to Md. 4 and go over the bridge. The first right turn on the other side leads into the town of Solomons, where you can bird the river and also visit a marine museum and have a seafood dinner.

If you still have daylight to squander, there are three possible stops within the next 10 miles: Cove Point (bay view and maybe hawks on a westerly wind), Calvert Cliffs State Park (with a nature trail probably better visited in the early morning), and the Calvert Cliffs Nuclear Power Plant, open 9:00 A.M. to 5:00 P.M., with fine views over the bay at the point at which the warm water from the plant is discharged into it. The area of upwelling can be a spectacular magnet for water birds in very cold weather.

From this point Md. 4 will bring you right back to Washington.

The Eastern Shore

Almost any time of year the very best area to see the greatest diversity of birds in a single day's outing from Washington is a 15-mile stretch of impoundments and marsh, fields and woods near Dover, Delaware. There must be few avid birders in these parts whose life lists have not been substantially lengthened by happily remembered expeditions to **Bombay Hook National Wildlife Refuge** and **Little Creek Wildlife Area**.

From the tollbooths of the Chesapeake Bay Bridge, take U.S. 301 northeast about 34 miles and turn right on Md. 300, which runs east through farmland and small villages some 15 miles to Kenton, Delaware. From mid-July to mid-September Upland Sandpipers are in the short-grass fields and pastures; in winter Loggerhead Shrikes sit on the wires and Brewer's and Yellow-headed Blackbirds may be among the blackbird flocks in the cornfields; in a wet spring any muddy patch or rain pool may attract shorebirds.

At the traffic light in Kenton go right on Del. 42, which ends after 9 miles in Leipsic, crossing U.S. 13 en route. This rather heavily populated stretch of road is remarkably birdy and has yielded in recent years a Barnacle Goose (among thousands of Canada Geese in cornfields in December), three Ruffs (with yellowlegs and Pectoral Sandpipers in wet pastures in April), and a Mew Gull (with Ringed-bills in a field being plowed in March).

Go left (north) in Leipsic on Del. 9 1.5 miles to the Bombay Hook entrance sign and turn right. In winter and early spring the fields on both sides of the road between the highway and the first farmhouse are sure to have Horned Larks in them and may have Lapland Longspurs; from mid-March to early May they are frequented by Lesser Golden Plovers, which blend equally well with corn stubble and freshly plowed earth. The entire entrance road is good for migrating and wintering sparrows, and the skies should be scanned for hawks, notably Rough-legs, Northern Harriers, and falcons.

The second road to the left (Road 329) is also rich in sparrows and runs straight into the best warbler spot in the refuge—at the (locked) back gate to Finis Pool, before it turns sharply left. In May and September it pays to bird these woods by the gate before going on to the refuge visitor center.

Bombay Hook is open from sunrise to sunset except when the refuge dykes are too soggy to drive on. At the visitor center you will find rest rooms, a manned information desk, refuge maps, bird and mammal lists, and a sheet of recent sightings. The fields around the

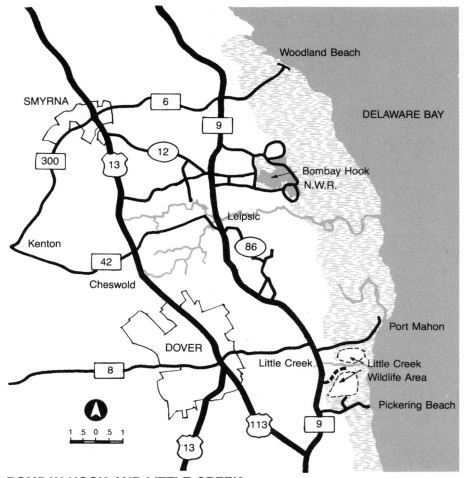

BOMBAY HOOK AND LITTLE CREEK

center are good for sparrows and Bobolinks in season and Ring-necked Pheasants all year.

The refuge roads run along and around three impoundments, Raymond and Sheerness Pools and Bear Swamp, all with observation towers, all with foot trails into nearby woods (the one by Raymond taking you beyond into interesting marsh habitat), all bordered on the east by tidal flats and marshes. Extension roads lead to Finis Pool, essentially a huge swampy arm of Sheerness, and through cornfields to another locked gate.

The most famous resident species is the pair of Bald Eagles that usually nest on the west side of Sheerness Pool but may be seen soaring anywhere. From September to April, with a lull in January and most of February, the numbers of waterfowl are spectacular, especially the tens of thousands of Canada Geese in late November and early December. (Look for Greater White-fronted Geese among them.) Snow Geese prefer the marshes, but the impoundments are packed with all the dabbling ducks, most of the diving ducks, and all three mergansers.

Shorebirds begin to appear in late March, are present until early June, and return again in July, continuing up to November. The tidal flats are always reliable, but in wet summers there may be no shorebird habitat in the impoundments until September. Raymond Pool is particularly noted for its large, lingering flock of Avocets and its attraction for Wilson's and Northern Phalaropes, all five "peep," and an occasional Curlew Sandpiper, while Ruffs prefer rain pools in the refuge cornfields and the flats of Bear Swamp in late April and May.

Double-crested Cormorants, Common Gallinules, and a wide assortment of rails, herons, egrets, ibis, and terns show up in the warmer months; Purple Gallinules have been known to nest in Finis Pool. Woodland birding is excellent in migration in the woods north and west of Sheerness and around Finis Pool, and Blue Grosbeaks often nest near the Bear Swamp loop. Be alert for the sight and sound of Barn, Screech, Great Horned, and Barred Owls, which are all resident.

In winter only, when you leave the refuge (or before you visit it), go north on Del. 9 0.1 mile and take the first left fork toward Smyrna (Road 12). The second road on the left, Road 326 at 1.4 miles, takes you by a farmyard on the right, noted for Brewer's Blackbirds, and fields that often hold Water Pipits and sometimes Lapland Longspurs. Be sure to do all your birding from the road; trespassers are widely disliked. (The next left returns you to Road 12.)

Useful Facts

1. At Bombay Hook the light for viewing the impoundments is best in the morning, though the tidal flats are backlit then. Afternoon birding is disappointing except on a cloudy day.
2. Hunting is allowed in a large part of the refuge much of the period from late October to late January, and the roads beyond Sheerness Pool are frequently closed to visitors in those months except on Sundays.
3. Birding is relatively dull in the refuge in June and early July.
4. Mosquitoes and biting flies are *absolutely terrible* from June (or earlier) through September. Spray from head to toe before you leave the visitor center.
5. If you would rather be deprived of money than sleep and still be at Bombay Hook for early morning birding, take note that Dover, 4

miles south of Del. 42 on U.S. 13, has several good motels in a wide price range and at least two all-night restaurants.

6. Leipsic, like the rest of Delaware, is a notorious speed trap, especially in the summer.

Little Creek Wildlife Area is the inevitable afternoon complement to a morning of birding at Bombay Hook National Wildlife Refuge. Only 8 miles down Del. 9 from Bombay Hook, it provides surprisingly different birds and habitats. Most vantage points ask for eastward viewing, so it rarely pays to work the area before noon except on a cloudy day.

Starting from the village of Leipsic, you can either zip straight down the highway, which carries too much traffic to dawdle on and inadequate shoulders to pull off on, or you can go part of the way via a very peaceful back road. Go east on Second Street, the extension of Del. 42, into the village to the stop sign on Main Street, and turn right. Then take the first left on Road 86, which runs east, bends south and finally west, rejoining Del. 9 just above the Octagonal Schoolhouse (a historical landmark), 2.3 miles north of the junction of Del. 8 and Del. 9 at the north edge of the village of Little Creek. This 4-mile loop will take you past fields and pastures, often with rain pools, through a small swampy woods and across a tidal creek. Hawks, shorebirds, shrikes, warblers, blackbirds, and sparrows are all possible in season; it's well worth exploring.

The Wildlife Area has three points of access. The northernmost is well-marked Port Mahon Road, the only road that runs east from Little Creek, off Del. 9 just above the Post Office. About 0.9 mile east, opposite six oil storage tanks on the left, a gravel road on the right leads to the northwest corner of the north impoundment (usually called the **Port Mahon** impoundment).

If cars are up on the dyke (there is room for two), park in the field below; otherwise you can park on the dyke and bird from your car as you eat lunch, if so inclined. Walking the dyke is easiest in winter and spring before the reeds grow too high to make it worthwhile.

Like the south impoundment discussed below, this huge area, a mixture of open water, acres of marsh, and, sometimes, freshwater flats, is a paradise for dabbling ducks. (Look for Eurasian Wigeon when the American Wigeon are in.) Harriers, falcons, and Rough-legged Hawks hunt here; gulls rest and feed on the flats, with a rare Black-headed Gull or an occasional Little Gull among the Bonapartes. All the tern species on the Delaware list are apt to be here in summer, and one or two White-winged Black Terns appeared for long periods in three recent years. This is the northernmost area in the East where Black-necked Stilts nest regularly and is a favorite shorebird concentration point in dry years. Sedge Wrens often nest west of the north-south dyke in the saltmeadow grass, while Marsh Wrens bubble reliably in the reeds.

If the tide is low enough to expose some flats, continue east on Port Mahon Road out to Delaware Bay. You will soon cross, then run parallel to a creek that attracts herons and Clapper Rails. Scan the marshes to the north for egrets and ibis from spring to fall, Northern Harriers, Rough-legged Hawks, and Short-eared Owls (especially at dusk or on a dark day) in winter. The marshes are also prime habitat for Seaside and Sharp-tailed Sparrows.

Just before the road bends left along the bay shore, a foot bridge on the right crosses the creek. If the bridge is in good repair (as it sometimes is) and there are no fresh "No Trespassing" signs, cross the creek and walk right along the dyke on the far side. If water levels are not too high, you will soon find yourself in excellent shorebird, gull, and tern habitat at the northeast corner of the impoundment. Dyke walking can be difficult, but memories of dozens of Little Gulls, a Ruff, and a Curlew Sandpiper in this area in various Aprils lure birders back again and again.

Immediately beyond the bend, the creek spills out into the bay. The flats here at low tide can be packed with every probable species of shorebird and gull (and an astonishing Little Stint was photographed here in May 1979); the branch on the other side of the road lures rails out to feed until the traffic gets too heavy or the tide too high.

The poorly maintained bayside road is partly protected by a metal sea wall. Both along the open shore and inside the wall you are likely to find shorebirds, especially peep, Red Knots, and Ruddy Turnstones. In winter the fishing pier provides an ideal platform for viewing diving ducks and sea ducks and gulls out in the bay. Explore the shoreline for about a mile beyond the creek mouth; you can turn around at Conley Hardware, Inc., the long white building with oystershell piles beside it. To the east a marshy point jutting south often provides a resting place for Royal and Common Terns.

On your return to Del. 9 a left turn takes you after 1.5 miles to the main entrance to the Little Creek Wildlife Area, on the left. Follow the entrance road (frequented by wintering White-crowned Sparrows) past the headquarters buildings (there is no reason to stop) about 1.3 miles to a small parking lot. A boardwalk leads to an observation tower over the south impoundment, with much more water and much less marsh than the north impoundment. Consequently, this is the most likely spot to see huge concentrations of waterfowl—most spectacular in March, when drifts of Snow Geese swirl along the far shore as the first Glossy Ibis coast in from the south, over crowds of Ruddies, mergansers, scaup, and a dozen other species of duck.

A closer look is available from the road beyond the parking lot, which is open to pedestrians despite the "No Entry" sign and leads to more ill-defined and overgrown dykes extending into both north and south impoundments. In drought summers there can be stupendous flats to the right, but you will be looking into the sun.

Back on Delaware 9 turn left; after 0.9 mile go left again on Pickering Beach Road. After 1.6 miles you will see a sign for Little Creek Wildlife Area on the left. Turn in and follow a twisty, bumpy road to the south edge of the south impoundment. You park at the junction of two dykes, one running north and one running east out to the bay. Both provide access to far-off birds, but the latter also leads to a marsh area popular with waders (including both bitterns) and long-legged shorebirds when the water in the impoundments is too deep for them. You may find the Black-necked Stilts here when they seem to be nowhere else.

Pickering Beach, at the end of the paved road, is a good place to look over the gulls and ducks on the bay in winter; shorebirds like it at low tide, especially in May. Be alert for the Sedge Wrens and Henslow's Sparrows that sometimes nest near the road.

The last stretch of Del. 9, two miles south to U.S. 113, is at its best when there are rain pools in the fields and the grass in the pastures is short. In September look for Lesser Golden Plover and Buff-breasted Sandpipers, and from mid-July on, check for Upland Sandpipers in the field north of the junction of the two highways.

In the winter months, if you have covered Little Creek with an hour to spare before sunset, you may want to dash south to Broadkill Marsh, described at the end of chapter 27.

From the junction of Del. 9 and U.S. 113, drive south 11.8 miles, fork left on Del. 1, and continue 13 miles to Del. 16. Turn left and drive to the marsh.

23 Northern Delaware

Whether keeping state bird lists is one of the games you play or whether you simply like to expand your stock of splendid birding areas, northern Delaware offers a wealth of delights you shouldn't miss. It is worth noting that Wilmington is no farther from Washington than Bombay Hook, and traveling between the two destinations is but a leisurely, shunpiking drive of an hour or so, if you do not make the suggested stops.

The recommended route can be taken in either direction, but it is desirable to bird the Wilmington area in the morning if you can.

If you begin in Leipsic—the village just south of Bombay Hook—with a few detours you will be following Del. 9 north as far as Delaware City. This is a lovely back road, twisting through fields and marshes, passing patches of swamp and stands of pine, crossing tidal creeks, and going by handsome old farmhouses (interspersed

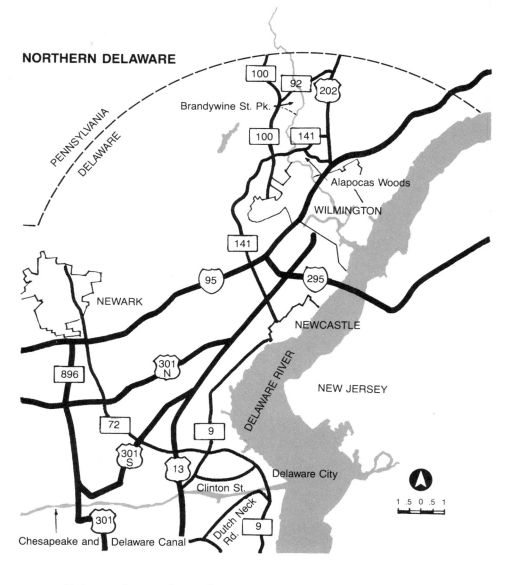

NORTHERN DELAWARE

Brandywine St. Pk.

Alapocas Woods

WILMINGTON

NEWARK

NEWCASTLE

DELAWARE RIVER

NEW JERSEY

Delaware City

Clinton St.

Dutch Neck Rd.

Chesapeake and Delaware Canal

PENNSYLVANIA
DELAWARE

with increasing numbers of examples of Nondescript Modern). It is at least as rewarding a road in fall and winter as in spring (owls in the pines, hawks over the fields, blackbirds feeding in corn stubble, and waterfowl in the creeks and marshes), and is always more interesting than bustling U.S. 13.

Measuring from the junction of Del. 9 and Del. 42 in Leipsic, after 7.5 miles you go through 0.5 mile of swampy woods that can be rich in warblers. Stop and bird the shoulders here if you have time. (At the end of the woods a left turn on Road 317 will take you to Council's, a good, plain seafood restaurant that is about the only place to eat en route.)

Continuing north, turn left on Road 456 at 15.1 miles as far as the wooden bridge over Beaver Branch (15.5 miles). This stretch is apt to be good for Screech and Great Horned Owls, Red-tailed and Red-shouldered Hawks, as well as migrant and nesting land birds.

Out of season, **Augustine Beach**, up Del. 9 (at 24.9 miles), is a good place to scan the Delaware River for waterfowl and look for sparrows in the edges. A little beyond lies the old village of Port Penn; 2 miles north of it looms the high bridge over the Chesapeake and Delaware Canal. Just before the road rises to the bridge turn left at the sign for Dutch Neck Road (27.6 miles). You will soon come to the canal bank, where a right turn will lead to the south jetty of the canal entrance, an excellent spot for loons, grebes, and gulls in the colder months. On your right, a long, brushy, man-made hill is excellent for sparrows in fall and winter and has been known to shelter both the occasional Lincoln's and Clay-colored Sparrow as well as more common species.

A left turn along the canal takes you past the **Thousand Acre Marsh**, a vast freshwater pond to the south, which is a superb shorebird area in a dry summer (Ruffs and Marbled Godwits have been found here as well as the more routine migrants) and a fine waterfowl lake in winter. From the T-junction at the canal a drive of 1.2 miles west will take you past a marshy pond with water lilies and spatterdock, which is especially good for Common Gallinules and Least Bitterns. The whole area is a loafing ground for gulls and terns in late summer.

Retrace your route, go over the bridge and into Delaware City, and turn left at the traffic light onto Clinton Street. At 0.9 mile along this road, park and look out over **Dragon Run Marsh** on your right, where a famous pair of Purple Gallinules nested a few years ago. It is always worth a check to see if they have returned, and you can enjoy the number and variety of herons, egrets, and ibis that use the marsh all summer.

If you cross the road and climb the embankment on the left by means of a path just ahead, you will look down into a large impoundment popular with dabbling ducks and coots.

Continue another 2 miles, where, just past the school, you turn right on Road 378. In 0.5 mile you will cross **Dragon Creek**. If you don't have to share it with fishermen you have a good chance to see King and Virginia Rails as well as other marsh birds and transient Bobolinks.

After 0.8 mile turn left on Del. 72, passing the Getty refinery, and turn right after 1.6 miles onto U.S. 13. In the course of the next 8 miles you will find plenty of motels, but they fill up early and it is wise to have a reservation. It is the most convenient stretch to stop for the night, for the morrow's early birding.

Your principal target will be **Brandywine State Park**, which is easily reached by taking Del. 141 north (toward Newport), a turn from the right lane off U.S. 13, 8.1 miles north of U.S. 72. Stay on Del. 141 for 7.3 miles, turn left on Del. 100 for 2.7 miles (until it makes a sharp left turn), and there turn right at the conspicuous park sign onto Adams Dam Road. After 0.3 mile turn left onto the entrance road and drive to the nature center.

This wonderful park consists of 433 acres of rolling hills sloping down to Brandywine Creek. There are large stands of ancient tulip trees broken by overgrown fields, with maples, box elder, and tangles of honeysuckle along the creek, and an always birdy marsh in the southeast corner. The highest ground is kept mowed and a park road leads up to the well-marked Hawk Watch, often manned by Delaware birders in the fall.

It is perhaps the single best place in Delaware for upland species, both migrant and resident, and the diversity of flycatchers, warblers, and sparrows is astonishing in spring and fall.

There is a steep fee of $4 for nonresidents from Memorial Day to Labor Day, but entrance is free the rest of the year. The other restriction is that the park is not open until 8:00 A.M., but there are two convenient and productive areas to while away the earliest birding hours.

The closest is on the other side of Brandywine Creek. Where Del. 100 turns left and Adams Dam Road runs right, you can continue straight ahead on Del. 92, which lies along the west boundary of the state park. On the far side of the Brandywine is the entrance to another park on the right, apparently accessible only on foot. Park by the roadside and walk in. A trail bearing around to the left will take you up to a ridge covered by overgrown fields that is often alive with passerines at dawn.

Alternatively, you may continue on Del. 141 (instead of turning left on Del. 100). Just 0.5 mile beyond the crossroad, turn left at a traffic light, still on Del. 141, and in 0.7 mile go right onto unmarked Alapocas Drive. In the course of the next 0.9 mile, you will be driving along the edge of **Alapocas Woods**, a county park with two or three entrances leading to parking spots and trails. You can walk along several stream valleys that often provide shelter for migrant thrushes in the brushy understory, while the deciduous woods overhead are noted for their warblers and vireos in spring migration.

Delaware birders doing Big Days in May often begin their birding in Alapocas Woods, a sure sign of fruitfulness that out-of-staters can profitably heed.

Take note that Del. 141 is easily accessible from Interstate 95, whether you are heading toward or away from Washington, and that the intersection of Del. 141 and Del. 100 is only 6 miles north of the interstate, mostly on a new freeway.

24 Kent County, Maryland

Among the richest birding areas in the colder half of the year, Kent County is no farther from Washington, D.C., than popular refuges like Bombay Hook and Blackwater, but is much less frequently visited. Waterfowl, raptors, blackbirds, and sparrows and their kin can occur in spectacular abundance, and the rolling, open country of the upper Eastern Shore, dotted with handsome old houses built by three centuries of farmers, adds an aesthetic dividend to the exhilaration of seeing birds.

The starting point is Chestertown, 72 miles from the Washington Beltway, via U.S. 50, U.S. 301, and Md. 213. At the second light beyond the bridge over the Chester River, start measuring your mileage as you turn left onto Md. 20. (Mileage figures assume you will take all recommended side roads.)

At 2.3 miles a left turn onto Brice's Mill Road will take you down an ancient sunken farm road with sparrowy hedgerows. It ends at a T-junction at 4.2 miles; turn right, and at 5.6 miles continue across a tricky intersection that jogs slightly left. Look for feeding Canada Geese and Whistling Swans in the fields beyond, White-crowned Sparrows along the road, and Red-tailed Hawks and Bald Eagles in the sky.

Park by **St. Paul's Church** at 7.8 miles, do a little land birding around the spillway you have just passed, and check the pond behind the cemetery for ducks. In the spring Warbling Vireos nest in the churchyard.

Go straight on (not right around the church) and at 8.1 miles turn left onto the road to **Remington Farms main pond**, well sign-posted and immediately visible. Remington Farms is a private waterfowl management area, but this part is always open to the public and can be packed with Canada Geese and dabbling ducks. A White-fronted Goose may often be present, and such rarities as Garganey Teal and Barnacle Geese, of unknown provenance, have been found in recent years.

The light is good only in the morning. You are required to stay in your car, from which viewing is excellent and photography easy.

Make the mandatory U-turn, go back to the road and turn left. The high hedgerows are full of birds, and the area abounds in deer at twilight.

At 9.9 miles the road ends at Md. 20. Across the road, a little to the left, is the entrance to the **Remington Farms tour**, open except from October 1 to February 1. The tour deserves at least an hour of your time, as it is delightful for buteos, ducks, and sparrows in winter and for nesting Ospreys, Blue-winged Teal, Wood Ducks, and migrating warblers in spring. You may be lucky enough to see a King Rail, but they are as elusive here as elsewhere.

The tour ends on Md. 21, on which a right turn takes you in 0.8 mile to Md. 20, where another right turn takes you back to the starting point of the tour in 1.1 miles.

If the tour road is closed, you will have turned left onto Md. 20 (at 9.9 miles). At 13.7 miles turn left at the light in the village of Rock Hall on Md. 445 (Main Street), and at 14.9 miles take a detour right on **Allen's Lane**. Beyond the houses the woods on the right have a resident pair of spooky Great Horned Owls and are also good for Screech Owls, woodpeckers, Hermit Thrushes, and Pine Warblers.

The lane ends at 15.6 miles at the bay, where you can scan for loons, Whistling Swans, both scaup, Canvasbacks, Oldsquaw, and all the scoters.

Back on Md. 445 continue south, looking for bluebirds, and turn left at 16.7 miles on Grays Inn Road, a short spur to a marsh and public landing especially good for grebes and sparrows.

The highway now runs between narrow strips of wood and hedgerow that are always birdy, especially in migration when they offer the best cover on the shoreline. Keep an eye out for the Cooper's Hawk at 20.7 miles.

At 21.3 miles you come to the bridge over Eastern Neck Narrows, the boundary of **Eastern Neck National Wildlife Refuge**. Park on the far side and linger to study the resting gulls (a Lesser Black-back has been seen among the Ring-bills recently) and the shorebirds on the tidal flats, Whistling Swans, Canada Geese, Ruddy Ducks, Canvasbacks, Redheads (uncommon), Wigeon, both American and Eurasian (rare), and both scaup. You may squeak up a Marsh Wren.

Drive on to Tubby's Cove on the right at 22.1 miles, where a boardwalk leads out to an observation tower. This walk provides the best views of the resident Mute Swans, all three mergansers, King and Virginia Rails.

At 22.6 miles turn left on Bogle's Wharf Road, which leads down to a county-maintained public landing. (Don't blame the refuge for the state of the rest rooms!) Here you have fine afternoon views over the Chester River, especially attractive to Common Loons, Bufflehead, Common Goldeneye, and scoters. Check the waters in the cove as well.

At all times in the refuge remember to look for raptors, both in flight and perched. Both vultures, Red-tailed and Red-shouldered Hawks, Sharp-shins, Bald Eagles, and Northern Harriers are reliable winter residents; Golden Eagles, Cooper's Hawks, and Rough-legs are possible, while Ospreys are present from spring to fall.

Ingleside Recreation Area at 24.3 miles is closed from October to April except to those who get permission and a key from refuge

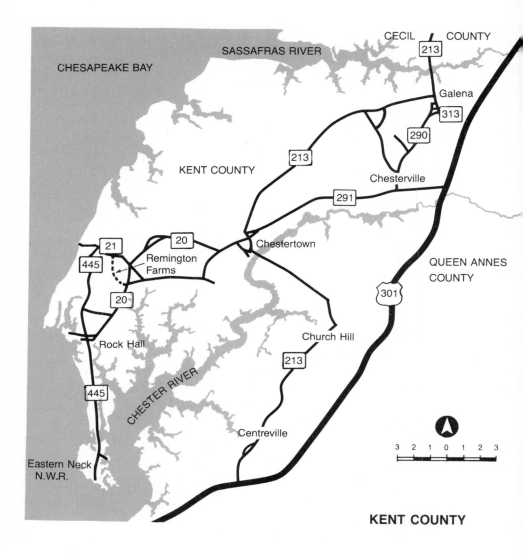

CECIL COUNTY

SASSAFRAS RIVER

CHESAPEAKE BAY

213

Galena

313

290

213

KENT COUNTY

Chesterville

291

20

21

Remington Farms

Chestertown

QUEEN ANNES COUNTY

445

301

20

Church Hill

Rock Hall

213

445

CHESTER RIVER

Centreville

Eastern Neck N.W.R.

3 2 1 0 1 2 3

KENT COUNTY

headquarters, open only on weekdays. It is worth a visit for its northward views over the bay, especially for Whistling Swans, scoters, and Oldsquaw.

The wildlife trail, just beyond on the left, rarely yields interesting birds, but you may see the Wood Ducks, Eastern Bluebirds, and the endangered Delmarva Fox Squirrel. It is the only area in the refuge, other than the boardwalk, where you may walk out of sight of the road without permission.

The next road to the right, at 24.5 miles, leads up through sparrowy fields to refuge headquarters, a working office (not open on weekends) rather than a visitor center. If you have the time, ask for access to the trails to Cedar Point and Shipyard Creek, interesting open-country walks in the southeast part of the refuge. At least drive to the end of the public road, a high point from which raptor watching is excellent.

Retrace your route to Rock Hall and start measuring mileage again from the intersection of Md. 445 and Md. 20 (mile 0.0). A right turn onto Md. 20 will take you straight back to Chestertown, passing the entrance to the Remington Farms tour road.

Alternatively, go straight north on Md. 445 through fields attractive to winter flocks of blackbirds, where the sharp-eyed may pick up an occasional Brewer's or Yellow-headed Blackbird among the Red-wings and cowbirds.

At 1.0 mile there are woods with responsive nighttime Screech Owls. Another good owling road runs east at 2.0 miles, but the next daylight stop is the marsh that borders the left side of the road from miles 2.6 to 3.0. Sedge Wrens turn up here in winter, Common Snipe winnow in the spring, and rails, Glossy Ibis, and egrets may be around in the warmer months.

Check the snags off to the right at 3.5 miles for Bald Eagles and take note that the woods at 4.2 miles shelter both Chuck-will's-widows and Whip-poor-wills in spring and summer.

You can drive down to the bay shore at 4.9 miles by turning left on Md. 21 or get back to Md. 20 and thence to Chestertown by turning right. The first mile east on Md. 21 can be wonderful for migrant warblers in season.

A different part of Kent County also deserves a winter visit. Take U.S. 301 for 23 miles beyond Md. 213 and turn left to Chesterville. In Chesterville, at 0.0 miles, turn north (right) on Md. 290, and park at 0.6 mile by the sign for **Angelica Nursery**. If it is early enough in the winter, the nursery brush pile will be unburned and full of sparrows. This spot is famous among area birders for the Lark Bunting that lingered there for several weeks one recent winter.

Continue north to an unmarked paved road to the left at 1.5 miles and take it as far as the railroad tracks at 2.8 miles. (You can turn around on the far right-hand side of the tracks.) The fields on either side are good for Water Pipits, Horned Larks, and sometimes Lap-land Longspurs and Snow Buntings, especially when the earth is largely covered by snow.

Go back to Md. 290, turn left, then bear left again at the junction with Md. 313 (6.9 miles). Be alert for Rough-legged Hawks, Northern Harriers, Short-eared Owls, and the same field birds, as well as feeding Canada Geese and Whistling Swans, and great swarms of blackbirds.

In Galena (7.6 miles), turn left on Md. 213 and left again at 10.3

miles on Vansant Corner Road. The road ends at a T-junction opposite a house with a large goose pond behind it. Turn left and head
south back to Chesterville. A final left turn at the end of the road (14.4
miles) takes you back to U.S. 301.

Note: The landowners of Kent County are not hospitable to trespassers. Ask for permission whenever you feel you must invade
private property.

25 Blackwater and Hooper Island

Among the classic winter field trips for the Washington birder is an
all-day expedition to **Blackwater National Wildlife Refuge** and
Hooper Island in Maryland's Dorchester County. The best period of
all runs from mid-November to Christmas, though birding can be
good much longer in a mild winter and is interesting most of the year.

Your starting point is the junction of westbound Md. 16 and U.S. 50
just south of Cambridge, where there is a conspicuous sign for the
refuge. Three roads—Maple Dam Road, Egypt Road, and Md.
335—run south from Md. 16 to the refuge. **Egypt Road**, 2.7 miles
west of U.S. 50, is the traditional birder's route; it has the virtues of
being mostly straight and untraveled and lined by fields attractive to
swans and geese, Horned Larks and Water Pipits, blackbird flocks
and sparrows, and, in a wet spring, a variety of shorebirds. Look for
Eastern Bluebirds and American Kestrels on the wires and raptors in
the skies.

In spring and early summer stop in the swampy woods 3.5 miles
down Egypt Road for warblers (Prothonotaries nest there) and take a
detour to the west down Old Field Road 0.8 mile farther along (it
continues to Md. 335) for more mixed-woodland habitat.

The last half-mile or so of Egypt Road is good for predawn owling
(Screech and Great Horned Owls may respond to a tape). The point
where the road ends at unmarked Key Wallace Drive is a prime spot
to watch and listen for *peent*ing Woodcock in courting season before
the sun is up.

Key Wallace Drive runs more or less along the north boundary of
the refuge from Maple Dam Road to Md. 335. If you have arrived after
7:30 A.M. (9:00 A.M. on Sunday) for your first visit, go right 1.3 miles to
the Wildlife Interpretive Center, pick up a refuge leaflet and a bird list,
and look at the sighting list and the excellent table-top map.

White-crowned Sparrows winter in the hedgerow around the building and thousands of geese may be just beyond it. Snow Geese, both

blue and white, will be easy to spot among the Canadas, but a rare White-fronted Goose is worth searching for.

Next head east 1.6 miles to the start of the Wildlife Drive, a 5-mile route. A left turn beyond the first pond takes you by a picnic area and a nature trail, out to a tall observation tower overlooking the vast marsh that borders the Blackwater River. The pine woods around the picnic area often shelter Pine Warblers and Brown-headed Nuthatches, but you should not expect to see a Red-cockaded Woodpecker in spite of its optimistic inclusion on the refuge bird list. (In recent years they were seen only in 1976, in a closed part of the refuge several miles away.)

When you return to the drive, you will be confined to your car except for a woodland nature trail. Beyond the trail you will be in sight of water most of the way, much of it covered with geese, with more of them filling the skies. Among the dabbling ducks, Mallards and Blacks, Green-winged Teal and Shovelers, Pintail and Wigeon and Gadwall can all be sorted out; the attentive hunter of rarities scans diligently for Eurasian Wigeon. Diving ducks are less common, but may be seen in the ponds at the beginning of the drive.

The abiding excitement of visiting Blackwater is not the seasonal certainty of waterfowl, however, but the possibility of seeing at least one of the resident Bald Eagles. The quest is not necessarily an easy one; it requires patience above all, good luck, and systematic effort. A spotting scope is nearly mandatory for a satisfactory view. The eagles are easiest to see when they are perched on the snags along the wildlife drive, but they are as likely to be sitting out in the marsh, where they are visible only from the observation tower, or soaring out in the immense sky. It is important to check every birdlike lump in the trees at the edge of the marsh or out in the peaty flats.

The Blackwater area is superb for raptors generally; Northern Harriers, Red-tailed and Rough-legged Hawks all winter there; Ospreys nest there, and Golden Eagles show up every year, though it is easy to mistake immature Bald Eagles for them. Turkey Vultures are abundant, and Black Vultures not uncommon.

After completing the Wildlife Drive, loop back to the east again along Key Wallace Drive, past the refuge headquarters building. The marshy flats on the left (at low tide) are the best place to see wintering Common Snipe; they also attract other shorebirds, gulls, terns (in season), ducks and herons, and the surrounding reeds shelter Marsh Wrens.

Key Wallace Drive ends at a road that is not signposted; to the left it is known as Maple Dam Road, but to the right it becomes **Shorter's Wharf Road**. Take your mileage at this point (mile 0.0). Turn right and bird the logged-over woods on the left for bluebirds, woodpeckers, and, in summer, Blue Grosbeaks.

BLACKWATER AND HOOPER ISLAND

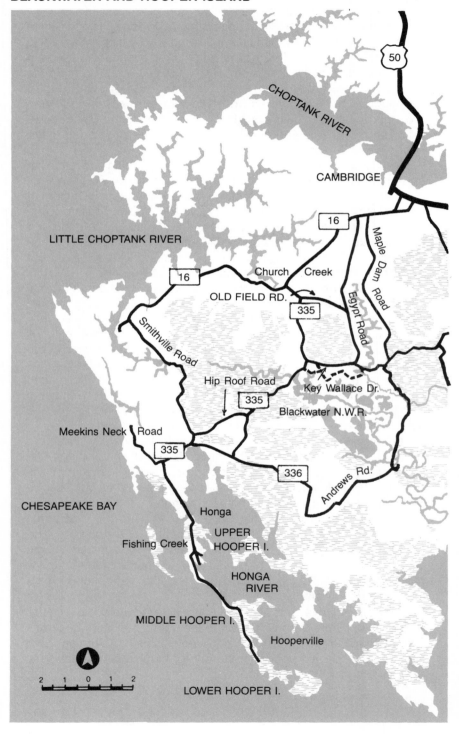

ELLIOTT ISLAND

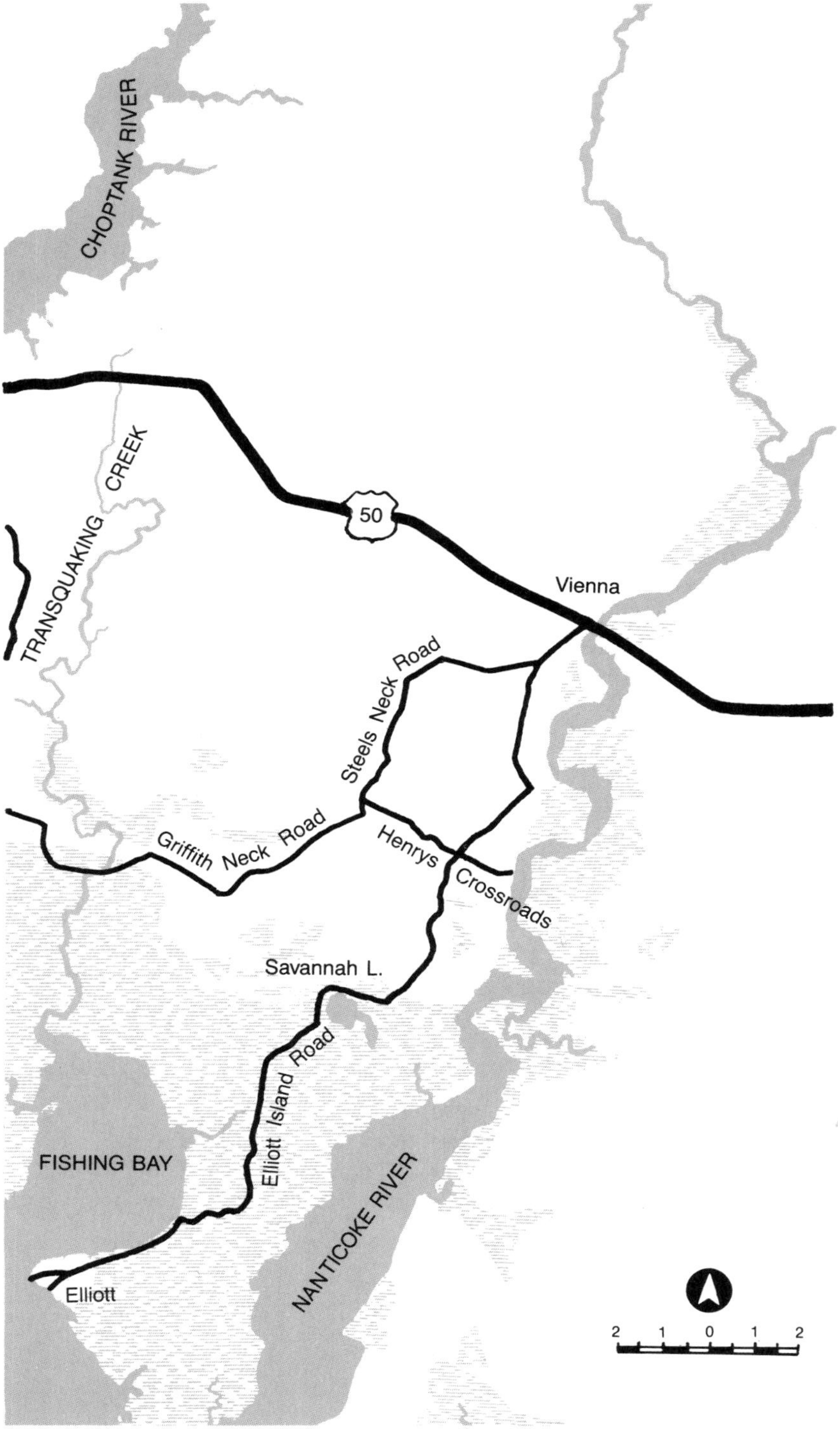

CHOPTANK RIVER

TRANSQUAKING CREEK

50

Vienna

Steels Neck Road

Griffith Neck Road

Henrys Crossroads

Savannah L.

Elliott Island Road

FISHING BAY

NANTICOKE RIVER

Elliott

2   1   0   1   2

The road soon leaves woods and farmland and runs through a magnificent stretch of marsh and pine that not only provides another chance to look for all the refuge specialties but includes fine shorebird habitat, especially in spring if water levels are not too high. Farther south the habitat becomes suitable for Prairie Warblers and Field and Swamp Sparrows. Having mysteriously become Andrews Road, the highway ends, at 10.1 miles, at Md. 336.

Turn right and head west and, at 14.9 miles, south on Md. 335. This road leads to **Hooper Island**, which is really a chain of islands, covered by small watermen's communities, interspersed with coves and harbors and extensive views of the Chesapeake Bay. Explore every side road you see (they are few and short) and scan the waters wherever you can. In winter, loons, grebes, swans, diving ducks, Old-squaw, scoters, mergansers, gulls, and eagles may be seen any-where. Terns and oystercatchers and a variety of herons nest on islands west of the villages of Honga and Fishing Creek, the nearest of which can be scanned from the road on a clear day. From the northernmost bridge to the end of the road is less than 9 miles.

Heading north again, 2.7 miles above the Hooper Island bridge, a left turn onto **Meekin's Neck Road** by a red-painted shed will take you all the way to the bay if the last quarter-mile is not too sodden. Most of the way is firm and dry. It is a good road for land birding, for hawk watching in migration (notably over the great marsh on the south side), and for observing duck movements up and down the bay (keep right at the Twin Willows sign).

Back on Md. 335, go left on Smithville Road 1.5 miles farther north and, a half-mile later, right on Hip Roof Road, a pretty stretch of marshes, woods, and fields especially good for herons and raptors. At the end, turn left onto Md. 335 again and follow it all the way back to Md. 16 in the village of Church Creek. Though you may encounter a lot of traffic on this route, you can usually find a shoulder to pull off on beside the marshes. Farther north, next to the fields, which may be seething with flocks of blackbirds, a patient searcher may some-times find Yellow-headed and Brewer's Blackbirds. If it is too dark for blackbirds, linger along the marshes instead and listen for rails and Marsh Wrens.

Beautiful as this country is, you will find it marred by more "No Trespassing" signs than anywhere else in the world. (My favorite adds "Survivors Will Be Prosecuted.") Obey them fervently.

When goose hunting starts after Thanksgiving, avoiding the inces-sant sound of gunfire on Saturdays will enhance your pleasure con-siderably.

If you first visit Elliott Island when the sun is high on a summer day, its compelling attraction for birders will mystify you. Elliott Island, like all the great Delmarva marshes, is beautiful and full of birds, but in spring and summer it requires more of its devotees than most nonbirders could imagine anyone submitting to.

The best hours to be there are from about two hours before sunset to two hours after sunrise, including at least an hour or two in full darkness. The most sought-after bird in the marsh, the Black Rail, is least difficult to see and hear (though never a sure bet) between 10:00 P.M. and 2:00 A.M. in May and June.

Not only must you turn your schedule upside down but you need special equipment, the most important item being superstrong insect repellent, best applied before you dress and again just before you reach the marsh. You also need a tape recorder, a tape of rail calls, preferably with long sequences of each species, possibly a tape of the calls of other birds you want to see, and a good flashlight.

Why go through all this effort? To see and hear birds you may encounter in no other way and to savor the beauty of a unique landscape.

If you cannot be persuaded to sample Elliott Island's summer pleasures, wait until November or later when there are no mosquitoes, and Rough-legged Hawks, Northern Harriers, Bald Eagles, and waterfowl can all be seen in the middle of the day. Your trip can easily be combined with a visit to Blackwater National Wildlife Refuge.

The road to Elliott Island begins in Vienna, Maryland, on U.S. 50, half-way between Cambridge and Salisbury. Just before the Exxon station, fork right into the village on Race Street and then turn right onto Market Street at the Maryland National Bank. From this point (mile 0.0) to the end of the road is a 19-mile run and the only decisions you need to make are the stopping points.

The first 8 miles run through fields and deciduous woods. Stop, look, and listen frequently for Summer Tanagers and Blue Grosbeaks, and notice the intersection at Henry's Crossroads at 5.4 miles. (It is actually the road on the right that is called Henry's Crossroads, while the one to the left is Lewis Wharf Road.)

From this point on be punctilious about staying on the public road, and avoid parking beside any occupied house. Residents here find birder behavior threatening or irritating or both, and courtesy, inconspicuousness, and scrupulously lawful behavior are essential.

Stop at 7.4 miles opposite the sign for Weston Farms and listen for

Henslow's Sparrow

Henslow's Sparrows and Sedge Wrens. Stop again for the same species just beyond the complex of buildings around the Dietrich mailbox.

From now on you are in loblolly pines, through which Brown-headed Nuthatches wander. Chuck-will's-widows call after dusk; they rest on the road and their red eyes may be picked up in the headlights. A tape of their call may bring one in to fly around the car.

At 8.2 miles you will pass a buff-colored house on the left at a bend in the road. The next quarter-mile is usually excellent for Henslow's Sparrows.

At 8.9 miles you come out onto the marsh, where a sign announces a single-lane road, with wider passing points, for the next 6 miles. Traffic is normally very light, but you must avoid delaying other cars. Move promptly to a passing point when you see someone approach; park only in these spots, never on a soggy shoulder.

Sedge Wrens (notoriously unpredictable as to nest sites and arrival dates) are often found along the next mile. Take note of their favored habitat and look for it elsewhere. The area just beyond the bridge immediately after the sign is especially promising.

Savannah Lake on the left is normally empty in summer (though herons may line the shore), but waterfowl are sometimes abundant there in the colder months.

Beyond the lake you are in rail country. If you do not have a tape, the slam of a car door may start them calling after nightfall, but only a recording of the voice is likely to pull nearby birds out onto the road.

Seaside and Sharp-tailed Sparrows and Marsh Wrens sing far into the evening. If you arrive in daylight, look for the Marsh Wrens among the tall reeds along Pokata Creek, which winds through the marsh, sometimes close to the road.

The only nesting shorebird in the marsh is the Willet, but in migration the shallower pools along the road attract small numbers of other sandpipers—mostly yellowlegs, dowitchers, and peep.

In the deeper ponds and creeks dabbling ducks, Common Gallinules and Pied-billed Grebes are often in sight and herons and egrets fish along the edges.

At dusk or dawn park out in the middle of the marsh, watch the changing light, look for the flights of egrets or night herons flying to or from their roosts, and listen for the booming of bitterns, the cuckooing of grebes, and the cacophony of the night birds and frogs chorusing against the chatter of the daylight singers.

The mustard-colored house on the left at 11.4 miles marks the start of the best stretch for Black Rails; the bridge at 13.0 miles marks the end of it, though they may be heard well to the north and south of those points on a calm night in a good year.

Beyond this point the marsh is broken at intervals by islands of pines, home to House Wrens, Pine Warblers, Catbirds, Brown Thrashers, and Rufous-sided Towhees. At 14.8 miles a short road to the left runs through woods with a resident Great Horned Owl, where Yellow Warblers, White-eyed Vireos, and Yellowthroats sing along the edges.

At 15.7 miles the road runs close to the open water on the right. In daylight in the warmer months, terns sometimes hunt close to shore and in winter diving ducks can be observed at close range.

There is no point in going farther unless the sun is up, since you leave the marsh and enter the outskirts of the village at 17.7 miles. Though it lacks architectural interest, it is attractively open and peaceful, and its residents show none of the hostility so manifest north of the marsh.

At 18.2 miles, a road to the left takes you down to the harbor, while the main road ends close to the water at 19.0 miles in an interestingly swampy patch of woods. Both roads are worth taking for the opportunities they offer of scanning Chesapeake Bay, again much more rewarding in winter than summer.

Elliott Island is not a place to bird in a hurry. Go prepared, and enjoy it. If you have arranged your trip to combine it with a visit to Blackwater, the linking road is the one to the left (as you head back to Vienna) at Henry's Crossroads.

Take every possible left turn (there are three more) except the one into the checking station at the humpbacked bridge over Transquaking Creek. In 15.1 miles you will find yourself at the beginning of Key Wallace Drive where a right turn will take you in 1.0 mile to the start of the refuge wildlife drive. En route you pass through fields, woods, and marsh, all good for birding, especially for soaring Bald Eagles.

At high tide the road east of Transquaking Creek may be flooded, but rarely deep enough to prevent a slow transit. Stop on top of the bridge for a splendid marshland view.

---

27 From Salisbury to Broadkill Marsh

Most birders who are not beach bound themselves stay well clear of the Atlantic resort communities and parks in Maryland and Delaware from Memorial Day through mid-October. The towns are full of people and the parks charge high fees, while the coastal birds are easier to find on Assateague Island or around Bombay Hook and Little Creek.

The most popular time for birders to visit the coast from Ocean City to Broadkill Beach is November-April, when they have the best hope of finding wintering raptors and the rare northern water birds that sometimes mingle with the more dependable ducks and gulls.

Here is a classic birding run up the Maryland and Delaware coast that can stand on its own or be combined with a pelagic trip out of Ocean City or a day at any of the Delmarva refuges for a satisfying winter weekend.

If you go prepared physically for the coldest winds and psychologically for a total dearth of rarities, you are likely to find much to enjoy. Start early to fit everything in.

The tour begins with a quick visit to the **Salisbury dump,** variously signposted as the Brick Kiln Road Landfill and the Newland Park Landfill. At the western end of Salisbury, turn right at the first traffic light you come to as you head east on U.S. 50, onto Md. 349. Fork right in less than 0.2 mile and right again at 0.6 mile. At 1.6 miles you reach the dump. Follow the trucks through the gate to the right, announcing your purpose to the guard if he is there. The thousands of gulls present will be obvious; the most likely rarities are Lesser Black-backed, Glaucous, and Iceland Gulls, among the abundant Ring-billed and Herring Gulls. Park well out of the way of the trucks.

BROADKILL BEACH TO OCEAN CITY

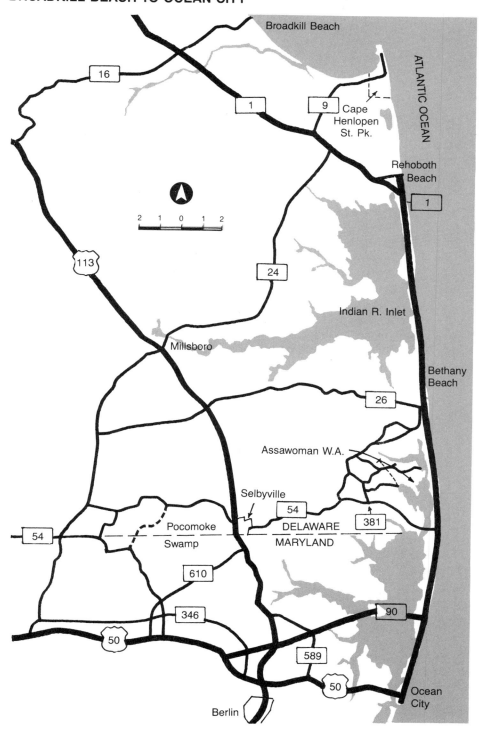

Then continue east to the intersection of U.S. 50 and U.S. 113 near the town of Berlin. Take the exit for U.S. 113 south and, exactly 0.5 mile from U.S. 50, park on the shoulder of the ramp. Fifty yards to the right are two sewage lagoons separated by a dyke. Scope them from the road for ducks and gulls. Then make a U-turn at the next crossover and return to U.S. 50, (mile 0.0)

At 2.4 miles turn left (north) off U.S. 50 onto Md. 589 and, at 2.9 miles, go left again on Griffin Road. Three ponds are on the left before the road bends left at 3.6 miles. If you round the bend, you will be able to study the birds on the far side of the sandbar in the third pond.

If you continue north on Md. 589 0.3 mile beyond Griffin Road, you cross over a creek that sometimes has ducks and gulls right beside the bridge. You can study them safely from Gum Point Road, a right turn just beyond the creek.

The next stop, **West Ocean City Pond,** is on Golf Course Road, which runs north from the traffic light on U.S. 50 by an Exxon station 3.7 miles east of Md. 589 and just west of the bridge into Ocean City. The pond, 0.4 mile north on the left, is quite large, with inaccessible corners. Do not trespass on adjacent property, no matter what has just swum out of sight.

This pond is noted for its hundreds of Whistling Swans and Canvasbacks, but may easily turn up a dozen other species from herons to gulls, and the other ponds may have quite different populations. It pays to check all of them.

On entering Ocean City, turn right immediately onto Philadelphia Avenue, follow it to the end and turn in (only in winter) at the entrance to the Oceanic Motel. The little harbor on the right sometimes has loons, grebes, cormorants, and gulls, and at high tide Purple Sandpipers and Ruddy Turnstones may be resting on the rocks and the pier.

Drive on through the motel and straight ahead to the north jetty of **Ocean City Inlet.** You can scan the inlet, ocean, and south jetty from your car, or park in the lot and walk carefully out along the rocks.

Winter regulars here are Common and Red-throated Loons; Horned Grebes; Gannets; Brant, Greater Scaup, Oldsquaw, Red-breasted Mergansers; all three scoters; Purple Sandpipers; Ruddy Turnstones; and Bonaparte's, Herring, Ring-billed, and Great Black-backed Gulls. To see and identify them all, a spotting scope is essential. Only a few are present on any one visit.

The rarities that show up at the inlet most often are Harlequin Ducks, King and Common Eiders (usually on the south side of the south jetty), Black-legged Kittiwakes, and Little, Black-headed, Glaucous, and Iceland Gulls. Expect none of these, but scour the area thoroughly and you may sometimes come up with one or two.

Leaving the inlet, you will be heading north on Baltimore Avenue. At the onion dome of the town hall, turn left on Third Street and follow it to its end at Sinepuxent Bay. You will be at the best vantage point for scanning the **"Fourth Street Flats,"** tidal flats that actually run from Second to Seventh Streets.

At low tide hundreds of gulls (including all the inlet species), terns, shorebirds, and geese rest here and feed in the adjacent waters. They are easy to study in morning light but become silhouettes on a sunny afternoon.

You can work your way easily enough north along the bay to Ninth Street, at which point condominiums start getting in the way. If you have time to spare, explore the bayside shoreline for several miles north, looking for points of access, since these waters are popular with a variety of loons, grebes, and diving ducks.

The main road north is Philadelphia Avenue. Above 115th Street there are on the left several open, filled areas as yet undeveloped, and these are worth tramping for Horned Larks, wintering sparrows, Snow Buntings, and Lapland Longspurs. (The best find to date is a LeConte's Sparrow.)

At the Delaware state line go left on Del. 54 for 4.0 miles and turn right on Road 381 (mile 0.0). Bear right at 2.1 miles, right again at 3.0 miles, right again at 3.2 miles, and left at 4.3 miles. At 4.9 miles turn right into the entrance to **Assawoman State Wildlife Area,** a beautiful preserve of pine woods, swamps, impoundments, and bay waters laced with firm, sandy roads that should all be investigated.

Mute Swans, Red-headed Woodpeckers, Brown-headed Nuthatches, and Pine Warblers are all resident here, and many ducks and land birds spend the winter. Passerine migration is rich in the spring, and Chuck-will's-widows are abundant then along the roads at dusk. (The area is open from 7:00 A.M. to 8:00 P.M.)

When you leave Assawoman, turn left, and then keep right at every fork and T-junction (disregarding all side roads). After 6.7 miles you will find yourself at the traffic light on Del. 1, onto which you will turn left. (If you do not go to Assawoman, you will reach this same point on the main road north from Ocean City, 6.1 miles above the turnoff onto Del. 54.)

After 4.6 miles you will come to the bridge over **Indian River Inlet.** Exit right before the bridge and drive to the far end of the big parking lot. This inlet is much narrower than Ocean City's, and you can examine both sides of both jetties. It has all the same possibilities for birds, but is seldom as productive. It is worth your while to drive west under the bridge to the marina at the end of the road and to check the marshes, sandbars, and open water all around. To continue north on Del. 1, you must return to the point at which you left it, on the east side of the highway.

From the inlet to the town of Rehoboth Beach is a fast 6.5 mile run, but keep your eyes open. Roadside birds reported along this stretch include Rough-legged Hawks, an American Bittern, a Short-eared Owl on a signpost, a flock of Snow Buntings, and another of Common Redpolls.

When Del. 1 bears left, go straight instead down Bayard Avenue toward Rehoboth Beach for the sake of seeing all the gulls and waterfowl in Silver Lake, about a half-mile ahead on the right. It is a good spot to eat lunch and look for Redheads among the Canvasbacks.

Continue straight to the end of the road, which has become Second Street, where a left turn will take you back to Del. 1 north of town. About 3.3 miles north from the junction of Del. 1 and Alternate Del. 1, fork right by the Sunoco station and follow the signs to the Lewes-Cape May ferry. The open fields in this area can be teeming with blackbird flocks, and with patience and luck you may find Brewer's or Yellow-headed Blackbirds among the Redwings.

Just before a high bridge looms up ahead, turn right at the Gibbs Paint and Chemical Company. Just beyond it on the left is the "Paint Pond," which birders regularly check for resident Black-crowned Night Herons and a constantly changing waterfowl population. Return to the highway, continue to the visitor parking area at the ferry slip, and scan the neighboring waters for loons, grebes, cormorants, and sea ducks. Then drive on toward **Cape Henlopen State Park** (free in the winter, but horrendously costly for nonresidents from Memorial Day to mid-October).

Just inside the park, immediately beyond a barrackslike two-story building marked "University of Delaware—College of Marine Studies," a left turn will take you to an eroded parking area beside a long pier. Scan the beach and water on either side and walk out on the pier as far as you can. The breakwater beyond the pier, especially the tower at the left end, is a fairly reliable resting place in winter for both Great and Double-crested Cormorants, and the pier has been known to shelter eiders and even, once, a Western Grebe.

Back on the main park road you will pass a huge playing field that is much visited in migration by grass-loving shorebirds. Leave it to your right and take any open road left as far as you can go, beyond the pine-encircled radar tower to a parking area that gives you a view of the whole cape and access to its dunes and beaches.

A closed nesting area for terns and skimmers in summer, the dunes may host in winter a Short-eared Owl or two, the Ipswich race of the Savannah Sparrow, Snow Buntings, Lapland Longspurs, and occasionally Common Redpolls and Pine Siskins. The beach, especially at low tide, offers hope of all the birds listed for the Ocean City inlet and flats (except Purple Sandpipers) and the joy of a walk by the sea besides.

The entire cape with its pines, myrtles, and scrubby vegetation is worth birding for any wintering species from falcons to shrikes to crossbills, but you may be running out of time.

Retrace your route past the ferry turnoff, over the high bridge, and back to Del. 1, on which you head north for 8.0 miles. At that point the highway crosses Del. 16, the best route back to Washington. Follow the signs for the Bay Bridge.

If you reach that intersection before dusk, turn east instead and drive out to the great marsh west of Broadkill Beach. The best place to park and see the entire marsh is by the bridge at 2.8 miles.

Noted in summer for its Henslow's Sparrows and Black Rails, in winter **Broadkill Marsh** is quartered at sunset by Northern Harriers, Rough-legged Hawks, and Short-eared Owls, while skeins of Canada Geese snake in thin, black lines against the reddening western sky, their calls mixing with the hoots of the Great Horned Owl in the nearby woods. It is a perfect place to end the day.

Pocomoke Swamp and Deal Island 28

Cypress Swamp Conservation Area, a sanctuary on the Delaware-Maryland line owned by Delaware Wildlands, Inc., is widely known to East Coast birders as **Pocomoke Swamp.** Hordes of bird clubs from Massachusetts to Virginia converge on the most accessible stretch of this beautiful swamp during the first three weekends of May.

The drawing power of these dates is the excellent chance of seeing a variety of migrant songbirds in addition to the nesting species that are the main attraction. If you can manage a weekday visit in this period, you will enjoy birds rather than people. If you do not mind missing the migrants, which can be found as readily elsewhere, come in late April or from late May to early July, when you can study in peace the nesters and perhaps their endearingly curious fledgling young.

If you arrive before sunrise, Barred Owls may still be calling. Nonpasserines are likely to include Green Heron, Red-shouldered Hawk, Yellow-billed Cuckoo, and Pileated Woodpecker. Great Crested and Acadian Flycatchers, Eastern Wood Pewee, Wood Thrush, Blue-gray Gnatcatcher, and White-eyed, Yellow-throated, and Red-eyed Vireos are near certainties.

It is the warblers, though, that are the magnet: Black-and-white, Prothonotary, Worm-eating, Parula, Yellow-throated, Pine, Ovenbird, Louisiana Waterthrush, Kentucky, Hooded, and Redstart are the common ones.

The most sought-after of all is the Swainson's Warbler, here at its most northerly breeding grounds on the East Coast. In the past few years the three or four pairs (at most) that have tried to settle in here to nest have been unmercifully harassed by tape-playing birders yearning to bring them into view. The Maryland Ornithological Society now posts an urgent plea for the Swainson's to be left in peace. You still have a good chance to see one if you memorize the song before you go; whether you succeed or not, you can hardly call the morning a failure with so many other species to see and hear.

The easiest route to the swamp from the west is from U.S. 13, where it crosses the Maryland-Delaware state line. Go east at that point (mile 0.0) on Del. 54 for 9.1 miles. When Del. 54 turns north, continue east on Bethel Road, bearing right at the fork at 11.2 miles. At 11.9 miles turn left on Sheppard's Crossing Road.

Shortly after entering the swamp you will cross the Pocomoke River at 12.6 miles. Park near it and do a little birding on either side of the road. Then continue to 13.1 miles, and turn left on an unpaved road. When you cross the next bridge, at 13.4 miles, park somewhere safe, either on the road ahead (north) or the one to the right (east).

Bird along both roads and explore any little trails you see. The Swainson's Warblers are most likely to be along the north road. There is a trail along the stream you have just crossed that can be rewarding.

Most birders spend their time in this part of the swamp. If you continue another 0.7 mile you will be out of the woods and out of Maryland at 14.1 miles. When you enter the next woods at 14.8 miles you will have a long stretch of swamp, probably all to yourself, a good trail by the Delaware Wildlands sign on the right at 15.0 miles, and all the same birds except the Swainson's Warbler.

Emerging from these woods at 15.6 miles, you meet Del. 54 at a T-junction at 16.1 miles. Turn right if you are going to the coast and drive once more through the swamp, birding at will along the highway. (A left turn, of course, will return you eventually to U.S. 13.)

At 21.8 miles fork left on Del. 54 if you are heading east or north; otherwise continue straight until you meet U.S. 113 at 22.4 miles.

The reverse route from the junction of U.S. 113 and Del. 54 (mile 0.0) in Selbyville, Delaware, is even easier. Drive west on Del. 54 through the swamp and go left at 6.2 miles just before the curve sign. This is the unpaved road that first winds through the Delaware swamp and then runs through the Maryland swamp.

You will reach U.S. 50 by leaving the swamp at the south end. Turn left on Sheppard's Crossing Road (mile 0.0) and turn right at 1.8 miles. Continue south to Md. 610 at 3.3 miles and bear right; you will run into U.S. 50 at 4.5 miles.

All the same species can be found in Pocomoke State Park 3.5

miles west of Snow Hill, Maryland, on U.S. 113 and in the adjacent Pocomoke State Forest to the west. Investigate the trails that run back into the woods on the north side of the highway in the first two or three miles west of the park entrance.

While many birders combine a morning at Pocomoke with an afternoon on Assateague or around Ocean City, the rest of the day can also be spent profitably on an excursion to **Deal Island Wildlife Management Area,** dominated by a colony of Great Blue Herons and home to nesting Least and American Bitterns; Bald Eagles; Northern Harriers; Ospreys; Pied-billed Grebes; Gadwall, Blue-winged and Green-winged Teal; Common Gallinules; Coots; Marsh and Sedge Wrens; and Sharp-tailed and Seaside Sparrows.

It is intensively used as a feeding area by all the herons and ibis nesting in nearby colonies and by the Forster's Terns that breed on the little marsh islands offshore in Chesapeake Bay. Normally, water levels in spring are too high to attract any shorebirds but yellowlegs and occasional Black-necked Stilts, but both species of dowitchers and White-rumped Sandpipers may turn up in the fall, and Common Snipe winter in the marsh. One year when the impoundment was drained, thousands of shorebirds poured in.

In winter it shelters large numbers of dabbling ducks and is a popular spot to look for Eurasian Wigeon among the American Wigeon, though the search is rarely rewarded. In addition to the Harriers and Bald Eagles, likely raptors include Red-tailed and Rough-legged Hawks, Peregrines, Merlins, and Short-eared Owls.

To reach Deal Island take U.S. 13 south from Salisbury to Princess Anne and turn right on Md. 363. Drive 9.5 miles and fork left at the Deal Island WMA sign. Keep right where a road branches left after 1.2 miles and continue to the chain across your path at 1.4 miles. The limited view here out over the marshy impoundment is best in morning light, but you may find Sedge Wrens and both bitterns along the road at any time of day.

Go back to Md. 363 and continue west 2.2 miles to Dame's Quarter, where you take the first possible left (mile 0.0), onto Riley Roberts Road, which goes through a small settlement, then gradually deteriorates but is always navigable. You might park by the chained-off road on the left, at 1.7 miles, and walk as far as you like along the north side of the impoundment. Then continue to the end of the road by the Chesapeake Bay at 3.3 miles; you will have driven along the west side of the impoundment. If you are in the mood to hike eight or nine miles you can circumnavigate the impoundment on foot.

When you leave the wildlife management area, do not miss the opportunity to see the quintessential watermen's communities along the highway to the west. After passing through Chance and Deal

Island, the road ends in 6.7 miles at Wenona, where you can look out to Little Deal Island and over the Chesapeake Bay. In November dozens of loons may be seen from here (hundreds of them through a scope on a clear day), and perhaps Gannets plunging into the water far offshore.

If you while away the hours until nightfall, the marshes can be full of the sounds of Rails: King, Clapper, Virginia, and Black, all in similar abundance. You are unlikely to see any without the aid of a tape recorder.

Before you set out be aware that the marshes of Somerset County can be infested, day or night, with unbearable numbers of mosquitoes. An ample supply of concentrated insect repellent may be as crucial to your pleasure there as binoculars.

29 The North End of Assateague

Until very recently the only way that law-abiding birders could reach the north end of Assateague Island was by boat. The only stretch of wilderness beach in Maryland was otherwise inaccessible public land with a southern bay-to-ocean boundary, a mile or so wide, in private hands.

Happily, conditions have changed; the formerly private land is now open to the public, and the National Park Service has wisely decided to limit access to hikers (and boaters) only. This policy means that it is now possible to reach the best shorebird area in Maryland, the best spot to watch peregrine migration, and the only good vantage point for birds lurking on the south side of the south jetty of Ocean City inlet.

The price that must be paid is a healthy walk up the beautiful beach, at least 3 miles to the nearest shorebird flats and at least 6 miles (some say 7.5) to the inlet. On summer weekends you must pay $3 to park in the nearest lot, the day-use parking area in Assateague State Park, or else add 1.5 miles each way to park free in the National Seashore lot at North Beach.

It is all worth it. Take a picnic, take a swim, take a nap en route, but by all means take the trip and plan to spend all day. Start off soon after dawn, preferably on a day when low tide is scheduled for 10:00 to 11:00 A.M.. You definitely do not want a high tide in the morning.

If you go in summer, take plenty to drink, a hat, sunscreen, a good insect repellent, and maybe a bathing suit. Be prepared for wet feet.

Your starting point is reached by taking Md. 611 south from U.S. 50, 0.8 miles west of the west end of the bridge into Ocean City. After

OCEAN CITY TO SOUTH POINT

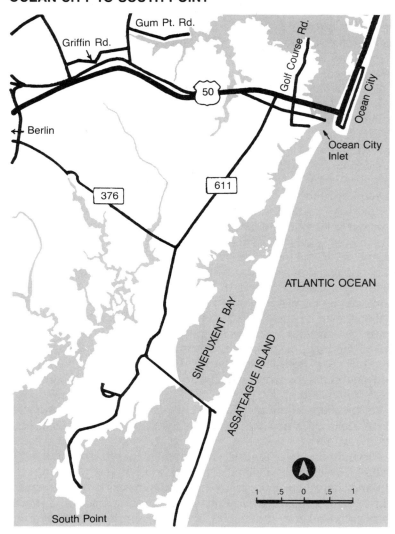

crossing the high bridge onto Assateague Island continue straight past the toll booth and into the day-use lot of the state park, on the right. Park immediately, close to the large brown buildings, and head out to the beach.

Walk north along the surf. In 1.75 miles you will pass a large green house and, 10-15 minutes later, a sign for a hike-in campsite. Ahead are three thick posts, the first well back to your left, the other two out on the beach and conspicuous.

Measure your time between the campsite sign and the third post, and walk as far again, keeping an eye on the housing development across the bay on the left. When you have almost passed it, look for a marshy swale that cuts across the island, the first real break in the bushes that run up the center. Turn left and cross to the west side.

Flushing Willets, Seaside Sparrows, Boat-tailed Grackles, and Red-winged Blackbirds (in summer) as you go, you will come upon a major tidal flat, likely to be crowded with shorebirds, egrets, ducks, and gulls. Just off the shore beyond are islands where Laughing Gulls, a few Herring Gulls, Clapper Rails, Willets, and Oyster-catchers nest; all of these species are as readily found on Assateague itself.

Working your way north around a tidal gut or two (the pony tracks are good paths to follow), you will reach the bay shoreline, an alternating sequence of beach and flats. Look for Piping Plovers on the dry sand, Wilson's Plovers on the wet flats. Assateague is the northernmost point along the coast where Wilson's Plovers regularly nest, and the only place to see them in Maryland. Look for them from May to August. In the winter months the sandy washovers attract Snow Buntings and grassier flats Lapland Longspurs, which one year were joined by a handful of Smith's Longspurs.

In addition to breeding and migrant shorebirds, other species often loaf on the shore and the flats: Royal, Gull-billed, Common and Least Terns, gulls of every species on the Maryland list, ducks and geese. Out in the bay and along the ocean front Common Loons may be found all year; Red-throated Loons, Horned Grebes and sometimes Red-necked Grebes, diving ducks and Red-breasted Mergansers are there from fall to spring.

Visitors from a nearby island where colonial water birds nest include flocks of Glossy Ibis and all the egrets and herons. Some linger far into winter.

The northern tip of the island used to lie against the south jetty of Ocean City inlet, but it is migrating westward 40 feet a year because of sand starvation, caused by the jetties blocking the alongshore current. As a result, a growing sandy beach bulges out into the channel, while the connection of island and jetty is increasingly tenuous. The beach is a popular gathering point for gulls in winter when the jetty attracts Double-crested and, rarely, Great Cormorants, all three scoters, Harlequin Ducks, King and Common Eiders, and Purple Sandpipers. Loons, Horned Grebes, and Oldsquaw feed in the inlet, as do flocks of Bonaparte's Gulls with occasional Little and Black-headed Gulls to be found among them.

At the north end, thickets of bushes provide shelter for migrating land birds, while several man-made spoil piles make habitat for nesting Least Terns in summer and good lookouts for birders to watch for migrating Peregrines and Merlins from mid-September to late October. (The National Park Service would be pleased to have a minimum of visitors around the tern colony from late May to mid-July.)

Your walk back along the ocean will be more fruitful if you wait until the sun is in the west. In summer and fall the beach may be thick with Sanderlings, Piping and Black-bellied Plovers, Whimbrel and Knots, while late August marks the arrival of southbound gulls.

In October, November, March, and April, Canada and Snow Geese, scoters, scaup, and mergansers pass by overhead or off-shore in long lines. All winter long Gannets may be seen out to sea, particularly when the wind is from the east.

The most exciting birding is apt to be during or just after a major coastal storm when such pelagic species as storm-petrels, shearwaters, jaegers, and alcids may be seen from the beach. (All of these are at least as likely to be seen at Ocean City inlet as farther down the coast.)

If you tire of walking down the beach, you can cut inland at the green house (known as the McCabe House) and follow a firm dirt road back to the parking lot.

There is other good birding on Assateague that is much less strenuous. If you wait until the hordes leave after Labor Day, you can beat the bushes in the campgrounds for fall warblers and western vagrants, and sort through flocks of sparrows for a Clay-colored or a Lark Sparrow. Later, from November on, Snow Buntings and Snow Geese may be among the dunes.

In winter it is worth your while to look for owls in the pine woods 3.2 miles down the main road of the island (a right turn just before the toll booth). Turn in at Old Ferry Landing Road and park immediately. Access into the woods is provided by paths on the south side of that road and by a service road off the main road south of the ranger station. Old Ferry Landing Road and Candleberry Trail beside it also give you an easy way into the marsh, if you are looking for Clapper Rails and Seaside and Sharp-tailed Sparrows.

On your way to or from Assateague, several roads in the immediate vicinity deserve exploration.

The road to South Point, which begins just west of the mainland offices of the state park, runs through woods and fields with sparrowy hedgerows to a public landing with good views of the bay. It is most promising in fall and winter.

The road to Ocean City Airport, a left turn off Md. 611 1.5 miles south of U.S. 50, is noted for warblers in migration and Chuck-will's-widows on spring nights.

Finally, two roads in West Ocean City are excellent for afternoon birding, especially near low tide when flats are exposed. Turn east off Md. 611 at the first blinking light 0.4 mile south of U.S. 50 and follow the road to its end. You can walk out on the remains of an old bridge and scan on either side for shorebirds, gulls, and the other species that turn up in Ocean City inlet.

Then go east on U.S. 50 and turn off just before the bridge over the bay at the sign for Shantytown. Beside this little shopping area is a parking lot perfect for birding from your car, directly opposite a tidal flat.

Should you decide to try to reach the north end of Assateague by boat, be warned that the boat rental marinas in West Ocean City charge $16-20 for four hours, and some rent only to fishermen. You would do well to take along at least a fishing rod and a cooler if you have them, even if you do not plan to spend much time with a line in the water.

30 Chincoteague

Chincoteague National Wildlife Refuge may be the best place on the Atlantic coast to see a succession and combination of virtually all the eastern loons, grebes, cormorants, herons, ibis, swans, geese, ducks, falcons, shorebirds, gulls, terns, and skimmers, along with land birds ranging from resident Fish Crows, Brown-headed Nuthatches, Pine Warblers, and Boat-tailed Grackles to breeding Seaside Sparrows, and wintering Ipswich (Savannah) Sparrows and Snow Buntings.

If you enjoy a world of marsh, pine woods, wild beach, and open ocean, it is a beautiful and fascinating place to visit and bird all year-round, with abundant and convenient tourist accomodations. It is an easy area to bird by car, but gives its greatest rewards to the birder with the time and energy to explore it on foot.

Allow a solid three hours to drive from the Washington Beltway via U.S. 50 east to U.S. 13 in Salisbury, U.S. 13 south to Va. 175, and Va. 175 east to Chincoteague.

If you arrive when the tidal flats are exposed, begin your birding along the causeway from the mainland, just before you cross the second bridge. A short spur road on the right, 1.4 miles from the west end of the causeway, provides close views of a bed of Chincoteague's justly famous oysters, where you should find at least two, perhaps a hundred American Oystercatchers, as well as other shorebirds, egrets, Laughing Gulls, and Forster's Terns in summer, and Brant, gulls, and perhaps Horned Grebes, Double-crested Cormorants, and diving ducks in winter.

Immediately east of the bridge, pull carefully over to the shoulder on the north side of the road and park in front of the first billboard. The extensive mud flat attracts not only Brant, gulls, terns, and oystercatchers, but Black-bellied Plover, Willets, Short-billed Dowitchers, Dunlin, and "peep," mainly Western Sandpipers.

The same shorebirds may be on the flats beside the northside pull-off 0.3 mile farther east.

Drive on through the village of Chincoteague, which is on Chincoteague Island, to **Chincoteague Refuge,** the Virginia end of Assateague Island. (Part of the refuge is managed by the National Park Service under the name of Assateague National Seashore.) Follow the signs to Assateague and you will be in the refuge. Stop first at the Refuge Information Center, the first left turn after the first bend, and pick up the available handouts, including a bird list. Check the wildlife sighting list hung on a nail outside the door. Look and listen for Brown-headed Nuthatches and Pine Warblers around the parking lot.

If you arrive after 3:00 P.M., you can take your car around the 3-mile **Wildlife Drive** (open only to pedestrians and bicyclists earlier in the day), which loops around Snow Goose Pool and through pine woods. When water levels are high, usually November to June, it is full of waterfowl; as it dries up in July and August, it is a mecca for feeding egrets and ibis and for resting gulls, terns, and skimmers. When mud flats appear, it becomes prime shorebird habitat, first for yellowlegs, Short-billed Dowitchers, Stilt Sandpipers, and an occasional Ruff, then for Pectoral Sandpipers and "peep." In drought years (about two out of five), Snow Goose Pool dries up entirely and attracts "grasspipers" like Lesser Golden Plover and Buff-breasted Sandpipers. The shorebirds are magnets for migrating Peregrines and Merlins in September and October. The pine woods halfway around may shelter a flock of Brown-headed Nuthatches and are sometimes swarming with warblers in migration. A morning walk around the Wildlife Drive allows you to see in good light areas that are backlit in the afternoon.

Back on the main road, keep your eyes open for White-tailed and Sika Deer, feral ponies, and cars stopping suddenly to look at them.

Black Duck Marsh, the first impoundment on the left, is especially attractive to Snow Geese, Green-winged and Blue-winged Teal and other dabbling ducks, and is a good spot to look for Eurasian Wigeon in October and November. In summer it dries up earlier than the other impoundments and is often the best area for egrets and ibis in June and July. In these months, particularly at dawn, you may see dozens of Gull-billed and Forster's Terns hawking for insects over the shallow water.

A little before you reach the marked entrance to the Pony Trail on the right there is an unmarked dirt pull-off on the left from which you have the best views of the southwest part of Swan Cove. You will need a good telescope and afternoon light. Waterfowl and herons often shelter from northerly winds behind the little islands, while terns, mostly Black Terns, and shorebirds rest on the mud flats. In late summer and early fall, Avocets and Hudsonian and Marbled Godwits feed in the shallows.

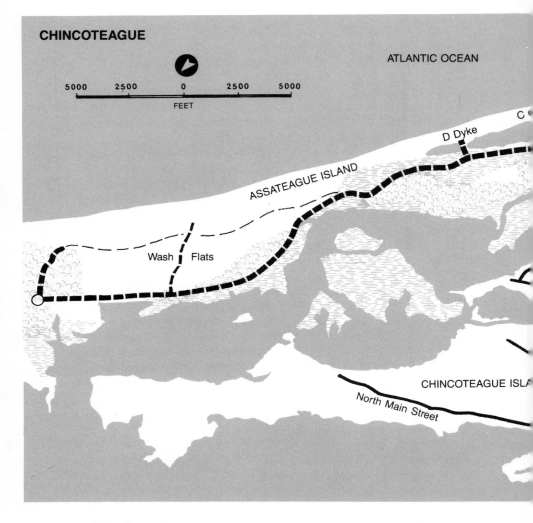

CHINCOTEAGUE

ATLANTIC OCEAN

5000   2500   0   2500   5000

FEET

D Dyke

ASSATEAGUE ISLAND

Wash Flats

CHINCOTEAGUE ISLA

North Main Street

The Pony Trail is so lovely that it is a pity that insects make it unbearable for most of the summer. If you get up early enough to be the first to take this 1.6-mile loop you are quite likely to meet a Sika Deer face to face, get a close view of a Delmarva Fox Squirrel, and stare down a herd of ponies blocking your path. It is the best area on the refuge for migrant and wintering land birds.

Along the trail are two areas once prepared as parking lots. If you go around the loop clockwise, you will find a path running off to the left just beyond the first of these lots (nearly halfway around). Follow it almost no distance to the beach on the east side of Tom's Cove, which you will probably have to yourself. A walk toward the point on

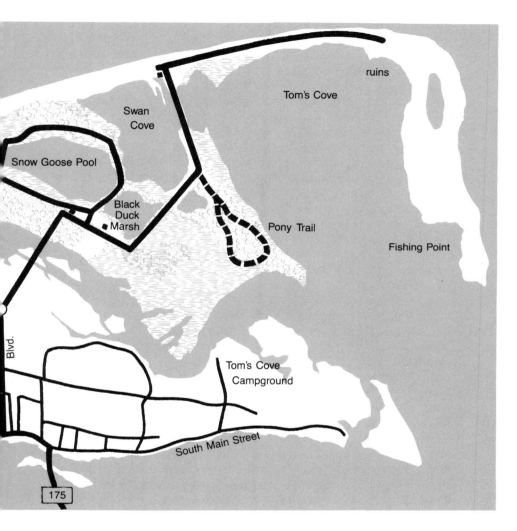

your right can be a delight, particularly in spring migration, for both water birds and land birds.

The causeway between the east half of Swan Cove and the north end of Tom's Cove, a tidal bay, is usually worth a number of stops. Look for Mute and Whistling Swans, Canada Geese, Ruddy Ducks, and Pied-billed Grebes to the left, and Common Loons, Horned Grebes, Brant, and Red-breasted Mergansers to the right. You may see Double-crested Cormorants and Ospreys on the pilings and hunter's blinds, American Oystercatchers, Ruddy Turnstones, and Black-bellied Plover on the oyster shells and tidal flats, Whimbrel, Clapper Rails, and Seaside Sparrows in the salt marsh, and yellowlegs, dowitchers, "peep," gulls, and terns anywhere. Especially near dusk in summer look for Black- and Yellow-crowned Night Herons and Black Skimmers along the ditches.

The road to the beach ends at a small circle. Go left to the Tom's Cove Visitor Center where an interesting and useful assortment of books are for sale, and to parking lot A, which is an excellent spot to study and photograph gulls, mainly Laughing and Ring-billed, in all their plumages, at close range.

Access by car to the entire area south of this point is currently (late 1982) unpredictable. The paved road that used to extend two miles down the beach behind the dunes was buried in sand in the winter of 1981-82, and forecasts based on studies of beach dynamics predict continuing instability and erosion along the thin neck of land leading to the south end of Assateague.

Whether you can drive part way or must walk the entire 5 miles to Fishing Point, this is a hike to take if you can. The area of greatest interest on both sides of the island lies south of the ruins of the old fish canning factory in Tom's Cove, about 1.5 miles south of the T-junction.

In September and October, the wires, bushes, and sandy patches along the beach road are heavily used by migrant passerines, especially swallows, flycatchers, orioles, and sparrows. Check them carefully for Western Kingbirds, Clay-colored Sparrows, and Lark Sparrows.

From mid-May to early June, horseshoe crabs lay their eggs on the Tom's Cove beach from the factory ruins to Fishing Point, and the sand may be almost invisible because of the dense numbers of feeding Sanderlings, Red Knots, Ruddy Turnstones, Semipalmated Sandpipers, Dunlins, Short-billed Dowitchers, and Laughing Gulls. (Walk this stretch only near low tide, or be prepared to wade.) The cove beach, except for the last half-mile, is much less interesting the rest of the year, though the loons, grebes, and sea ducks in the cove itself will keep you entertained from fall to spring.

The walk down the ocean beach is almost always interesting, though the birds that nest, feed, and rest along it suffer constant disturbance from Memorial Day through Labor Day, mostly from oversand vehicles. A protected nesting area at Fishing Point has a precarious future because of its limited cost-effectiveness; species breeding in and around it include Piping and Wilson's Plovers, American Oystercatcher, Willet, and Common and Least Terns. Great Black-backed, Herring, Ring-billed, and Laughing Gulls, and Royal, Caspian, Forster's, and occasionally Sandwich Terns loaf on the sand and feed beyond the surf. Aside from Sanderling and Whimbrel, which are regularly found the length of the beach, most of the migrant shorebirds are concentrated on the flats around Fishing Point, sometimes numbering in the thousands. Common species at the Point include Semipalmated and Black-bellied Plovers, Ruddy Turnstone, Short-billed Dowitcher, Dunlin, and Semipalmated, Least, and Western (fall only) Sandpipers; every now and then Lesser Golden Plovers, Marbled and Hudsonian Godwits, and White-rumped Sandpipers drop in as well. Common and Red-throated Loons and Double-crested Cormorants often gather in the inlet, and Brant feed along the shore at the point.

If the mosquitoes are not too fierce and the rainfall has not been excessive, the marshy flats and the ponds behind the dunes should be investigated. Birds normally on the ocean beach and the tidal flats move into this area if there are strong onshore winds, while herons, ducks, and yellowlegs are regularly present.

A sea watch is best mounted up the beach, near the visitor center. Birds are most likely to be seen from October to May, or after major storms. Look for loons, gannets, scoters, Red-breasted Mergansers, Oldsquaw and, under ideal circumstances (stormy weather and strong easterly winds), shearwaters and jaegers.

The ultimate Chincoteague bird walk is the 14-mile round trip to the top of the Wash Flats, one that can be shortened by 3.5, 4.5, or 7 miles if you take the Safari Wagon (reservations at the Information Center) to the south end of the Flats, the west end of the crossdyke, or all the way to the end of the service road. In winter the Safari Wagon does not run and you have to walk the whole distance to see the thousands of waterfowl that fill the 3-mile-long divided impoundment. In any case, it is a very long trip and it is worth your while to acquire current information about the abundance and variety of birds present before you set out. The Wash Flats can be the most exciting place in the refuge, depending on water levels, with a July or August day producing most of the long-legged waders, shorebirds, and gull and tern species on the refuge list, and a day in September or October likely to provide you with more Peregrine Falcons than any other site on the East Coast. It is a reliable spot for Buff-breasted Sandpipers in late August and September, and it is known for such one-shot rarities as a Pomarine Jaeger, a Long-billed Curlew, and a Mountain Plover.

If you make a day of it, starting at dawn, taking a picnic lunch and as much to drink as you can bear to carry, and perhaps packing a bathing suit, you should find the trip enormously rewarding—but skip it if the forecast is for sunny skies and temperatures over ninety degrees or if mosquitoes and green flies are rampant. If it is good hiking weather, the most interesting route is to go one way along the service road and the other along the beach and the east side of the Wash Flats, choosing the beach route to coincide with the hours nearest low tide.

Assuming low tide is in the morning, park at the Refuge Information Center, walk left up the Wildlife Drive, and go through the stile next to the gate at the north corner of the drive. You are now on the service road. After about 0.3 mile, take the first road right, which goes across "C" Dyke to the beach. Walk left up the beach about 2.5 miles until just after you pass kilometer post 7 and then cross the dunes and climb over the metal gate at the east end of the crossdyke. Not far ahead you can cross the ditch on the right side of the road. Zigzag north, surveying both the water's edge to the west and the grassy flats to the east, the latter being where Buff-breasted and Baird's Sandpipers and Lesser Golden Plover are most likely to occur.

Continue past the Osprey nesting pole and platform at the north end of the flats to the road that winds west through the woods to the turnaround at the end of the service road. The latter runs south along the west side of the Wash Flats, giving excellent views of bayside tidal flats en route. After you pass the gate at the south boundary of the Wash Flats, you can either follow the fence east over to the beach again or continue south along the road back to the Wildlife Drive. The route is easily reversed; you need only to know that "C" Dyke is marked by a large "C" sign and is the second vehicle crossover south of the Wash Flats. If you don't have the energy to go to the top of the flats, make the crossdyke your northern limit; you will save 5 miles but miss some good birds.

When you leave the refuge, several other stops are worth making. The easiest place to see Clapper Rails is along the road just east of the bridge to Assateague, at the edge of the marsh on either side. They are most likely to be seen, spring to fall, when low tide coincides with dawn and dusk. Lie in wait for them at the end of the tidal gut on the north side of the road.

In the likely event that you do not see a Yellow-crowned Night Heron in the refuge in May and June, drive to Tom's Cove Campground at the southeast corner of Chincoteague Village and ask politely at the office if you may visit the heronry. They will, we hope, continue to give directions to the unrented campsite in which the tall pines have been usurped by the Yellow-crowns.

Main Street, which runs along the west side of Chincoteague Island, is worth cruising in the morning or on an overcast afternoon. At the north end is a narrow marsh lined by loblolly pines where Black-crowned Night Herons sometimes roost, mostly in winter. The porch of the Crab House Restaurant behind the Exxon station provides good views of Chincoteague Channel and the tidal flats beyond, where Brant, gulls, and shorebirds can be studied as they feed or rest.

As you leave Chincoteague, pull in behind the motel just west of the drawbridge and scan the sound west of it for ducks, loons, and grebes in winter, terns in summer, and gulls all year-round. Red-necked Grebes, Harlequin Ducks, and both King and Common Eiders have turned up here, and it would be a pity to bypass such possible gems.

The Virginia Eastern Shore 31

The Eastern Shore of Virginia south of Chincoteague offers minor and major birding pleasures that rival those of the refuge itself. Two of them require investments of funds and advance planning, both of which are fully justified.

Mileages at points on U.S. 13 cited below are the distances, without the recommended detours, from the Maryland-Virginia line (mile 0.0).

The **Saxis marshes** lie west of Temperanceville (7.8 miles). Turn right off U.S. 13 on Road 695. After 8.6 miles, turn left on Road 778, drive south 0.5 mile, and park on the shoulder. The broom sedge in the marsh on both sides of the road is reasonably dependable for Sedge Wrens and Henslow's Sparrows in late spring and early sum-mer; try the hours close to dawn. Beyond Road 778, Road 695 runs out into open marsh, where you can expect Clapper and Virginia Rails and Seaside Sparrows. Black Rails have been found here, but not regularly. If you are here by day, go on to the end of the road in Saxis and observe the ways of this single-minded crabbing village.

The **Holly Farms lawns.** At 8.7 miles, U.S. 13 passes the Holly Farms chicken-processing plant. Its extensive lawns can be scanned from the highway or from a road along the south side of the property. Gulls are always present and Black-bellied and Lesser Golden Plover, and Upland, Baird's, and Buff-breasted Sandpipers have been seen there in fall.

The **farm fields** between Accomac and Quinby warrant a detour to the east to look for shorebirds in a wet spring. Leave U.S. 13 (at 20.7 miles) on Business 13 into Accomac, and turn left in 2.3 miles on Road 605. After 3.8 miles, turn left on Road 647, a loop road that returns to Road 605 in 3.4 miles in Locustville. If rain pools are standing in the bare fields, many hundreds of shorebirds, mostly Black-bellied Plover, Semipalmated Plover, Ruddy Turnstone, Short-billed Dowitcher, Dunlin, and Semipalmated Sandpiper, will all be feeding in the soft earth.

The same conditions may exist here and there along the road as far south as Quinby, 8.4 miles from Locustville. At that point take Va. 182 west 3.8 miles back to Painter on U.S. 13 (34.4 miles). En route you will cross the beautiful marshes of the Machipongo River, worth a detour at any time of year.

The Virginia Coast Reserve. The high point of a trip to this part of Delmarva should be, at least once, an expedition to one or more of the barrier islands, most of which are owned and managed as the Virginia Coast Reserve by The Nature Conservancy. If you do not have your own boat, you may be able to rent one in Wachapreague or negotiate for transportation with a waterman at one of the harbors.

The easiest and most rewarding solution between mid-May and early October is to form a group of four to six people and arrange for one of the tours run by The Nature Conservancy on weekdays only. The tour, in an open boat, leaves from reserve headquarters near Nassawadox and goes out to Hog Island and the marshes nearby, a prime area to see breeding herons, shorebirds, gulls, terns, and skimmers, plus all the coastal migrants. You will be informed, entertained, and relieved of all logistical problems. To acquire more details or to make reservations, write or call: Captain Barry Truitt, Virginia Coast Reserve, Brownsville, Nassawadox, Virginia 23413; telephone (804) 442-3049. An excellent fact sheet on the tours and a natural history guide for the islands, including a bird list, are available.

If you have never had the opportunity to visit a barrier island inhabited only by thousands of nesting or migrating birds, virtually undisturbed by human beings, do not miss this one. Depending on when you go, you may see huge flocks of Red Knots massed along a peaty shore, herons on their nests in the marsh elder bushes, an enormous herd of downy Royal Tern chicks bunched together by an inlet, Wilson's Plover families running in spurts across the mud, or Peregrines and Merlins shooting across the marshes. Rarities on the 260-species checklist include Brown and White Pelicans, Magnificent Frigatebird, Anhinga, White Ibis, Long-billed Curlew, and Roseate Tern; but you need no rarities to make this an exhilarating experience.

If you cannot manage the boat trip, try to visit Brownsville, the old estate that serves as reserve headquarters. The handsome residence built in 1806 is worth a look, and birding on the property can be rewarding, probably more so in fall and winter. In Nassawadox (43.3 miles) go east at the flashing light 0.2 mile on Road 606, then north (left) on Road 600 for 0.2 mile. A right turn onto Road 608 will take you to the entrance to Brownsville in 1.2 miles.

Kiptopeke. If you are making this trip in September or October, take advantage of the fact that the Kiptopeke Bird Banding Station, close to the tip of the peninsula, is operating and is open to visitors, and plan to spend the night in one of the several motels between Cheriton and the Chesapeake Bay Bridge-Tunnel.

Just south of the Quality Inn at 65.8 miles, Road 704 slants off to the southwest (66.0 miles). This divided highway, no longer maintained, used to run to the entrance for the pre-Bridge-Tunnel ferry. Take this road and move over to the south side of the median. Just before an obvious former motel on the left, turn left up a dirt drive and follow it to the point where you see parked cars or their traces in the dust. Take one of the trails into the woods on your right; you should immediately come upon the bander's camp. If it is late in the day and no one is around, leave and come back the next morning a little after dawn. If you see anyone, ask for the BIC (pronounced "bick"), i.e., the Bander in Charge, a title that rotates from week to week among a half-dozen or so banders.

The banding operation usually runs from dawn to late afternoon, depending somewhat on the rate at which birds are coming into the mist nets and on the BIC's concept of quitting time. If you know how to take birds out of the nets you will be particularly welcome; if you don't but want to learn, someone is likely to teach you if you are patient. If you just want to watch and enjoy seeing what birds have been caught, you will feel right at home. The basic requirement is to follow the BIC's house rules and to refrain from distracting her (or him) at busy moments.

In addition to the great variety of small landbird migrants you will see in the hand, you may coincide with a wave of swallows or hawks or Bobolinks migrating overhead and movements of herons and egrets around the edges of the farm land surrounding the banding station.

If you want to do some independent birding in the area, the trees along the waterfront west of the America House Motel, just north of the Bridge-Tunnel tollbooths, can be superb for catching all the migrants that have followed the coast south as far as possible and prefer turning the corner and heading north again to flying out over the ocean. Be sure to check the golf range at the motel for Golden Plover and Upland and Buff-breasted Sandpipers. Scan the ruins of the old ferry slip for cormorants, gulls, and terns. Even a Brown Pelican is possible.

The Chesapeake Bay Bridge-Tunnel. To reach Norfolk and points south from Delmarva, the only direct route is via the 17-mile highway over and under Chesapeake Bay. Whether you want to end up on the south side of the bay or not, a birding expedition on the bridge-tunnel can be worth every penny of the costly toll except, perhaps, in calm midsummer weather. At least ten days in advance, write a polite letter to: Executive Director, Chesapeake Bay Bridge and Tunnel District, Post Office Box 111, Cape Charles, Virginia 23310. (If you have not left time for an exchange of letters, call the north office, if you are heading south, at (804) 331-2960 or the south office, if you are heading north, at (804) 464-3511, as far in advance as possible.)

In your request for permission to stop on the bridge-tunnel islands "to observe seabirds and waterfowl," be sure to specify the day you plan to cross and the number of cars in your party. Permission should come promptly in the mail, along with certain restrictions (no children in the car, for example), enabling you to stop, park, and circumnavigate on foot the three northern islands at the ends of the two tunnels.

Show your letter to the collector at the tollbooth (69.3 miles), and keep it handy for the patrol officers, who will leave you alone or treat you kindly if you follow the rules.

If you do not obtain this written permission in advance, you will be able to stop only on the southernmost island along with the rest of the general public, and the odds are 3 in 4 that the most interesting birds will be on or around the islands closed to you.

What will you see? Much depends on the season and on the force and direction of the winds—best when they are strong and easterly. In spring and fall hope for shearwaters, jaegers, and storm-petrels, and expect cormorants, shorebirds, gulls, and terns, plus a variety of small landbird migrants in the grassy areas on the roadway. In waterfowl season you are almost certain to see Greater Scaup, Oldsquaw, Red-breasted Mergansers, and all the scoters. You may find Great Cormorants, Harlequin Ducks, and Common and King Eiders, mostly from December to February. Look among the flocks of gulls for Lesser Black-backed, Thayer's, Iceland, and Glaucous; if Bonaparte's Gulls are present a Little or Black-headed Gull may be among them. In winter months Ruddy Turnstones and Purple Sandpipers are inevitable among the rocks below you, and Gannets may be fishing nearby.

South of
Chesapeake Bay

The southeast corner of Virginia is known to Washington birders mainly for two southern specialties, Red-cockaded Woodpecker and Swainson's Warbler. Less familiar are the numerous outstanding birding areas, all within a few miles of each other, that make a weekend around Norfolk exceptionally fruitful in most months of the year.

In southern Virginia the **Red-cockaded Woodpecker** is at the northern limit of its range. The state's annotated checklist reports a shrinking population, with fewer than fifty birds estimated for all of Virginia in 1978. Most colonies are unpublicized; the location pinpointed below has remained reliable for years.

It lies along U.S. 460, a major truck route between Petersburg and Suffolk. From the only traffic light in Waverly, drive east 5.7 miles and park in front of the billboard announcing "Virginia Diner, 2 miles." (This same spot is 2.1 miles west of the only traffic light in Wakefield.) Scout both sides of the road for mature pine trees with nest holes, around which sap has oozed heavily down the bark. You will be able to assess which ones are reasonably fresh. They are typically within 100 yards of the road, less than one-fourth mile west of the billboard.

When the parents are feeding young (late May to mid-June), you may have some luck seeing them at any hour of the day. The rest of the year the only times that you can expect to see them near the holes, where they roost as well as nest, are at dawn and dusk. (You can waste hours attempting to disprove this assertion.) During the daylight hours they wander far afield.

Hog Island, a state game refuge, lies due north of Wakefield. From the traffic light (mile 0.0) go north on Va. 31 and after 0.4 mile, keep straight on Road 617 for Bacon's Castle. Road 617 crosses Va. 10 at 19.0 miles and ends at Road 650 at 20.4 miles. Turn left and drive 5.0 miles to the refuge entrance, keeping left at all forks, passing the nuclear plant on the right. The gate opens at 8:00 A.M.

This peninsula jutting into the James River has shallow impoundments, cultivated fields, and stands of loblolly pines. It attracts large numbers of Canada Geese, dabbling ducks, Hooded and Common Mergansers, and Ring-necked Ducks in winter, and shorebirds and terns in fall. Brown-headed Nuthatches are resident. Rarities have included White Pelican, Wood Stork, White-fronted Goose, and Fulvous Whistling Duck.

The Great Dismal Swamp, southeast of Suffolk, deserves a visit from late April to mid-May, after the Swainson's Warblers have arrived to breed and while the migrants are still moving through.

SOUTHSIDE VIRGINIA

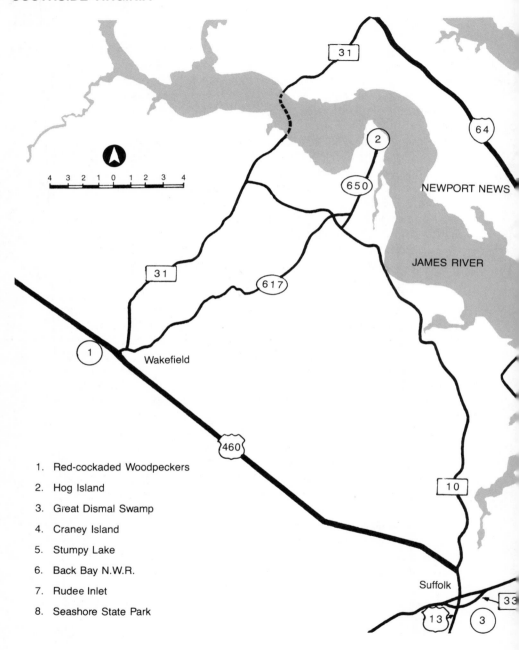

1. Red-cockaded Woodpeckers
2. Hog Island
3. Great Dismal Swamp
4. Craney Island
5. Stumpy Lake
6. Back Bay N.W.R.
7. Rudee Inlet
8. Seashore State Park

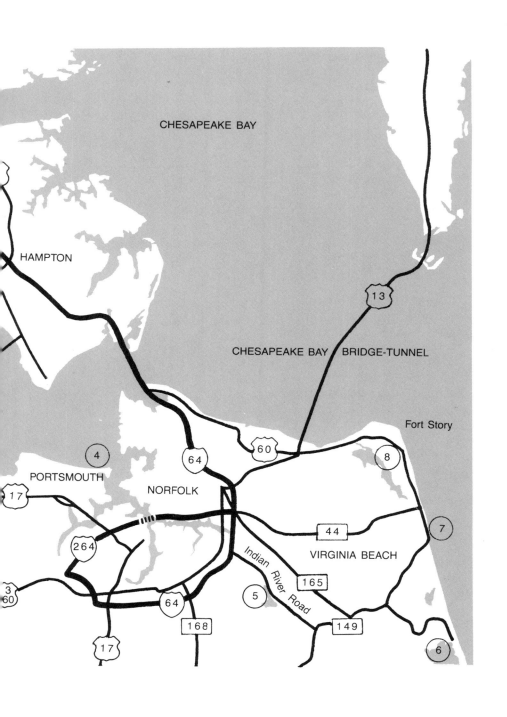

CHESAPEAKE BAY

HAMPTON

13

CHESAPEAKE BAY BRIDGE-TUNNEL

Fort Story

4

60

64

8

PORTSMOUTH

17

NORFOLK

264

44

7

3
60

VIRGINIA BEACH

Indian River Road

165

5

64

168

149

17

6

This famous swamp, surveyed by George Washington, is now a National Wildlife Refuge. Refuge headquarters is on U.S. 13, 2.2 miles south of its junction with Va. 32. The office is on the left, at the south end of a big blue metal building. From 7:30 A.M. to 4:00 P.M. on weekdays you can pick up maps and bird, mammal, and plant lists, and ask questions.

The best birding area in the swamp is reached via Va. 337, Washington Street, which crosses U.S. 13 and Va. 32 0.7 mile south of the junction of the two routes. Go east on Va. 337 0.8 mile and turn right on Whitemarsh Road. Go south 0.8 mile and turn left at the refuge sign onto Jericho Ditch Lane, an unpaved road. After 1.0 mile park at the locked gate, taking care not to block the road. Walk another mile to Jericho Ditch, turn left and go as far as the next corner. When you get back to the intersection, continue south on Lynn Ditch as far as you have time for.

In addition to Swainson's Warbler, breeding species include Woodcock, Chuck-will's-widow, Whip-poor-will; Acadian Flycatcher; Fish Crow; Brown-headed Nuthatch; Yellow-throated Vireo; Prothonotary, Worm-eating, Yellow-throated, Hooded, and Kentucky Warblers; Summer Tanager; and Blue Grosbeak. Of particular interest is the southern race of Black-throated Green Warbler, Wayne's Warbler, which arrives to nest in early April.

Craney Island Landfill, a superb area for water birds, is open weekdays only from 8:00 A.M. to 4:00 P.M. From the junction of U.S. 17 and I-264 in the city of Portsmouth, head northwest on U.S. 17 for about 3.5 miles until you see a sign for Churchland Park. Turn right at that point onto Cedar Lane and follow the signs to Craney Island Landfill, turning left after 1.9 miles onto River Shore Drive and then right after 1.0 mile onto Hedgerow Lane, which will take you to the gate. Register at the Corps of Engineers office and then drive around the enormous impoundment formed from the spoil dredged from the great harbor beyond. You may go anywhere your car or feet will take you provided that you keep out of the way of the work trucks. A few tongues of dykes stick out into the impoundment, most of which are worth exploring, and sometimes you will want just to run up onto the peripheral dyke to check what may be below.

What you should find, in their season, are hundreds, maybe thousands of waders, waterfowl, shorebirds, gulls, terns, and skimmers. Along the west side of the impoundment are endless tidal flats (where there were 401 precisely counted Avocets one August day) and a cove where a Western Grebe lingered one winter. Look for phalaropes and godwits, Ruffs and Curlew Sandpipers, or Snow Buntings and Lapland Longspurs if you do not get there until November. Offshore in the colder months you may see Horned Grebes, Shovelers, Gadwall, Canvasbacks, Wigeon, Ruddy Ducks, and Red-breasted Mergansers.

Like all impoundments in these parts, water levels are dependent on rainfall, and the spots where the birds are cannot be predicted. Explore for yourself. Be careful not to disturb the nesting species.

Stumpy Lake. From I-64, take Indian River Road east about 3.4 miles, turn right at the sign for Stumpy Lake Golf Course, and drive to the end. Park only by the clubhouse. The swampy, man-made lake is bordered by pines and deciduous woods and provides good birding all year.

Red-headed Woodpeckers, Brown-headed Nuthatches, and Pine Warblers are resident, and Yellow-throated Warbler is a nesting species. Common and Hooded Mergansers and Ring-necked Ducks winter in the lake; Rusty Blackbirds and sometimes Orange-crowned Warblers in the adjacent woods. In late summer look for herons, terns (especially Caspian), and shorebirds. Anhingas have been resident in recent years, but are not likely to be easy to find, even if they endure.

Keep to the edges of the golf course and try not to distract the golfers.

Back Bay National Wildlife Refuge. From I-64 take Va. 44, the Virginia Beach Expressway, east to the first exit. At the foot of the ramp, turn left onto Newtown Road south, and left again in 0.2 mile onto Va. 165, Princess Anne Road. At the T-junction in Princess Anne, turn left on Va. 149 (mile 0.0) and follow the signs to the refuge. Bear right at the fork at 1.9 miles; turn left on Sandbridge Road at 2.6 miles and left at the T-junction at 4.8 miles. When you reach the community of Sandbridge, turn right on Sandpiper Road (at 8.1 miles) and drive to the refuge (entrance at 12.4 miles, parking lot at 13.6 miles).

The refuge is on a bay that can be scoped from a point close to the parking lot, but most of it is accessible only to the hiker. A loop road of about 7 miles encircles the three impoundments, and a spur road at the south end leads down to False Cape State Park. The west side of the loop is the better surface to walk on. To reach the beach, cross the dunes only on the road running east from the parking lot.

Back Bay has essentially the same species as Chincoteague, but the landscape and its relative isolation make a visit an entirely different experience. A sea watch here can be particularly interesting.

Rudee Inlet, at the south end of the ocean front of Virginia Beach, where U.S. 60 and Va. 149 meet, is a narrow channel lined by rock jetties. It is accessible by car on both sides and is worth scanning for Purple Sandpipers, Common and King Eiders, Harlequin Ducks, and the more common jetty species. (See Ocean City Inlet, page 146, for possibilities.)

Seashore State Park is north of Virginia Beach and just inland from Fort Story at the entrance to Chesapeake Bay. From U.S. 13 take U.S. 60 about 4.5 miles east to the park entrance on the right.

Access is free between the Labor Day and Memorial Day weekends. Largely preserved as a natural area, this park includes habitats ranging from lake shore through swamp, pine and deciduous woods, and dune thickets to open beach and Chesapeake Bay. Among the 27 miles of footpaths, Bald Cypress, Long Creek, and Main Trails offer perhaps the greatest variety. Brown-headed Nuthatches are resident, but the time to visit is in migration, from early April to mid-May and from early September to late October. Excellent in spring, it is superlative in fall for thrushes, vireos, warblers, and tanagers. Be sure to check the beach for shorebirds, gulls, and terns and the dune scrub and thickets and the marshes for sparrows and other passerines.

33 The North Carolina Outer Banks

Of course there is no need to go nearly as far afield as North Carolina for wonderful birding. The birds and the landscape of the Outer Banks barrier islands are, however, just different enough and just close enough to beckon many Washington birders that far south at least once every year or two.

Species that are much more common on the North Carolina coast than in Virginia and Maryland include (in season) Brown Pelican, White Ibis, Wilson's Plover, and Sandwich Tern, plus longed-for pelagic species like Audubon's Shearwater, Black-capped Petrel, and Bridled Tern, and occasional visitors like Fulvous Whistling Duck, Swallow-tailed Kite, Long-billed Curlew, and Gray Kingbird.

The Banks are interesting all year and the beach crowds from June to September may fill the motels and campgrounds but never overrun the birding spots.

If you can, take a four-day weekend. It is about a six-hour drive to the top of the Banks, via I-95, I-64, Va. 168, and U.S. 158. If you are bored by interstate highways, leave I-95 at Fredericksburg on U.S. 17, which connects with I-64 at Newport News; it takes a bit longer, but it is a pretty and quiet route with little traffic north of Yorktown.

From Memorial Day to Thanksgiving you should have motel reservations. The most convenient accomodations for birders are in Nag's Head, Manteo, Hatteras, and Ocracoke.

Measurements begin at the east end of the long bridge across Currituck Sound to the Banks, and detours from the highway are not included in the cumulative mileage.

At 0.5 mile, note the crossroad with Duck Elementary School on the northeast corner and a Union 76 station on the southwest corner.

NORTH CAROLINA OUTER BANKS

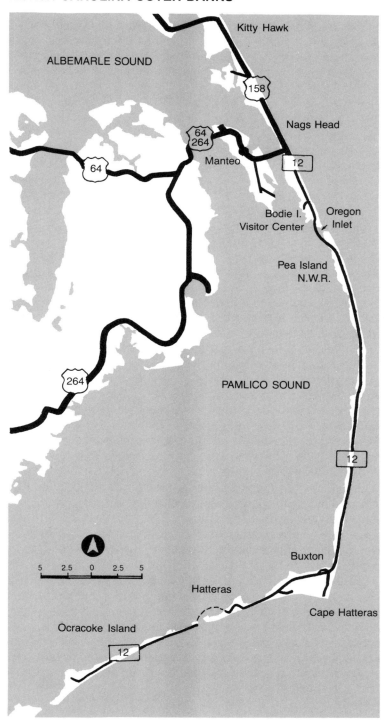

ALBEMARLE SOUND

Kitty Hawk

158

Nags Head

64
264

Manteo

12

Bodie I.
Visitor Center

Oregon
Inlet

Pea Island
N.W.R.

64

264

PAMLICO SOUND

12

5   2.5   0   2.5   5

Buxton

Hatteras

Cape Hatteras

Ocracoke Island

12

In migration (mainly mid-April to mid-May and September-October), transient woodland passerines can be abundant both north and south of the intersection for a mile or so. Park anywhere along the side road and see what you can find, investigating any tracks, trails, or clearings. Swainson's Warblers have nested in the canebrakes along the stretch south of the filling station; they may disappear as the land is developed.

Northwest of the school a canal parallels the road about 100 yards to the left. You cannot see it from the road, but a walk downhill and through the woods to its edge will pay off in views of herons, woodpeckers, sparrows, and surprises.

In summer the woods are often quiet and in winter almost birdless.

Continue to the point (at 1.4 miles) where Business 158 forks left, Bypass 158 right. Bear left off Business 158 toward Duck and take the first right. The **Kitty Hawk fishing pier** is immediately obvious on the left. At this writing it is closed because of storm damage, but you should check for its reopening. On any visit from October to April, a walk to the end of the pier provides a wonderful chance to study loons, grebes, gannets, sea ducks, gulls, and early and late terns, all typically at close range.

Return to Bypass 158 and continue to the entrance to **Wright Brothers National Monument** at 7.5 miles. The monument is worth a visit for itself alone. In addition, the well-mowed grass attracts Lesser Golden Plovers and Upland, Pectoral, Baird's, and Buff-breasted Sandpipers in fall migration and Horned Larks and Water Pipits in winter.

At 16.0 miles, the highway becomes N.C. 12 as it enters the **Cape Hatteras National Seashore** at the intersection with U.S. 64 and U.S. 264.

Beginning at 18.9 miles, a series of shallow ponds line the west side of the road. The first, often the most productive of interesting birds, is set well back and is easy to overshoot. Sedge Wrens and wintering Common Snipe live in the marsh grass; ducks and gulls linger in winter, and shorebirds are abundant in spring and fall if the water levels are low.

Two of the larger ponds have small observation platforms and paved parking pullouts. Check them all if you have time and the light is right.

At 21.9 miles, a left turn leads to Coquina Beach, a popular picnic area and bathing beach, and a right turn takes you to **Bodie Island Visitor Center** with its lighthouse and pond. The mile-long entrance road, lined with pines, is very attractive to land-bird migrants, but the glory of Bodie Island (which has not been an island in living memory) is its huge pond with marshy edges and islands. It is overlooked by two observation platforms, one 8 to 10 feet above the marsh and the other at the water's edge.

Depending on season and water level, the pond is unsurpassed for its Whistling Swans, dabbling ducks, herons and egrets, freshwater rails, shorebirds, and gulls, and a favorite hunting ground for falcons and accipiters. Marsh and Sedge Wrens, Swamp Sparrows, and Yellowthroats haunt the edges; Rufous-sided Towhees mew in the shrubbery; and Brown Creepers have been known to spiral up the lighthouse. Visit on a cloudy day or in the afternoon.

At 24.0 miles, detour into the **Oregon Inlet Marina** and drive along its east side to the end of the road. It is a good spot to check for loons, grebes, and bay ducks in winter, shorebirds, terns, skimmers, and Brown Pelicans in the warmer months.

Continue over the Oregon Inlet bridge onto Hatteras Island and into **Pea Island National Wildlife Refuge.** At 27.1 miles, turn sharp left toward the Coast Guard Station. This detour takes you in 0.5 mile to a hard-to-find path through the shrubbery on your left. Park on the right shoulder and duck under the branches. Behind the wall of bushes you will discover a large pond that shelters resident Black-crowned Night Herons, wintering American Bitterns, and a variety of waterfowl.

Just beyond, take the gravel road on the right out to the edge of the inlet for excellent views of seabirds swimming and fishing in the channel.

Down the highway again, at 29.9 miles pull off into the eroding little parking lot on the right and take your scope out to the observation platform that overlooks excellent shorebird flats on the right and the north end of North Pond on the left. The northern tips of the long islands in North Pond are a heron roost in summer and this dyke is an exciting place to end the day. Shorebirding is excellent along the east side of the pond. In winter, swans, Snow Geese, and both dabbling and diving ducks are common from end to end; the energetic birder may find the 4.5-mile walk around the periphery worthwhile, since the islands hide many birds from the nonwalker's view.

At the southeast corner of the pond there is another parking lot, along with rest rooms and an observation platform with fine views of the south end of North Pond and the north end of the New Fields impoundment. This latter area is superb for shorebirds in summer, especially the more long-legged species like Avocet and Black-necked Stilt, attractive to ibis and herons, and full of geese and dabbling ducks in winter. Between the impoundment and the road, marshy fields are planted for Canada and Snow Geese, occasionally joined by White-fronted Geese and once or twice by a Ross's Goose.

Across from the rest rooms a trail leads to a platform high in the dunes, a prime spot for an afternoon sea watch. In summer you may not see much but shorebirds and terns, but in winter you can almost count on loons and gannets, scoters and mergansers, and an assortment of gulls. With patience and luck you may see a Pomarine or

Parasitic Jaeger, a Great Cormorant (on the remains of a shipwreck below you), or even a Black-legged Kittiwake far offshore.

Parking on the shoulder gets really risky toward the south end of New Fields; there are a few firm spots on the east side of the highway a little beyond the dyke that divides New Fields from South Pond. At 32.5 miles, a sand road for pedestrians only runs off to the west around the north end of South Pond, which is just as birdy as the two impoundments to the north, though with less shorebird habitat.

Hikers may prefer to park at refuge headquarters at 33.8 miles, where a refuge leaflet and map and a bird list are available and a sighting list is displayed. From there a trail leads northwest down to South Pond and the road around its rim, a loop of 4 miles or so.

Most birders drive nonstop from this point to the turnoff to **Cape Hatteras Lighthouse** at 62.8 miles, a high-priority stop even when the birding is slow.

From the entrance, drive past the sometimes interesting pond on the left to the intersection at 0.9 miles. A left turn takes you to the visitor center (rest rooms, good exhibits, interesting bookstore) and the lighthouse. Climb it at least once in your life; the view of the clashing currents around the Cape point is stupendous.

A right turn at the intersection takes you past the start of an interesting nature trail to a Y-junction. The left-hand road leads to a small pond best viewed from the hood of your car; the right-hand road leads to a campground that is worth cruising in winter for Snow Buntings and Lapland Longspurs.

Straight ahead, a jeep trail leads out to the beach. If you do not have a four-wheel-drive vehicle, walk, at least as far as the huge tidal pool that is conspicuous from the top of the rise.

The entire beach around the point is so deeply rutted by fishermen's vehicles that walking is very unpleasant. If you can endure it, though, a hike out to the very point can pay off, at least in autumn, in spectacular counts of seabirds, including shearwaters, gannets, jaegers, and pelagic terns, while shorebirds may thread their way through the fishing poles. The concentration of gulls, terns, skimmers, ducks, and shorebirds around the tidal pool almost always yields a rarity or two.

(If you have a four-wheel-drive car, your perspective will change completely and you can have the time of your life birding the beaches both here and farther south, around the tip of Hatteras Island and on the beaches of Ocracoke Island.)

Drive on from here to the town of Hatteras at 71.2 miles, from which Paul DuMont and Bob Ake run their deservedly popular pelagic trips in spring and fall. (Make your reservations well ahead.) Check the pilings in the harbor on the east side of the highway for cormorants, pelicans, gulls, and terns.

The road ends at 73.9 miles, at the slip for the free ferry to **Ocracoke Island.**

If you have an extra day, spend it on Ocracoke (especially if you have four-wheel-drive). It is an island small enough to explore on your own. Land birding can be outstanding around the village in September and October.

With only half a day to spare, take a round trip on the ferry. It is wonderful, with birds all the way, flying around the boat, swimming in the sound, or resting on the numerous spoil islands along the way. Brown Pelicans are a certainty but anything may turn up, from a Wilson's Storm-Petrel to a Kittiwake. If you have time, take an hour on Ocracoke to bird the pond 300 yards up the road from the ferry slip on the left and the flats and marshes off the track to the right, just opposite the pond.

A single note of warning; exercise extreme caution in driving any unpaved road or parking along road shoulders. Bare or sparsely covered sand is lethal to ordinary cars, and grassy stretches can be treacherous. Timid imitation of the clearly successful parking behavior of other two-wheel-drive cars will minimize your risks.

Special Pursuits

The single reason that birders from all over the continent come regularly to this region is the opportunity to take boat trips out into the Atlantic Ocean. These trips, geared exclusively to enable participants to observe seabirds and mammals, offer the chance to see species that can rarely, if ever, be seen from land away from their breeding grounds.

Trips out of **Ocean City, Maryland,** are typically scheduled at least once a month all year long and include a Christmas Bird Count. Conditions permitting, the 65-foot boat goes 60 to 70 miles out to the canyons at the edge of the continental shelf, where upwelling nutrients tend to attract feeding flocks of birds and mammals.

Winter species seen regularly are Gannet and Black-legged Kittiwake; other possibilities include Fulmar; Manx Shearwater; Great Skua; Glaucous, Iceland, and Thayer's Gulls; Atlantic Puffin; Razorbill; and Dovekie. This is the least promising season for sea mammals.

In spring and early summer the winter species gradually disappear and are replaced by Greater, Sooty, Manx, and Cory's Shearwaters; Wilson's Storm-Petrel; Northern and Red Phalaropes; all three jaegers; and, sometimes in June, South Polar Skua. Sea mammals in this period may include Fin, Sperm, Minke, and Right Whales, Pilot Whales, and Common, Bottle-nosed, Risso's, and White-sided Dolphins.

Late summer and early fall typically produce Cory's and Greater Shearwaters, Wilson's Storm-Petrel, and the phalaropes and jaegers. Rarities that may turn up include Audubon's Shearwater, White-faced and Band-rumped Storm-Petrels, Black-capped Petrel, White-tailed Tropicbird, Sabine's Gull, and Bridled and Sooty Terns. Fin and Minke Whales, Pilot Whales, and Bottle-nosed, Risso's Spotted, and Striped Dolphins are all possibilities.

By late fall most of the warm-weather migrants have departed, although some shearwaters and jaegers are often still around; but several of the winter species can be expected, including Gannet and Kittiwake.

The trips out of Ocean City can be enormously exciting or fairly dull. Most pelagic species are likely to be seen far off-shore, with only intermittent sightings during the five hours or more between the harbor and the canyon. You should take a pelagic trip only if you are prepared to be cold, wet, possibly seasick, and sometimes bored. The rewards can be great enough to compensate for all the discomfort.

Trips are also scheduled out of **Hatteras, North Carolina,** four times a year: the Memorial Day weekend, a mid-August weekend, Labor Day weekend, and Columbus Day weekend.

Species that can reasonably be expected on all four trips are Cory's, Greater, and Audubon's Shearwaters, Wilson's Storm-Petrel, and Northern Phalarope. Sooty Shearwater and Leach's Storm-Petrel are likely only in spring, Red Phalarope only in fall. Bridled and Sooty Terns may have gone by October; they are mainly late-summer birds. Jaegers are most likely in May and October. The Black-capped Petrel, until recently considered very rare, has been seen in increasing numbers on most trips (eighty-two of them in October 1981).

Rare possibilities include Fulmar (May and October), Manx Shearwater, White-faced Storm-Petrel, White-tailed Tropicbird, Long-tailed Jaeger, South Polar Skua, Sabine's Gull, and Arctic Tern.

Though an expedition to Hatteras is much more of an undertaking than one to Ocean City, the birds, in compensation, are much closer to shore. Typically, the boat reaches the Gulf Stream, its destination, in about two hours. The sea, however, is not necessarily calmer, nor the voyage drier.

All trips from either location are scheduled with alternative weather dates the same weekend. The ship captain makes the final decision as to whether conditions are safe for a voyage; often the weather at the dock or close to shore is deceptively benign when the sea 20 miles out is too hazardous to venture on.

Both the Ocean City trips and the ones out of Hatteras are run by knowledgeable and experienced leaders who provide an abundance of useful information to participants, both before and during the voyage. To acquire the current schedules and prices, write:

Ocean City: Ron Naveen, Post Office Box 9423, Washington, D.C. 20016; *Hatteras:* Robert L. Ake, 615 Caroline Avenue, Norfolk, Virgina 23508; or Paul G. DuMont, 4114 Fessenden Street, NW Washington, D.C. 20016.

Since names and addresses may not always be the same, if the ones above do not produce the information you hoped to receive, write instead to the Audubon Naturalist Society, 8940 Jones Mill Road, Chevy Chase, Maryland 20815. The leaders of these palagic trips advertise regularly in the society's newsletter.

Washington residents are exceptionally fortunate in the ready access they have to the major routes of migrating raptors. Nationally famous hawk-watching spots like Hawk Mountain and Cape May Point are only a half-day away; outposts along the easternmost Allegheny ridges and the western shore of Chesapeake Bay are much closer; and the grounds of the Washington Monument or a back yard close to the Potomac are, on occasion, excellent places to lie on one's back and stare at the sky.

Generally, any winds from the northern half of the compass mean good hawk-watching weather in autumn at one lookout or another, but the best conditions are found a day or two after a major cold front has pushed through, lasting as long as the wind is blowing from the northwest. Strong northwest winds along the coast cause migrants to keep closely to the shoreline, rounding Cape May or Cape Charles and heading north on the eastern side of Delaware or Chesapeake Bay until land is easily visible to the west. Then they cross over and head south again.

Fall migration begins in August, peaking in September for Broadwings, Bald Eagles, Ospreys, and American Kestrels and the end of the month for Peregrines. In October Sharp-shinned and Cooper's Hawks and Merlins reach their highest numbers, while the first of November is prime time to look for Red-tails, Red-shoulders, Northern Harriers, Turkey Vultures, Goshawks, Golden Eagles, and Rough-legs.

For those who do not dedicate their entire autumn to raptors, perhaps the best strategy is to aim for nearby mountains in early September, Cape May in late September, Assateague in early October, and Hawk Mountain in late October or early November.

Spring hawk migration is largely ignored by local birders; the most intensive studies in this area have been conducted only recently by observers at Fort Smallwood Park (see below). In the spring of 1981 surveys were taken two days out of three from mid-March to mid-June, averaging twenty-nine birds an hour! Peak counts for most species occurred in late April, and the best conditions were provided by southwest winds.

Hawk-watching is a sociable sport in which more viewers mean more birds seen by all. The lulls between birds are brightened by tips on identification, arguments about field guides, tales of adventure, birding gossip, and the chance to meet birders from all over the country.

Unless you are going to one of the observation points manned throughout the season by experienced raptor enthusiasts, it pays to round up some friends to keep you company. Hawk-watching requires patience and attentive scanning, and it takes unusual dedication to sustain this kind of behavior for long by yourself.

Dress more warmly than you think necessary, take along thermoses of hot drinks, and never forget a thick cushion for mountain rocks.

Listed below are ten favorite spots with Washington area birders.

HALF-DAY OUTINGS (one hour or less from the Washington Beltway, I-495):

1. **Fort Smallwood Park, Maryland,** at the mouth of Baltimore Harbor. Take the Baltimore-Washington Parkway north 16 miles from the beltway to Md. 176. Go east 5 miles (toward Glen Burnie). At Md. 3 go south 0.6 mile to Md. 100, then east 7 miles to Md. 607, Hog Neck Road. Follow Md. 607 north 1.1 mile to Md. 173, Fort Smallwood Road. Turn right and drive 3 miles to the park entrance. In the park, take the rightmost road, go through the closed but unlocked gate and park. If the gate *is* locked, walk around it and out to the beach. Hawks come from North Point across the mouth of the Patapsco River on west to northwest winds. Especially good for Kestrels, Sharp-shins, Ospreys, Northern Harriers, Red-tails, some Cooper's, occasional Merlins, and Peregrines. Usually manned when the wind is right. Outstanding for spring hawk migration, too.

2. **Washington Monument Knob, Maryland.** Take I-270 north from the beltway 31 miles, I-70 west 4 miles to U.S. 40 Alternate (note the sign to Washington Monument State Park), U.S. 40A 10 miles to top of South Mountain, and turn right opposite Old South Mountain Inn. Drive 1 mile to the parking lot and walk 1,100 feet to the monument. The best view is from the top of the monument (thirty-five steps); the best winds west to north. All species, but not many falcons. Usually manned.

FULL-DAY TRIPS (less than three hours from the beltway):

3. **Linden, Virginia.** Take I-66 west from the beltway 55 miles to the Linden exit. Go back east on Va. 55 to the village of Linden, then north, on unpaved Road 638, 5 miles to the fire tower or 3 miles farther to a field with good views west. Access to the top of the fire tower, with good views except to the west, is obtained by a call in advance to the Fire Warden at (703) 667-3282. Request

that he open the Tri-County fire tower of District 7 so that you can watch migrating hawks. Good for winds in northern half of the compass; choose a site facing into the wind. Buteos, accipiters. Not regularly manned.

4. **The Pulpit, Pennsylvania.** Take I-270 north from the beltway 31 miles, I-70 west 29 miles, I-81 northeast 13 miles, U.S. 11 north 3 miles, Pa. 16 west 12 miles, Pa. 75 north 6 miles, and U.S. 30 west 6 miles to crest of Tuscarora Mountain. (This is the scenic route. You can continue on I-81 to U.S. 30 and go west through Chambersburg, which is a congested city strung out along the highway.) Park where you can, heeding the "No Parking" signs, and follow the trail that begins south of the highway on the west side of the ridge, just below the building marked "Snack Bar." The trail leads to the observation point, normally manned by experts. Excellent for most species, including Golden Eagles and Goshawks, in west, north, and east winds. (Note: The Pulpit may have been usurped by hang-glider devotees by the time you read this.)

5. **Waggoner's Gap, Pennsylvania.** Take I-270 north from the beltway 29 miles to U.S. 15, U.S. 15 northeast 50 miles to Pa. 94, Pa. 94 northwest 9 miles to Pa. 34, Pa. 34 7 miles to Carlisle, and Pa. 74 west 9 miles to Waggoner's Gap. Park on the left side of the road or in the lot up the steep rough road on the right. (Note: route signs in Carlisle are poorly placed. Turn left onto Pa. 74 at the sign for Opossum Lake and right on North College Street. Remember the route for your return trip.) If you are sure-footed and wearing shoes with good traction, take the short trail from the parking lot left of the one to the power station, bear right, and climb up the rock pile to the highest point. Early arrivals get the most comfortable rocks. Footing is secure, seating flatter, but watching less fruitful in the parking lot. Species like those at Pulpit; views are best west and north. Normally manned.

6. **Point Lookout, Maryland** (see Chapter 21). Take Md. 5 south-east from the beltway to the end of the road, about 70 miles. Put your back to the fence at the tip of the point. Look for the same species as at Fort Smallwood on west to northwest winds. Not regularly manned.

WEEKEND TRIPS

7. **Hawk Mountain, Pennsylvania.** About four hours from Washington via I-95, I-695, I-83, I-81 north, and I-78 east. Exit at Hamburg on Pa. 61, go north 7 miles, and turn right on Pa. 895. After 2.5 miles, turn right at the sign for Hawk Mountain Sanctu-

ary. Nationally famous, fantastically popular, with superb views. Try to be there for the two or three days of northwest winds after a cold front. Not many falcons or Cooper's Hawks but unsurpassed for most other species. Two lookouts, one close to the parking area, one a rocky 0.7 mile uphill. Always manned, with lots of experts, instructive displays at headquarters, a fine bookshop, weekend evening programs in autumn. It is worth a call in advance to check on the weather and current raptor movements: (215) 756-3431.

8. **Bake Oven Knob, Pennsylvania.** Fifteen miles northeast of Hawk Mountain, with the same birds, fewer people, easier walking. Stay on I-78 for 11 more miles. Go north on Pa. 143 and turn left on 309. After 2.0 miles go right on Road 39056 for 2.1 miles. Go left on an unmarked road next to a white house and, when it bends right, keep straight instead on unpaved Bake Oven Road. Follow it up a steep hill to the Bake Oven Knob parking lots (no sign). Two lookouts, usually manned, north (right) along the Appalachian Trail.

9. **Cape May Point, New Jersey.** About four hours away; it takes less time but more driving via I-95 and the Delaware Memorial Bridge (choose your own route down from there); the ferry to Cape May from Lewes, Delaware (pronounced *Lewis*), ties you to its schedule, but provides a bonus semipelagic trip. From the end of the Garden State Parkway (U.S. 9), drive south on N.J. 109 through Cape May. Bear right on Perry Street, which becomes Sunset Boulevard, for 2.2 miles. Go left at the stone pillars, immediately left again, right onto Lighthouse Avenue and, after 0.7 mile, left into the parking lot. The hawk observation point is straight ahead. *The* concentration point for Merlins and Cooper's Hawks, a likely spot for Peregrines, with a frequent skyful of American Kestrels and Sharp-shins, good numbers of buteos, Ospreys, Northern Harriers, and a few eagles of both species—360-degree visibility makes a deck chair ideal. Always manned. Recorded information, with the tape changed Mondays and Thursdays at 6:00 P.M., is available from the Cape May Bird Observatory at (609) 884-2626.

10. **Assateague Island, Maryland and Virginia** (see Chapters 29 and 30). Just west of Ocean City, Maryland, take Md. 611 south from U.S. 50 and follow the signs to Assateague National Seashore and State Park. Park as far north as you can and walk until you have a good view from bay to ocean. Alternatively, drive south from Salisbury, Maryland, on U.S. 13 to Va. 175 and go east through the village of Chincoteague to Chincoteague National Wildlife Refuge. Snow Goose Pool and the Wash Flats are the best raptor areas. The entire island attracts more Peregrines

than anywhere else on the East Coast, especially to open areas of grass, mud, or sand flats. Look for them just after coastal storms or on days with northwest winds. Other falcons, accipiters, and harriers can be common as well. Not manned, but Peregrine banders operate from a jeep on both the north end and the Wash Flats. Sit still, watch them, and they will locate the birds for you.

Finding Your Own Owls 36

For those who do not put away their binoculars after the Christmas bird counts and wait for the first reports of spring migration, one of the most challenging and rewarding birding pursuits is the search for wintering owls.

Because there is very little published information on finding owls, the average birder usually feels that setting out to see any owls on one's own is a hopeless enterprise. It is not, of course, though only rails require comparable initiative. You do not need to be led to an owl by the hand, though you can often see more of them that way (with the same owl and its habitat suffering more disturbance on each visit).

The favorite owling spots around Washington and some of the resident owls have long been overvisited by local birders, who sometimes pursue their goal with total disregard for the well-being of the birds or their habitat. As a result, field trips to see woodland owls have been discontinued and publicity is no longer given to sightings of any species but Short-eared and Snowy Owls. Accordingly, the only locations pinpointed in this book are for birds that are either unapproachable or relatively unflappable. Some areas to search in are recommended, though.

The following suggestions are designed to help you find owls independently with a minimum of harassment and environmental destruction.

1. Learn to recognize appropriate habitat. In particular, bone up on varieties of conifers, such as red pine, spruce, arbor vitae, that owls like most. Parks, state forests, reservoir borders, cemeteries, old nurseries, and even small roadside plantations are all good possibilities. Be alert for such areas all year long and work through them from December to March.

2. Acquire or borrow a strong flashlight, small portable tape recorder, and a tape with a minute or so each of calls of Screech, Barred, Barn, and Great Horned Owls. You may want to try a tape on Saw-whet and Long-eared Owls, but these migratory species are usu-

ally silent on their wintering grounds. You can make a tape, rather laboriously, from the Peterson records or cassettes, or, if you're lucky, copy one from an old owling hand.

OWLING BY DAY

1. Walk slowly and quietly through appropriate habitat, looking *down* on the lower branches and the ground for white droppings and the dark, usually oblong pellets of fur and bone that owls cough up daily.
2. When you find a tree marked by either or both signs look up into the tree for a dense spot that may hide or be an owl.
3. As soon as you spot an owl, back off immediately to the farthest spot from which you can see it. The owl is then more likely to relax, less likely to fly away.
4. If you're birding with others, make it a small group (the fewer the better) and avoid surrounding the owl. If it can't see all of you at once without turning its head, it will probably leave.
5. Be alert for the loud, frenzied scolding of birds mobbing a predator. Though they may be bedeviling a hawk or a snake, their target is just as likely to be an owl. The smaller birds from chickadees to jays gang up on Screech Owls; when crows join in, they are trying to drive off one of the large owls. Move in fast, before they succeed.

OWLING BY NIGHT

1. Choose a calm, dry night on a quiet road by a woodlot or forest, preferably well away from an occupied house, especially one with a barking dog!
2. In the dark, play the voice of each owl a few calls at a time, with pauses in between like a real owl, so that you can hear the response.
3. Unless you are trying to attract one particular species, start with the voice of a Screech Owl and gradually work up to a Great Horned Owl. Don't shift to a larger species until you give up on the previous one. (If you try to go from large owls to small ones, the latter will not respond since they can be preyed upon by the former.)
4. If and when you do get a response, do not continue more than five minutes longer. That should be enough to bring the owl in, and more playing is likely to be counterproductive.
5. Watch for the silhouette of the owl flying in to a branch overhead. If

you see or hear it, turn your flashlight on and shine it as accurately as you can. Waving the beam around a lot may drive the bird away. (Pinning an owl down in a light beam takes talent and practice.) Note: If you can learn to imitate owl calls passably, your need for equipment will be drastically reduced. As a dividend, Screech Owl imitations by day do wonders in attracting small passerines.

ABSOLUTE DONT'S

1. Don't destroy habitat or cover; move carefully.
2. Don't break branches and twigs for a photograph or a better view.
3. Don't flush an owl deliberately; *especially* don't throw things at it or its nest. Trying to drive a bird off its nest is inexcusable.
4. Don't climb or shake the tree.
5. Don't handle an owl, even an irresistibly tame one.
6. Don't make unnecessary noise, or overdo the use of tapes.
7. Don't reveal the location of an owl to anyone you don't know, especially to a nonbirder.
8. Don't go back often or spread the news widely (except for Short-eared and Snowy Owls).
9. Don't owl in large groups (i.e., more than a small carload).

HABITATS AND HABITS

Saw-whet Owl Winters mainly in the piedmont and west of Chesapeake Bay. Prefers arbor vitae, spruce, honeysuckle thickets in the woods. Sits tight on thin horizontal branches, usually near eye level unless frequently disturbed. Normally silent in winter. (To hear one calling, try Cranesville Swamp on the Maryland-West Virginia border in May and June.) Keep its presence hidden from strangers.

Screech Owl May be found anywhere year-round: all sizes of deciduous trees; young thick evergreens, including hemlock, spruce, arbor vitae; wood duck and owl boxes; woodpecker holes; knotholes. Best found by tapes and imitation at night, mobbing birds by day. Some are easily flushed, some very tame.

Short-eared Owl Winters in coastal marshes and weedy fields in which it rests by day. Not easily flushed (flies at 10- to 30-foot approach). Best seen when hunting at dusk or on dark afternoons, when it is entirely indifferent to large numbers of observers. Try Port Mahon and Broadkill marshes in Delaware; Elliott Island in Dorchester County, Hughes Road in Montgomery County, New Design Road in Frederick County, Maryland; Chincoteague and Saxis marshes, Virginia.

Long-eared Owl Roosts, often in groups of several birds, in conifers 15 to 40 feet high, usually in thick stands of red cedars, spruces, loblolly, red, white and Virginia pines. Sits tight in winter at 10 to 30 feet close to a trunk about its own thickness. Check trees all around you every few steps, from all angles. Normally silent in winter.

Barn Owl Resident in barns, silos, attics of abandoned buildings, and in red cedars and white and loblolly pines. Easily flushed from trees and buildings, less so from silos. When checking a building for the presence of a Barn Owl, one observer should stay outside to watch for it, as the inside observer may flush it unaware. Quite responsive to tapes.

Barred Owl Resident in both coniferous and deciduous trees, often large ones. In upland woods in winter more often than in summer. Common year-round in bottomland woods, especially along the Potomac and Patuxent rivers. Easily flushed from a considerable distance. Hoots mostly from February to April. Responsive to tapes.

Great Horned Owl Resident in medium to very large conifers and deciduous trees, using the bulky branches to hide its size. Often high in the crown, but may roost close to the trunk like a Long-eared Owl. Most vocal in winter because of its early courtship (December, January). Nests in January and February, and abandons eggs readily if disturbed. Responsive to tapes. May be mobbed by Red-shouldered Hawks.

Snowy Owl An occasional visitor to the area. Has turned up on government office buildings, suburban roofs, haystacks. Birds that linger more than a few days are usually found near salt water on high, open perches. So conspicuous that protection from the public is impossible, but harassment should be kept to a minimum. (Most likely to be flushed by photographers with inadequate lenses.)

Appendixes

Audubon Naturalist Society of the Central Atlantic States
8940 Jones Mill Road
Chevy Chase, Maryland 20815
(301) 652-9188

The oldest and largest society in the area, ANS has a vigorous schedule of field trips (preponderantly bird walks), field courses and activities for families and children, and an ongoing nature photography workshop. It cosponsors a lecture series with the Smithsonian Associates and the Friends of the National Zoo and a program of Natural History Field Studies with the Department of Agriculture Graduate School. It operates the Audubon Bookshop, specializing in natural history books and records. It sponsors the Voice of the Naturalist, a weekly telephone recording, (301) 652-1088, that combines a rare bird alert and other birding news and information.

Maryland Ornithological Society
Cylburn Mansion
4915 Greenspring Avenue,
Baltimore, Maryland 21209

MOS publishes the state ornithological journal, *Maryland Birdlife,* holds an annual weekend of intensive field trips in May, and operates wildlife sanctuaries across the state, several with accommodations for members. Of its fourteen local chapters, the Montgomery County chapter is one of the most active, attracting serious birders from all over the Washington area. There are monthly meetings from September to May and a regular schedule of field trips. To obtain current information about chapter officers (who can tell you when and where the chapter meets and what field trips are coming up), write the headquarters in Baltimore. Since there is no permanent staff, do not expect an instant reply. The Audubon Naturalist Society may be able to put you in touch with a chapter member; virtually all leaders of ANS field trips in Maryland are MOS members as well.

Virginia Society of Ornithology
Mrs. J. H. Dalmas, Treasurer
520 Rainbow Forest Drive
Lynchburg, Virginia 24502

VSO publishes the state ornithological journal, *The Raven,* conducts a week-long foray in early summer to a Virginia county to look for breeding birds, and schedules an annual convention in May and several birding weekends a year. It is possible to belong to a local VSO chapter without being a member of the state society, and vice versa. The Northern Virginia chapter has occasional meetings and a strong schedule of local bird walks. The staff of the Long Branch Nature Center in Arlington, (703) 557-2740, will tell you how to get in touch with the current chapter president.

Northern Virginia Audubon Society (Vienna, Virginia)
Prince George's Audubon Society (Bowie, Maryland)
Southern Maryland Audubon Society (Clinton and LaPlata, Maryland)

These three clubs, west, east, and south of Washington, respectively, are chapters of the National Audubon Society, which can tell you how to make contact with the chapter president or membership chairman. Call (202) 547-9009. All chapters have regular meetings and field trips. If you are a member of the national society, you are automatically a member of a local chapter if you live within its boundaries. If not, you may become a member of any chapter you choose by specifying that the appropriate part of your dues go to that chapter. Members receive *Audubon* magazine.

Delmarva Ornithological Society
Post Office Box 4247
Greenville, Delaware 19807

Washington birders usually join DOS to get the state ornithological journal, *The Delmarva Ornithologist,* since most society activities are in Delaware. Regular meetings and field trips are supplemented by a spring birding weekend and long-range censuses of tracts of ornithological importance.

Mid-Atlantic Bird Banding Group
C/o M. Kathleen Klinkiewicz
Bird Banding Laboratory
Laurel, Maryland 20708
(301) 776-4880, Ext. 203

This informal club, open to anyone interested in banding birds (mainly nongame birds), schedules frequent meetings and workshops near Washington or Baltimore, always on some aspect of banding, and an August weekend in the field.

MAPS

The District of Columbia and all the states provide free road maps on request. In addition, the states sell county maps, which are almost indispensable for thorough exploration of local areas. To obtain a state map and a price list for county maps, send a postcard to the appropriate address:

Delaware
> Department of Transportation
> Post Office Box 778
> Dover, Delaware 19901

Maryland
> State Highway Administration
> Map Distribution Section
> 2323 West Joppa Road
> Brooklandville, Maryland, 21022

Virginia
> Department of Highways and Transportation
> 1221 East Broad Street
> Richmond, Virginia 23219

To get the District of Columbia map, you must either collect it in person, or send a self-addressed, stamped 7" x 10" envelope to:
> Department of Transportation, Room 519
> 415 Twelfth Street, NW
> Washington, D.C. 20004

For the current postage required, call (202) 727-6562.

The best map of the city of Baltimore is not free, unfortunately. Inquire about the present cost and postage, or buy it in person from:
> Surveys and Records Division
> 200 Municipal Building
> Baltimore, Maryland 21202

Even more detailed, though rarely as up to date, are the topographic maps of the U.S. Geological Survey. An index and catalogue are available from:
> Branch of Distribution
> U.S. Geological Survey
> 1200 South Eads Street
> Arlington, Virginia 22202

The sales office at the above address is an easy and efficient place to do business, and parking space is ample. There is also a downtown sales office at 19th and F Streets, NW, in Washington.

All sorts of maps, including many local and regional ones, can be purchased at The Map Store, 1636 I Street, NW, on Farragut Square in Washington.

BOOKS

Halle, Louis J. *Spring in Washington.* New York: Atheneum, 1963.
A classic account of the spring migration of 1945 in and around Washington, dated only in detail. Magical writing, enhanced by drawings by Francis Lee Jaques.

Harding, John J., and Justin J. *Birding the Delaware Valley Region.* Philadelphia: Temple University Press, 1980.
All you need to know about birding Cape May, Hawk Mountain, and some seventy other major and minor locations within a two-hour drive from Philadelphia, including Brigantine and Tinicum Marsh. An outstanding bird-finding guide.

Harrison, George H. *Roger Tory Peterson's Dozen Birding Hot Spots.* New York: Simon and Schuster, 1976.
Useful information about Cape May, Hawk Mountain, and ten more of the best birding areas across the continent. Out of print.

Meanley, Brooke, *Birdlife at Chincoteague and the Virginia Barrier Islands.* Centreville: Tidewater Publishers, 1981.
————. *Birds and Marshes of the Chesapeake Bay Country.* Cambridge: Tidewater Publishers, 1975.
————. *The Great Dismal Swamp.* Washington: Audubon Naturalist Society, 1973.
Chatty and informative reports of field work by the author and other ornithologists.

Pettingill, Olin Sewall, ed. *The Bird Watcher's America.* New York: Thomas Y. Crowell, 1965.
Chapters on the Cheat Mountains of West Virginia, the Great Dismal Swamp, and Hawk Mountain.
————. *A Guide to Bird Finding: East of the Mississippi.* 2nd ed. New York: Oxford University Press, 1977.
The Washington area is given short shrift, but the general material on Maryland and the entire Delaware chapter are excellent, and many sites within and just beyond the limits of the present book are included.

Thomas, Bill and Phyllis. *Natural Washington.* New York: Holt, Rinehart and Winston, 1980.
A guide to "natural attractions" within 50 miles of Washington, among them many birding sites, nature centers, and neighborhood parks.

Virginia Society of Ornithology. *Where to Bird in Virginia.* Virginia
Society of Ornithology, 1981.
A looseleaf collection, still increasing, of site guides, covering
areas all over the state. Map, directions, habitats, seasonal populations, rarities.

JOURNALS

Of the publications below, only the first is obtained by subscription.
The rest are received as a benefit of membership (see Appendix
A). The regional editors of *American Birds* and the editors of the
state journals welcome well-documented records of unusual sight-
ings and reports on other matters of ornithological interest.
American Birds. National Audubon Society, 950 Third Avenue, New
York, New York 10022.
Birding. American Birding Association, Box 4335, Austin, Texas
78765.
The Delmarva Ornithologist. Editor, Lloyd L. Falk, 123 Bette Road,
Wilmington, Delaware 19803.
Maryland Birdlife. Editor, Chandler S. Robbins, 7900 Brooklyn
Bridge Road, Laurel, Maryland 20707.
The Raven. Editor, Frederic R. Scott, 115 Kennondale Lane, Rich-
mond, Virginia 23226.

CHECKLISTS

Robbins, Chandler S., and Bystrak, Danny. *Field List of the Birds of
Maryland,* 2d ed. Maryland Avifauna Number 2. Maryland Or-
nithological Society, 1977.
A marvel of compression. Accidental, extinct, and hypothetical
species are listed separately; the rest are coded for physiographical province and habitat, with bar graphs of seasonal abundance.
Fifty good birding areas in Maryland are very briefly described.
Virginia Society of Ornithology. *Virginia's Birdlife: An Annotated
Checklist.* Virginia Avifauna Number 2. Virginia Society of Ornithol-
ogy, 1979.
Accidental, extinct, and hypothetical species are incorporated into
the main text. For all species not in these three categories, sea-
sonal abundance, breeding information, and out-of-season records
are provided for each of the three major physiographical provinces.
A checklist for the birds of Delaware is in preparation.
All the books in print and the checklists are available from the
Audubon Bookshop, 1621 Wisconsin Avenue, NW., Washington,
D.C. 20007.

C Cooperative Birding Activities

For birders who enjoy putting their skills to use, there are dozens of activities throughout the year that depend on field observers with various levels of skill and energy. They range from the mailing of a postcard about a conspicuously marked bird to recording and analyzing all sightings in a given area over several weeks, months, or years. Many of these activities develop talents and interests that bring at least as much pleasure and satisfaction as seeing new species. Here is a sample:

May Counts. On the first Saturday in May, the Maryland Ornithological Society asks everyone birding in the state of Maryland to keep careful track of all birds seen on that date in each county. The results are compiled and published in *Maryland Birdlife*. MOS county chapters make a point of deploying their members for maximum coverage, and beginners are teamed with experienced observers.

On the second Saturday in May, the Audubon Naturalist Society has a similar count, rather less structured. Anyone birding anywhere in the region is invited to submit the day's tally to the count compiler. Details are published in the society's newsletter.

Christmas Counts. Dozens of counts are scheduled in this area during two weeks and three weekends in late December and early January. Volunteers are assigned to census a specific territory in the 15-mile diameter circle within which each count is conducted. Beginners are welcome; participants may take part in as many counts as time and stamina allow. Schedules and coordinators are listed in the Audubon Naturalist Society newsletter, and results are published in *American Birds.* Many local bird clubs sponsor one of the counts.

Breeding Bird Surveys. Birders who can recognize the songs and calls of the breeding birds of the region may volunteer to conduct breeding bird surveys in June: 25-mile routes with three-minute stops every half-mile to count every bird seen and heard at each stop. Routes are assigned by the Office of Migratory Nongame Bird Studies, Patuxent Wildlife Research Center, Laurel, Maryland 20708.

VSO Foray. Each year the Virginia Society of Ornithology engages in a week-long survey of breeding birds and summer visitors to one Virginia county. Participants are welcome for all or part of the period.

Maryland Breeding Bird Atlas. An ongoing project to map the distribution of breeding birds in the state. Each participant is assigned a block within a grid covering the state and makes several surveys within the breeding season. For information, get in touch with the office of Migratory Nongame Bird Studies (see above). Staying power is more important than expertise, which is acquired on the job.

Breeding Bird Census and **Winter Bird Census** Sponsored nationally by the National Audubon Society, the census of four local tracts is sponsored locally by the Audubon Naturalist Society in Rock Creek Park, Glover-Archbold Park, Cabin John Island (along the Potomac), and Dranesville Park. Intensive surveys of a small area in a well-analyzed habitat map all the birds observed within a period of several weeks and record the density of each species. Volunteers at all levels of experience are welcome to participate on survey teams. Call the Audubon Naturalist Society (301-652-9188) for more information.

North American Hawk Migration Studies. Birders who can identify hawks in flight can contribute to a continent-wide survey of hawk migration by making counts at given observation points and filling out standard reporting forms for the Hawk Migration Association of North America, Box 51, Washington, Connecticut 06793. Virtually all the sites listed in Chapter 35 except the ones in Pennsylvania and New Jersey are seriously undermanned.

International Shorebird Survey. Birders who can identify shorebirds can participate in an ongoing survey, begun in 1974, that censuses shorebird concentration points throughout eastern North and South America. A survey of the same area every ten days from April to early June and from July to October is requested by the coordinator, Manomet Bird Observatory, Manomet, Massachusetts 02345.

Reporting Marked Birds. Anyone seeing a bird painted a bizarre color or wearing a neck collar, a wing tag, colored leg bands, and so on, can perform a useful service by describing the species, its marking (as exactly as possible), the precise location and the date on a postcard and sending it in to the Bird Banding Laboratory, Laurel, Maryland 20708. If you find a dead bird with a metal band, send the flattened band in with the same information. You will eventually get a reply telling you when and where the bird was banded and marked.

North American Nest Record Card Program. Birders can obtain cards from the Laboratory of Ornithology, Cornell University, 159 Sapsucker Woods Road, Ithaca, New York 14850, on which they record information on each nest they find in the breeding season: species, habitat, location, number of eggs or young, and so on. The cards are easy to fill out and add useful data to the massive and accessible files at Cornell.

Constructing a Checklist. Few of the local parks have more than preliminary checklists at best, and most nature centers welcome help in compiling one. By far the most useful records for this purpose are those taken at frequent intervals all year, with numbers of each species seen and any evidence of nesting included. (Try to talk the staff naturalist out of putting the birds into alphabetical order.)

Map page numbers are in bold-faced type. The main entries describing birding sites are in *italics*. National Wildlife Refuge is abbreviated as N.W.R.

Ornithological Societies
Needwood, Lake, 65
Nest record cards, 201
New Design Road, 15, 17, 25, 29, 35,
    38, 67, **68,** *70,* 191
Nighthawk, Common, 23, 43, 55, 58,
    70, 71
Nolan's Ferry Recreation Area, **68,** *70*
Norfolk, 39, 169, **171**
North Carolina Outer Banks, *174–79,*
    175
Northern Virginia Audubon Society, 196
Nuthatch: Brown-headed, 27, 137, 142,
    147, 156, 157, 169, 172, 173, 174;
    Red-breasted, 27, 50, 66, 90, 99,
    101; White-breasted, 27, 47, 56

O

Oakland, 35, 93, **94, 96**
Ocean City, 9, 11, 13, 16, 17, 18, 19,
    20, 21, 22, 183
Ocean City Airport, road to, 23, 155
Ocean City Inlet, 10, 13, 19, 21, *146,*
    153, *154*
Ocracoke Island, **175,** *179*
Oland Road, 70
Old Angler's Inn, *57*
Old Ferry Landing Road, 155
Oldsquaw, 13, 65, 106, 119, 133, 134,
    140, 146, 154, 161, 166
Oregon Inlet Marina, 177
Oriole(s), 43, 53, 57, 58, 69, 70, 72,
    160; Northern (Baltimore), 35, 56, 58,
    71, 89, 90; Orchard, 35, 56, 66, 71,
    89, 99
Ornithological Societies, 195
Osprey, 15, 61, 69, 103, 110, 114, 115,
    133, 137, 151, 159, 162, 185, 186,
    188
Ovenbird, 33, 47, 83, 91, 149
Owl(s), 44, 45, 47, 65, 99, 101, 111,
    115, 155; Barn, 23, 66, 103, 125,
    189, 192; Barred, 23, 43, 47, 51, 56,
    62, 63, 70, 72, 109, 114, 116, 125,
    149, 189, 192; Great Horned, 23, 47,
    51, 66, 67, 109, 119, 125, 130, 133,
    136, 143, 149, 189, 192; Long-eared,
    23, 66, 109, 111, 114, 189, 192;
    Saw-whet, 23, 66, 93, 95, 189, 191;
    Screech, 23, 44, 67, 114, 125, 130,
    133, 135, 136, 189, 191; Short-eared,
    23, 70, 127, 135, 148, 149, 151, 189,
    191; Snowy, 23, 104, 189, 192
Owl-finding, 189–92
Oxon Hill Children's Farm, 24, 27, 28,
    39, *111–13,* **112**
Oystercatcher, American, 16, 140, 154,
    156, 159, 160

P

Paint Pond, 148
Pamunkey Creek, 75
Patapsco Waste Water Treatment Plant,
    107
Patuxent River Park, 14, 15, 114
Paul Friend Road, 24, *96,* **96**
Pea Island N.W.R., 15, **175,** *177–78*
Peep, 63, 102, 125, 127, 143, 156, 157,
    160
Pelagic trips, 183–84
Pelican: American White, 40, 164, 169;
    Brown, 9, 77, 164, 165, 174, 177,
    178, 179
Pennyfield Lock, 10, 11, 12, 17, 25, 35,
    52, *57*
Peregrine, 15, 106, 151, 154, 157, 161,
    164, 185, 186, 188
Petrel, Black-capped, 40, 174, 183, 184
Pewee: Eastern Wood, 25, 56, 149;
    Western Wood, 40
Phalarope(s), 172; Northern, 18, 71,
    125, 183, 184; Red, 18, 183, 184;
    Wilson's, 18, 50, 125
Pheasant, Ring-necked, 15, 70, 124
Phoebe: Eastern, 25, 56, 81; Say's, 40
Pickering Beach, **124,** *128*
Pickering Beach Road, 128
Piedmont, 4
Pintail, Northern, 12, 47, 137
Pintail, White-cheeked, 40
Pipit, Water, 29, 63, 69, 70, 71, 74, 106,
    115, 125, 135, 136, 176
Plover: Black-bellied, 17, 102, 155, 156,
    159, 161, 163; Lesser Golden, 17,
    45, 61, 63, 102, 123, 128, 157, 161,
    162, 163, 165, 176; Mountain, 40,
    161; Piping, 17, 103, 154, 155, 160;
    Semipalmated, 16, 161, 163;
    Wilson's, 16, 154, 160, 164, 174
Pocomoke State Forest, 30, 151
Pocomoke State Park, 150
Pocomoke Swamp, 30, 31, 33, 34, 36,
    145, *149–50*
Pohick Bay, 14
Pohick Bay Park, *51*
Point Lookout, 5, 10, 13, 15, 19, 21, 28,
    29, 35, 36, 38, *117–19,* **118,** 187
Point of Rocks, 26
Point Overlook, The, 83
Port Mahon, 19, 21, 22, 28, 38, **124,**
    126–27, 191
Port Mahon Road, 126
Potomac Overlook Park, 28, 29, 34, *53,*
    214–15
Potomac Park, East, 20, *45,* **214–15**
Potomac River, 9, 13, 15, 23
Potomac Village, **52,** 57, 61
Prince George's Audubon Society, 196

Voice of the Naturalist, 195
Vulture(s), 74; Black, 14, 44, 56, 69, 115, 137; Turkey, 14, 44, 69, 115, 137, 185

W

Waggoner's Gap, 187
Wakefield, 169
Warbler(s), 43, 44, 47, 50, 53, 57, 58, 61, 63, 65, 66, 67, 71, 81, 107, 112, 123, 126, 129, 131, 133, 135, 136, 155, 157, 174; Bachman's, 40; Bay-breasted, 33, 81; Black-and-white, 30, 47, 56, 83, 90, 149; Blackburnian, 32, 82, 83, 87, 91, 92, 94; Blackpoll, 33; Black-throated Blue, 32, 81–82, 83, 87, 94; Black-throated Gray, 40; Black-throated Green, 32, 82, 83, 84, 86, 87, 94, 172; Blue-winged, 31, 72, 90; Canada, 34, 82, 83, 87, 94; Cape May, 32; Cerulean, 32, 54, 56, 57, 58, 83, 86, 88, 90, 91, 93; Chestnut-sided, 33, 81, 86, 94, 95; Connecticut, 34; Golden-winged, 31, 72, 84, 86, 88, 90, 93, 94, 95; Hooded, 34, 47, 54, 83, 114, 115, 116, 149, 172; Kentucky, 33, 47, 51, 54, 56, 61, 66, 86, 90, 115, 116, 149, 172; Kirtland's, 40; Magnolia, 32, 87, 94; Mourning, 34, 84, 87, 90, 93; Nashville, 31, 86, 87, 95; Northern Parula, 31, 56, 57, 83, 84, 86, 91, 116, 149; Orange-crowned, 31, 173; Palm, 33; Pine, 33, 50, 67, 72, 84, 90, 91, 92, 114, 115, 119, 133, 137, 143, 147, 149, 157, 173; Prairie, 33, 50, 61, 66, 72, 82, 90, 115, 140; Prothonotary, 30, 43, 50, 54, 56, 58, 91, 114, 149, 172; Swainson's 30, 54, 150, 169, 172, 176; Tennessee, 31; Wilson's, 34, 90; Worm-eating, 31, 57, 68, 83, 86, 88, 90, 91, 149, 172; Yellow, 31, 47, 56, 58, 89, 90, 143; Yellow-rumped, 32; Yellow-throated, 32, 54, 56, 57, 58, 89, 91, 114, 115, 116, 149, 172, 173
Wash Flats, **158,** *161–62*
W&OD Trail (Washington and Old Dominion Railroad Regional Park), 36, **52,** *55,* 74
Washington Cathedral, 26
Washington Channel, 45
Washington County, Md., 15, 23, 26, 27, 30, 31, 32, 34, *87–92,* **88–89**
Washingtonian Country Club, 67
Washington, D.C. *See* District of Columbia
Washington Monument Knob, 186
Washington Sailing Marina, 46
Waterthrush(es), 58; Louisiana, 33, 44, 56, 74, 83, 90, 114, 115, 116, 149; Northern, 33, 90, 94–95
Waxwing, Cedar, 29, 66, 90, 110
Welch Road, *95,* **96**
West Ocean City, 155
West Ocean City Pond, 11, 12, *146,* **153**
Whales, 183
Wheatear, Northern, 40
Whimbrel, 17, 103, 155, 159, 160
Whip-poor-will, 23, 50, 67, 74, 90, 99, 103, 135
Widewater, 57
Wigeon: American, 12, 76, 99, 104, 126, 133, 137, 151, 172; Eurasian, 12, 126, 133, 137, 151, 157
Willard Road, 39
Willet, 17, 143, 154, 156, 160
Wilson Bridge, 13
Winter Bird Census, 200
Woodcock, American, 18, 50, 51, 61, 62, 82, 89, 103, 119, 136
Woodpecker(s), 50, 62, 70, 71, 114, 133, 137, 176; Downy, 24, 56; Hairy, 24, 56; Pileated, 24, 54, 56, 115, 149; Red-bellied, 24, 56; Red-cockaded, 24, 137, 169; Red-headed, 24, 50, 56, 61, 63, 66, 71, 96, 114, 147, 173
Wren: Bewick's, 27, 88, 90, 93; Carolina, 27; House, 27, 62; Marsh (Long-billed Marsh), 27, 47, 61, 62, 69, 103, 109, 112, 115, 119, 127, 133, 137, 140, 143, 151, 177; Sedge (Short-billed Marsh), 28, 115, 119, 126, 128, 135, 142, 151, 163, 176, 177; Winter, 27, 54, 81, 84
Wright Brothers National Monument, 176

Y

Yellowlegs, 63, 71, 102, 123, 143, 151, 157, 159–60, 161; Greater, 17; Lesser, 17
Yellowthroat, Common, 34, 47, 56, 62, 65, 82, 112, 115, 143, 177

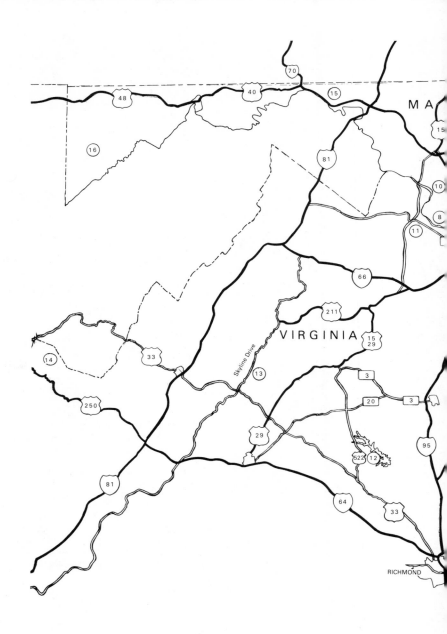

Circled numbers mark areas described in correspondingly numbered chapters.

National Capital Area

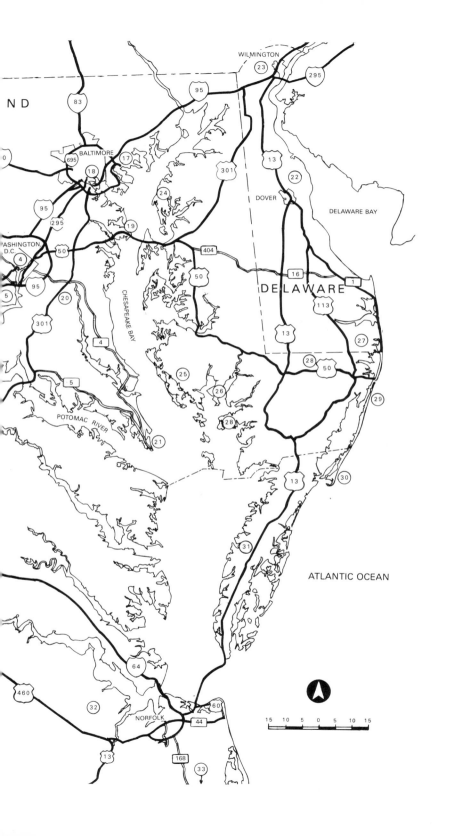

WILMINGTON

N D

BALTIMORE

DOVER

DELAWARE BAY

CHESAPEAKE BAY

ASHINGTON, D.C.

DELAWARE

POTOMAC RIVER

ATLANTIC OCEAN

NORFOLK

15 10 5 0 5 10 15

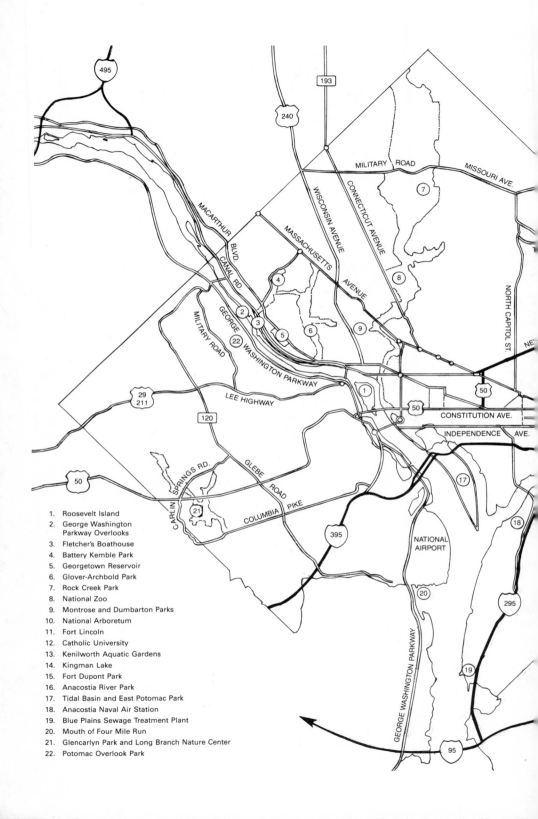

1. Roosevelt Island
2. George Washington
   Parkway Overlooks
3. Fletcher's Boathouse
4. Battery Kemble Park
5. Georgetown Reservoir
6. Glover-Archbold Park
7. Rock Creek Park
8. National Zoo
9. Montrose and Dumbarton Parks
10. National Arboretum
11. Fort Lincoln
12. Catholic University
13. Kenilworth Aquatic Gardens
14. Kingman Lake
15. Fort Dupont Park
16. Anacostia River Park
17. Tidal Basin and East Potomac Park
18. Anacostia Naval Air Station
19. Blue Plains Sewage Treatment Plant
20. Mouth of Four Mile Run
21. Glencarlyn Park and Long Branch Nature Center
22. Potomac Overlook Park

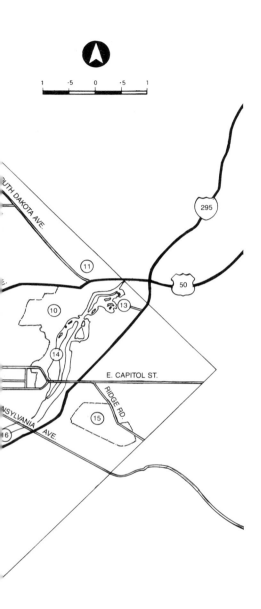

**District of Columbia
and Arlington County**